KANSAS CITY AND THE RAILROADS

KANSAS CITY

AND THE

RAILROADS

Community Policy in the Growth
of a Regional Metropolis

CHARLES N. GLAAB

UNIVERSITY PRESS OF KANSAS

First published in 1962 by The State Historical Society of Wisconsin. Publication of this reprint was made possible by a grant from the William T. Kemper Foundation, Commerce Bank Trustee.

Published by the University Press of Kansas (Lawrence, Kansas 66049), which was organized by the Kansas Board of Regents and is operated and funded by Emporia State University, Fort Hays State University, Kansas State University, Pittsburg State University, the University of Kansas, and Wichita State University

Maps are by Laura Kriegstrom Poracsky

Library of Congress Cataloging-in-Publication Data

Glaab, Charles Nelson, 1927–
Kansas City and the railroads: community policy in the
growth of a regional metropolis / by Charles N. Glaab.
p.   cm.
Includes bibliographical references and index.
ISBN 0-7006-0614-9 (cloth)   ISBN 0-7006-0615-7 (pbk.)
1. Railroads—Missouri—Kansas City—History.   2. Kansas City
(Mo.)—History.   I. Title.
HE 2781.K2G55   1993
385'.09778'411—dc20   93-16028

Printed in the United States of America
10 9 8 7 6 5 4 3 2 1

The paper used in this publication meets the minimum requirements of the American National Standard for Permanence of Paper for Printed Library Materials z39.48–1984.

TO THE MEMORY OF

REUBEN GLAAB

Contents

Illustrations

Preface to Reprint Edition

TO COMMENT ON a book I began in 1956 and published over thirty years ago requires search of memory. And probably any such search over that much time almost dictates reflection on the writing of American history in the latter part of this century. One of the common themes of contemporary historiography, often stated in the words of the great historian and defender of historical relativism, Carl Becker (1875–1945), is that "each generation writes its own history." In a number of brilliant essays, including his famous presidential address to the American Historical Association, "Everyman His Own Historian," Becker asserted that cultural demands of the time and prevailing conceptions shape all historical writing.[1] Since the 1970s, historians of radical persuasion have carried this view a step further and assert that nearly all historical writing of the past, from Francis Parkman through Henry Adams down at least to the time of the "new history" of the 1960s, simply embodies the prejudices and general wrongheadedness of the past that historians have escaped in our enlightened present. There is also the view that new sophisticated techniques of investigation and the accumulations of the computer have produced a better kind of current history, a history that outmodes the monographs of the past. Thomas Jefferson argued that all institutions should be examined and constructed anew every nineteen years. The passage of two of his generational periods since I began this study would seem to require at least some consideration of

---

[1] *American Historical Review* 87: 221–236 (January, 1932).

the viewpoints that underlie even a limited and not particularly theoretical monograph.

Kansas City and the Railroads began as a study in town founding,
railroad promotion, and city building. I sought to show, with considerable sympathy, how a group of business leaders with a major financial stake in what they were doing were able to organize a community,
win railroads, and make Kansas City a regional metropolis and a great
American city. Many historians of the 1950s, I among them, reacted
strongly against the economic determinism of Charles A. Beard and
other scholars that was incorporated in the texts we studied in college
after World War II. This book reflects the optimism about American
society that was a part of the postwar era and the positive view of the
"consensus school" of American historiography that emerged in the
1950s. And it is calculatedly undeterministic, emphasizing strongly
the possibility of human action shaping the course of events.

The book began as a doctoral dissertation at the University of Missouri. In the light of what real-estate people in the 1980s did to the
country through their urban promotions, I doubt that anyone today
would be inclined to submit a study quite as sympathetic to the
American business community as this one. It could be argued that I
accepted too heartily the view of the Kansas City entrepreneurs that
city building and city growth represented the triumph of civilization
and progress. I wrote during a time of hope for American cities, a
time that has probably passed. As I was completing the book at the
State Historical Society of Wisconsin, where I held a research position for a time and daily observed a tall clock made entirely of wood
that John Muir had constructed, I became interested in the work of
that naturalist, a pioneer in the American park and conservation
movements who had grown up in frontier Wisconsin. Since then, I
have gradually become aware that nineteenth-century city building,
though a dynamic and creative enterprise that contributed to the general material welfare, meant the destruction of resources and of nature in America. Viewing cities themselves, the American landscape,
and the accumulating pictorial evidence over the years—for example, the New York Museum of Natural History's brilliant 1992

photographic exhibition, "This Is the American Earth"—creates greater sympathy for Vernon Louis Parrington's conception of nineteenth-century growth, including urban growth, as "the great barbecue." And there are many lesser points in the book that reflect changing values. In writing the earlier preface, for example, I tried to satirize slightly the fulsome acknowledgments of wifely collaboration that I kept reading, but no one in academic circles today would dare put into print praise of a helpmeet for observing a "dutiful" and "proper division" of family labor.

One who has read monographs over the years might also detect, and I hope this would be the case, an old-fashioned mellowness of tone in the writing. (Critics would charge that this reflects the complacency of the period.) No longer do historians write their histories in clouds of pipe smoke while perhaps occasionally sipping Missouri bourbon or dry martinis and celebrating the good life of postwar America. Historians in those boom days of research grants, first-class air travel, generous book contracts, and seemingly unlimited professional opportunities often identified with society's people of power, including those in the past that they wrote about. And the American corporation, often quite willing to support historical research, seemed a much more benevolent institution than it did in the 1980s. The strident reform spirit of our time of intellectual Puritanism has radically changed the style of academic historical writing, and its tone now is closer to that of the sermon as historians tread resolutely forward in a moral crusade on behalf of the downtrodden.

But this kind of observation always encounters the truism that ultimately justifies the writing of history: fashion changes but humanity remains the same. As I tried in the early 1960s to turn a formal university dissertation into a readable book, I became less concerned with analysis of the dynamics of the shaping of community policy and more concerned with telling the story of a fascinating group of visionaries, town builders, real estate men, and promoters: Johnston Lykins, Theodore S. Case, Kersey L. Coates, William Gilpin, John W. Reid, and most notable of all, Robert T. Van Horn. A distinctive figure in western town promotion (in that he made no money from his successful efforts), a fine writer, and an intriguingly practical man, Van Horn, I found, had served as the leader of the town and in a sense was the hero of the early history of Kansas City. I was swept up in the telling of his story. And it is that story, a narrative about a group of players of that greatest of ninteenth-century games, town building, that has caused people now and then over the years to ask, "Where can I get a copy of *Kansas City and the Railroads?*"

The book owes its existence to an ambitious scholarly project of the postwar period, the History of Kansas City Project, organized in 1955 by R. Richard Wohl of the University of Chicago with the financial support of the Rockefeller Foundation.[2] Like Ralph Waldo Emerson's Utopians of a century or so earlier, every aspiring historian in those boom times had a project in his back pocket for new lines of investigation that would revolutionize historical understanding. Wohl, who was broadly trained in both the humanities and the social sciences and was recognized by his contemporaries as one of the more brilliant minds of his generation, sought to bring concepts from social science to create a new kind of urban history that would enable urban leaders more systematically to deal with the problems of the rapidly expanding cities of the postwar world. Wohl's early death in 1957 at the age of thirty-six prevented the realization of much of his ambitious design for a multivolume history of Kansas City that would embody his new approach, but the project was reorganized and continued until 1965 under the direction of Wohl's graduate student A. Theodore Brown, a scholar as broad in his outlook as his teacher. Over the years, numerous books and articles were written with project support; it also provided training for several graduate students who went on to develop urban history programs in several American universities at a time when few scholars called themselves urban historians and only a handful of urban history courses were taught around the country.

[2] A recent article provides a detailed assessment of the history of the project: Charles N. Glaab, Mark H. Rose, and William H. Wilson, "The History of Kansas City Projects and the Origins of American Urban History," *Journal of Urban History* 18: 371–394 (August, 1992).

My own experience demonstrates how the project provided practical training in a new field of inquiry. When I was hired as a research
associate in 1956, I had just begun a doctoral dissertation at the University of Missouri on twentieth-century political history, my intended field of research since undergraduate days when I had begun to
write about North Dakota Populists and Progressives. My first day
on the job, Brown handed me a stack of "urban biographies" (a term
that came to describe the histories of individual cities) and stated: "No
one knows what urban history is or how it should be written. Start
reading." Later, as I was assigned responsibility for the economic
aspects of Kansas City history, I became interested in Wohl's original
approach to the American businessman. I read widely in the new
Harvard entrepreneurial history and used some of its concepts when
writing an article on the Kansas City business community.[3] This experience of course influenced my effort to develop a study larger than
the "working papers" we turned out as project assignments, but there
could not be real specialization in the work of the project. The demands of trying to assess all aspects of a city's history precluded the
narrowness of approach that is a part of American university graduate
education.

It is unfair to single out examples from the many excellent urban
studies that were supported or sponsored by the project over the
years. But diversity, originality, and scholarly influence are particularly represented by William H. Wilson's study of planning in
Kansas City, which led to a later near-definitive account of the turn-
of-the-century city-beautiful movement in America, and by Lyle W.
Dorsett's study of the Pendergast machine, which led to several influential studies of political bosses. By the 1990s, comment on the emergence of urban history, now a well-established field of inquiry with its
own learned society and professional journal, occasionally suggested
the importance of a Kansas City school of urban history that had
emphasized the role of elites and business leaders in shaping the his-

[3] "Business Patterns in the Growth of a Midwestern City," *Business History Review* 33: 156–174 (Summer, 1959).

tory of American cities. A recent, excellent study of Jesse C. Nichols, the developer of Kansas City's Country Club District and its famous Country Club Plaza, seemed, for example, to find in Nichols many of the positive qualities found earlier in Van Horn and the town's other leaders.[4]

Wohl's death temporarily halted the History of Kansas City Project, but after its reorganization, financial support and cooperation from the project enabled me to enlarge my dissertation into a broader regional study, and the State Historical Society of Wisconsin published *Kansas City and the Railroads* in 1962 as part of a short-lived program in midwestern history that produced several excellent monographs. Generally, reviewers treated the book as a sound study of urban rivalry, praised the writing, but found no unusual interpretative themes. The edition of less than a thousand copies, a customary number for monographs at the time, was fairly quickly exhausted, in part because of the interest of the people at Kansas City in their own past. I searched elsewhere for urban promoters and urban visionaries and found them most everywhere I looked on the urban frontier, a vital part of the history of the American West in the nineteenth century.

The Kansas City story, and other similar stories, began to find their way into the texts. In a magnificent synthesis of American social history, *The Americans*, a tribute in a sense to the "consensus school," Daniel Boorstin told the Kansas City story and called my book "an important monograph on urban rivalry and community support of transportation." Scholarly railroad histories of the period incorporated portions of my research; for example, Arthur M. Johnson and

---

[4] William H. Wilson, *The City Beautiful Movement in Kansas City* (Columbia: University of Missouri Press, 1964), and William H. Wilson, *The City Beautiful Movement* (Baltimore: Johns Hopkins, 1989); Lyle W. Dorsett, *The Pendergast Machine* (New York: Oxford, 1968), and Lyle W. Dorsett, *Franklin D. Roosevelt and the City Bosses* (Port Washington, N.Y.: Kennikat, 1977); William S. Worley, *J. C. Nichols and the Shaping of Kansas City* (Columbia: University of Missouri Press, 1990), and my review in *Journal of Southern History* 58: 556–558 (August, 1992).

Barry E. Supple's *Boston Capitalists and Western Railroads* described the close relationship of Kansas City town builders and powerful investors in Boston, a connection that continued into the twentieth century. A rather casual interpretive essay of mine suggesting new approaches to urban history, based in large part on my Kansas City work, was anthologized in 1966 as a "valuable contribution to our urban past" reflecting new developments in "the craft of American history." Later, a chapter of *Kansas City and the Railroads* was included in a reader to represent one stage of the continuing urban frontier and the "importance of man's decisions in urban growth."[5]

In *A History of Urban America*, Brown and I attempted to apply a few themes derived from Wohl, ourselves, and the project to a general study of urbanization in America.[6] In writing the sections on the urban West and the growth of a national transportation network, I utilized, naturally enough, the Kansas City story as a major case study. Although *A History of Urban America* was written for a general audience and was initially published as a trade book, it was soon regarded as the first textbook in American urban history and came to be used in many of the courses in urban history that began to flourish in the 1970s. The work also appeared in several social science readers and was translated into at least one foreign language (Italian).

In the 1970s, histories of the American West often presented a relatively positive view of the town promoter and the urban prophets, recognizing particularly that their ideological outlook shaped the

[5] Daniel Boorstin, *The Americans*, Vol. 2, *The National Experience* (New York, 1965), 131–133, 458; Arthur M. Johnson and Barry E. Supple, *Boston Capitalists and Western Railroads* (Cambridge, Mass., 1967), 225–228; for a more recent account of the distinctive relationship between Kansas City and Boston investors, see Daniel Serda, *Boston Investors and the Early Development of Kansas City, Missouri* (Kansas City, 1992); Charles N. Glaab, "The Historian and the American Urban Tradition," *Wisconsin Magazine of History* 46: 13–25 (Autumn, 1963), reprinted in A. S. Eisenstadt, *The Craft of American History*, Vol. 2 (New York, 1966), 35–55; and Allen M. Wakstein, ed., *The Urbanization of America: An Historical Anthology* (Boston, 1970), 73, 108–113.

[6] Charles N. Glaab and A. Theodore Brown, *A History of Urban America* (New York, 1967; 3d ed., 1983).

character of nineteenth-century America. Later accounts, reflecting the tenor of the times, have sometimes returned to an older view of the booster as predator and exploiter. A recent brilliant examination of the American West focusing on Chicago suggests a synthesis. In writing about boosters, William Cronon observes that although "their unabashed optimism about progress and civilization has long since gone out of fashion," they played a critical role in shaping nineteenth-century thought about the Great West—a point well established, he writes, by "their chief historian."[7] Of course no striking influence on historical thinking can be assigned to a monograph that deals with only one city and its region over a fifty-year period. But it is the purpose of the monograph to have its findings woven into the fabric of American history, and *Kansas City and the Railroads* has, to my satisfaction, played that role over the years.

What are the general ideas about cities and their growth to be found in *Kansas City and the Railroads?* When I first began studying the early history of the city, I became convinced that systematic urban promotion played a creative and often positive role in nineteenth-century America—that the traditional kind of town boosters represented in literature by Mark Twain's Beriah Sellers and Sinclair Lewis's George F. Babbitt were distorted caricatures. Nor did I find the railroad leaders Kansas Citians had dealt with to be quite the robber barons and ruthless capitalists they were portrayed to be in so much of the historical scholarship of the time. In writing about such early leaders as Robert T. Van Horn and Kersey L. Coates, I tried to show that complex motives, many of them public spirited, were a part of town building and urban leadership. I also became concerned with demonstrating how Kansas City town builders used a vision of the

---

[7] For early positive views, see Richard A. Bartlett, *The New Country: A Social History of the American Frontier, 1776–1890* (New York, 1974), 417–422, and, for direct incorporation of Kansas City themes, Lawrence H. Larsen, *The Urban West at the End of the Frontier* (Lawrence, Kansas, 1978), 1–19. For later views of the promoter, see Richard White, *A New History of the American West* (Norman, Oklahoma, 1991), 416–429, and William Cronon, *Nature's Metropolis: Chicago and the Great West* (New York, 1991), 46, 396.

West that was essentially urban, derived from William Gilpin and others, as a positive ideology to organize their community behind their program. It is perhaps this theme, extending the non-Turnerian view of the urban nature of the frontier process, that has been most incorporated into later texts.

Obviously many sources shaped these conceptions. Contemporary theories of knowledge suggest how tenuous is the possibility of the invention of an idea in any field, including the sciences; new views in history are radically limited by the kind of questions asked and by the nature of the inquiry under way at any given time. When I first undertook this study, Henry Nash Smith's *Virgin Land*, with its brilliant evocation of how an idea of the West had always influenced American culture, was fresh in the historical mind. The contributions of business historians, with their scrupulous documentation of how business leaders had actually operated in the past, influenced my thinking as well. And, as part of the design of the History of Kansas City Project to apply social science to history, everyone who worked on the project became immersed in the scholarship of the time that studied power elites, urban oligarchies, and the organic nature of urban politics. But it has been gratifying over the years that my efforts to synthesize a few of these conceptions have found their way into general historical scholarship.

History teaches no lessons, but there is one other theme in *Kansas City and the Railroads* that may offer a bit of insight into the circumstances of urban America today. Kansas City leaders, after the initial success of their railroad program, used a version of local history— the triumph of the "Kansas City spirit"—to advance community programs over the years and make Kansas City a most livable place. In the early years, the Kansas City leaders dealt with a homogenous, cohesive, compact community. Now, of course, fragmentation of the metropolis and the flight of the elite to the suburbs have broken down the unity of the nineteenth-century city. Great ideological tensions divide urban communities today, but as Kersey L. Coates and Robert T. Van Horn recognized before the Civil War, as they stood on opposite sides of the greatest of all ideological divisions in American history, leadership often consists of abandoning divisive social ideology and, as I first wrote of the early Kansas City leaders, unreflectively getting things done.

Since I wrote *Kansas City and the Railroads*, a varied and substantial body of scholarship has greatly enlarged our knowledge of American railroad history, but no one, I believe, has tried to retell the often intricate story of the early Kansas City railroad program and its relation to the history of the city and the region. It is that story that may justify this reprint of my book. Accordingly, aside from the correction of a few errors, the original text remains intact. In order to clarify regional patterns of town and railroad developments I have added new maps and a list of the railroad companies referred to in the text.

A number of people have contributed greatly to the preparation of this reprint edition. I owe a special debt to David Boutros, Associate Director of the Western Historical Manuscript Collection, Kansas City, Missouri, who persuaded me, against my initial judgment, that a reprint of the book would be worthwhile and assisted greatly at every stage of its preparation. I would also like to thank Fred M. Woodward, Director of the University Press of Kansas, for his able editorial assistance and his early enthusiastic support of the project. My longtime friend Homer E. Socolofsky, Professor Emeritus of History, Kansas State University, carefully read the first edition and helpfully pointed out errors.

The generous financial support of the William T. Kemper Foundation, Kansas City, Missouri, made possible the publication of this reprint edition. I am particularly indebted to Jonathan M. Kemper, President of the Commerce Bank of Kansas City, who encouraged republication of the work and who has consistently supported the study of Kansas City history.

One of my hopes as I prepared this reprint was that new readers of the study might be moved to turn to other works that are part of Kansas City's rich tradition of historical writing—those connected with the History of Kansas City Project, of course, but also others extending back to the early days of the town. From the beginning, a sense of history has been a main ingredient in that powerful and enduring mixture of community sentiment called "the Kansas City Spirit."

CHARLES N. GLAAB

Toledo, Ohio
February, 1993

Preface to Original Edition

I N THESE DAYS of megalopolis, metropolitan under-represen-
tation, urban sprawl, and flights to and from suburbia, Americans, as in other eras, seem much concerned with their cities. Yet in
spite of occasional directives from within the craft to study the city,
professional American historians have continued to accept the restrictions of a tradition-bound national synthesis. To the extent that there
is an avant-garde in this most conservative of disciplines, it has
turned to social psychology, literary criticism, quantification of socio-
economic data, or even theology to find new approaches to the American past. Seldom though has anyone defended or speculated seriously
about the intensely particularistic study, which is developed in terms
of the realities that appear from within the internal history of the unit
studied and which does not represent the mere imposition of well
established national patterns upon a given institution or locality. Any
professional historian who examines the history of a single city risks
identification with a most pernicious species, the local historian, and
faces the prospect of intellectual exile to the laity of antiquarians,
permitted only to study inconsequential subjects in an inconsequential
manner.

I have assumed the risk, for this book represents a variety of ur-
ban-local history. It is about the rise of a leading western transportation center, Kansas City, from its beginnings in the 1850's as a trading post on the edge of settlement through its maturation as regional
metropolis in the 1880's. In no way, however, does this work provide
a full-scale, socio-economic history of the city; the task of preparing

Kansas City's biography, in a projected two volumes, is in the able hands of others. Instead, within a regional setting, I have attempted to develop one theme in the city's history—the story of railroad planning and promotion. This is a critical theme; in fact, in a very real sense, the central theme, as it is for thousands of communities in the West. During a period in which the location of railroads determined the location of cities, the principal concern of community leaders had to be the formulation and execution of plans to win railroads and make their hamlet, town, or city the trade, financial, and manufacturing center of a vast region—or if their propaganda were to be believed the metropolis of the world.

The importance of local aid and promotion of internal improvements as a factor in nineteenth century economic growth has increasingly become recognized, but the relationship between this energetic form of community activity and the development of cities has received only limited attention. The subject raises a number of questions. What forces within a community caused a systematic railroad program to develop? To what extent were notions and conceptions about the nature of the West and transportation translated into community ideology and how did this ideology affect community policy? How were local railroad programs organized and operated? Why did one community in a region win railroads while another with equal or even greater natural advantages fail? Can relationships between entrepreneurship, geography, and community policy that affected the patterns assumed by railroads and the location of cities be defined with some degree of precision?

In addition to providing a case study which explores these questions, I have also tried—since history deals with people—to tell the story of an intriguing group of railroad promoters, land speculators, and city builders who operated in the Kansas City region. Their lives do not provide object lessons that illustrate fine American traditions or even the professed ethical principles of capitalism. They simply took society as they found it and unreflectively got things done.

I have incurred a number of obligations in preparing this study. It began as a project "working paper" during my employment with the

History of Kansas City Project, Committee on Human Development, University of Chicago, which was supported through a grant from the Rockefeller Foundation. The late R. Richard Wohl, who conceived this project, acquainted me with the field of urban history, goaded me into trying to disentangle the complicated story of hundreds of local Kansas City railroad companies, and until his tragic illness and death provided inspired guidance. I hope that in a limited way this small work may provide some test of the provocative and brilliant hypotheses he constantly advanced about Kansas City and American urban history.

An earlier version of this study served as my doctoral dissertation at the University of Missouri. At different stages of its preparation, J. Neal Primm and Lewis E. Atherton supplied sympathetic and informed direction. Only a rare librarian has stood at the gates of knowledge saying, 'he shall not pass;' in general wherever I have worked I have received courteous treatment. I would particularly like to acknowledge the extraordinary special privileges accorded me by Richard B. Sealock and James Anderson. Miss Frances Berenice Ford, Mrs. Frederick James, W. D. Bryant, Howard F. Bennett, and Richard C. Overton kindly permitted me to use private materials in their possession. I am also grateful to Arthur D. McLane for permission to cite material from the Chicago, Burlington and Quincy archives. Miss Mildred C. Cox spent much time acquainting me with research sources available in Kansas City. Irvin G. Wyllie read a preliminary draft of the manuscript, suggested important lines of revision, and provided sound, rigorous stylistic criticism. I owe much to my former colleague, A. Theodore Brown, the present director of the History of Kansas City Project. During the several years we have explored the history of Kansas City together, he has freely extended to me the results of his own research, has provided project facilities whenever I asked for them, and has always taken time to bring his vast erudition to bear on any problem I have had. Throughout the preparation of this study, my wife Mary has dutifully observed a proper division of labor. She has kept children out from underfoot when there was work to be done, has served meals whenever I was there to eat them, and has endured with sympathy my long absences from home on research trips, late hours spent writing, and fits of ill temper.

Support from the research phase of the University of Wisconsin Urban Program under a grant from the Ford Foundation provided the time necessary to undertake a full-scale revision of an earlier, more limited version of this study. A grant from the American Association for State and Local History provided funds for travel and for the final preparation of the manuscript.

CHARLES N. GLAAB

Madison, Wisconsin
Spring, 1962

Railroad Companies

THE FOLLOWING RAILROAD companies are listed or discussed in the text and can be found in the Index. Many of these companies, organized for promotional purposes, existed only on paper (as their histories indicate), and others were consolidated and reorganized.

National and Regional Railroad Companies

Atchison, Topeka, and Santa Fe
Atlantic and Great Western
Central Pacific
Chicago, Burlington, and Quincy
Denver Pacific
Galveston and Red River
Hannibal and St. Joseph
Houston and Texas Central
Illinois Central
Kansas Pacific
Michigan Central
Missouri Pacific
New Orleans, Shreveport, and Kansas City
Pacific
Palmyra
St. Louis, Kansas City, and Northern
Union Pacific
Union Pacific, Eastern Division
Wabash

Kansas City and Local Missouri Railroad Companies

Atchison and St. Joseph
Kansas City, Arkansas, and Gulf
Kansas City, Clinton, and Memphis
Kansas City, Galveston, and Lake Superior
Kansas City, Hannibal, and St. Joseph
Kansas City, Independence, and Lexington
Kansas City, Memphis, and Mobile
Kansas City, St. Joseph, and Council Bluffs
Kansas City, Wyandotte, and Northwestern
Kansas City and Cameron
Kansas City and Keokuk
Kansas City and Memphis
Kansas City and Neosha Valley
Kansas Valley
Missouri, Kansas, and Texas
Missouri River, Fort Scott, and Gulf
Parkville and Grand River
Platte Country
Platte County
Tebo and Neosha

Kansas Railroad Companies

Atchison and Pike's Peak
Lawrence and Pleasant Hill
Leavenworth, Lawrence, and Fort Gibson
Leavenworth, Lawrence, and Galveston
Leavenworth, Pawnee, and Western

Introduction

The Legend of the Bridge

TODAY, Kansas City, Missouri, is an American metropolis and a national transportation center. Theories of city location and growth often make an individual city seem the creation of complex economic and geographic forces that focus in a time-space dimension; in terms of this type of analysis, the rise of Kansas City appears logical and perhaps even inevitable. But men have also played a part in making cities. Local historians of American cities emphasize this point—sometimes to the exclusion of any other—and, to explain a city's existence and its development, single out heroic actions by community leaders in times of crisis. The recorded history of Kansas City embodies this kind of interpretation of the city's formative years.

In an introduction to the most recent formal history of Kansas City, Roy A. Roberts, publisher of the *Kansas City Star* and a leading contemporary spokesman for the community, asserted that a distinct lesson could be learned from reading about the city's past. Why had Kansas City become a magnificent metropolis? "Enterprise, daring, above all faith pushed Kansas City ahead. Men, not chance did it." Specifically, he pointed to the battle for railroads, in which vigorous and wise leadership had won the struggle with rival communities for regional supremacy. To Roberts, the work of early city-builders in gaining railroads symbolized "what became known, and is still known as the 'Kansas City spirit'—not just a Chamber of Commerce slogan, but a living, meaningful thing." [1]

Scholarly analysis suggests that a complex of economic, social, and ecological relationships shape the nature of a city. But significant also in determining the "personality" and quality of life in any city are the legends, impressions, and evaluations that it uses to interpret its past. These stored social memories, when sharply focused, serve as a useful urban myth, which city leaders can invoke when making community decisions. In Kansas City, the principal community legend—complete with heroes, villains, a traitor, frantic journeys, and a dramatic confrontation of the enemy—concerns the coming of the railroads. The Hannibal and St. Joseph bridge, the first railroad bridge constructed across the Missouri River, has served as the city's special symbol. The winning of this bridge became, in Kansas City's self–evaluation, the key to its success and a tribute to the bold resourcefulness of a small group of inspired city fathers.

The significance that local chroniclers of the legend have assigned to the Hannibal and St. Joseph bridge reflects a generally accurate historical judgment. Railroads did make Kansas City a leading American city. In the 1850's the future metropolis was one of several small trading towns on the western edge of settlement. The Civil War nearly destroyed the community. But the 1867 decision of the Hannibal and St. Joseph–Chicago, Burlington and Quincy railroad system to support the building of a line from Cameron, Missouri, to Kansas City, and to bridge the Missouri River at the latter point, caused an immediate boom in the town and fixed the pattern of regional railroad connections permanently in its favor. Within a few years, Kansas City became the regional metropolis and began its rise as a major American meat-packing and transportation center. In the life of a city great events demand great legends. The winning of the bridge was of such consequence to Kansas City that the heroic legend began to take shape at a very early date.

On July 3, 1869, the Hannibal and St. Joseph bridge was opened to traffic. Because the powerful current of the Missouri and the shifting nature of the river's channel had created formidable engineering problems, two-and-a-half years had been required to build it. Twice the chief engineer, Octave Chanute, failed to establish a firm footing under the bridge's fourth pier. He eventually had to introduce new construction techniques from Germany to finish the work. But at last it was done, and Kansas City celebrated.[2]

A newspaper reporter from neighboring St. Joseph attended the July 3 festivities. Considering the years of intense rivalry between the two communities, he should have been less enthusiastic than local reporters. But he too was exuberant; the occasion, he wrote, was "without parallel in western celebrations." Forty thousand people were present. To the accompaniment of bands and artillery salvos, railroad employees drove a lavishly decorated train across the bridge. Ten thousand people marched to a grove south of town to hear the major address of the day. As more cannons boomed, a man named Holman made a successful balloon ascension from the public square. A mammoth barbecue followed in the late afternoon. In the evening, town leaders and visiting dignitaries attended a grand banquet at the Broadway Hotel, where in a series of toasts and responses, speakers commemorated the significance of the event. It was "such a spectacle," the St. Joseph writer observed, "as is not likely to be witnessed more than once in a lifetime." [3]

The occasion demanded full and enthusiastic treatment by the local press. "Today will live forever in the annals of Kansas City as the greatest event in her history," declared the *Kansas City Times*. The bridge was "truly the bridge of destiny," one of the paper's writers asserted. "Circumstances created it, and for a time fortune coquetted with it, and wafted it hither as a prophetic wand, now pointed towards Leavenworth, then towards Kansas City . . . ." Everything had depended upon obtaining the bridge. Had Kansas City lost out, it would have surrendered to Leavenworth and would have become a town of secondary importance. "Truly the present and future greatness of Kansas City turned on that day's work." The moral was plain. The victory demonstrated on "how slender a thread sometimes hang the fortunes of cities as well as men and nations." [4]

Although details differed, the newspaper accounts presented a common story of dramatic, vigorous local action in the achievement of the victory. From 1856 on, Kansas City leaders had realized the importance of building a connection northward to the Hannibal and St. Joseph Railroad—the first railroad completed into western Missouri. They had chosen Cameron, Missouri, thirty-five miles east of St. Joseph, as the terminus for a local project. Their Kansas City–Cameron company, organized in 1859, had made little progress when the Civil War stopped railroad building in the region. Right after the war, they resumed their efforts to raise money and to get the co-operation of the Hannibal and St. Joseph owners in Boston. But interests in the nearby Kansas town of Leavenworth, which had made tremendous gains during the war, also had organized a Cameron project. Quite by chance the news leaked out in 1866 that the Leavenworth promoters were about to close a contract with the Hannibal and St. Jo.—in fact, that they were already in Boston ready to sign. Immediately, Kansas City leaders called a meeting, and Charles E. Kearney, president of the Kansas City and Cameron, dispatched three powerful representatives of the local business community, Kersey L. Coates, John W. Reid, and Theodore S. Case, to Boston to try to delay these proceedings. The Hannibal and St. Jo. owners were astonished to learn of the interest of the Kansas Citians in building a Cameron connection. They favored the Leavenworth group, but Kansas City's superior geographical position, eloquently argued by the three Kansas Citians, persuaded them to delay the negotiations. Finally, the Boston people sent James Joy, the western representative of the Hannibal and St. Jo., to look over the situation firsthand. Joy had "studied the map" and recognized Kansas City's superior natural advantages. He ordered Kearney to go ahead with the Cameron road and the bridge. Because of this decision and the subsequent support by Joy of the city's interests, Kansas City would become the "metropolis of the Middle Missouri Valley." [5]

These initial newspaper accounts established two elements essential to the legend. First, there was the quality of sudden decision:

Leavenworth was about to steal the prize; only at the last possible instance did the people of Kansas City act. Secondly, the bridge decision was crucial in Kansas City's history: if the plan of Leavenworth had not been thwarted, all would have been lost to the rival town.

The first and in many ways the ablest of Kansas City's historians, William H. Miller, who as secretary of the board of trade in the 1870's and 1880's reflected the views of the local business community, added the remaining vital aspects of the bridge legend. First, he supplied the traitor. Before the war, Miller wrote, the Kansas City company had negotiated a contract with the Hannibal and St. Jo. promising its aid in building the Cameron line. John T. K. Hayward, a Hannibal and St. Jo. official who had been assisting the Kansas Citians in their effort, signed this contract for the Boston company. Then at some point between 1860 and 1866, Hayward had lost his position with the Hannibal and St. Jo. and had sold out to Leavenworth interests. He continued to represent himself to Kansas Citians as a Hannibal and St. Jo. man; at the same time he furthered Leavenworth's quest for its Cameron connection. His machinations accounted for the presence of Leavenworth negotiators in Boston and also accounted for their near success. For among the pre-Civil War officers of the Hannibal and St. Jo., only Hayward and John W. Brooks knew of the old contract. And Brooks, in 1866, was away in Europe! [6]

Miller also described some adroit Congressional maneuvering by local figures that helped make the eventual favorable decision possible. James Joy, in analyzing Kansas City's proposition, agreed to resurrect the old contract provided local leaders could get Congressional authorization for a bridge across the Missouri River. Upon receiving this news, Kearney immediately telegraphed Robert T. Van Horn, an editor of Kansas City's leading newspaper who was then serving as United States Representative, to push the required bill through Congress. Van Horn managed to get the Kansas City bridge authorization tacked on as an amendment to an omnibus bridge bill. The House voted to accept the amendment.

Just then, Kansas Congressman Sidney Clarke rushed onto the floor with an amendment to authorize a bridge at Leavenworth. But the previous question had been moved and seconded. Clarke was too late by minutes. Van Horn had turned the tide in Kansas City's favor.

Miller had obviously improved the dramatic quality of the legend. There was now a personal villain, John Hayward, instead of the more abstract enemy, "Leavenworth." The Van Horn episode in Congress strengthened the climax. The foiling of Leavenworth's dupe, the unresourceful Sidney Clarke, even added a bit of comic relief.

Later historians and journalists in recounting the bridge victory relied largely on Miller's account. But in rewriting the story, they often portrayed the events as high melodrama. The "dirty work" in hated Leavenworth, the treachery of Hayward, the frantic trip to Boston, the "fast political footwork" and "lightning-like" procedures in Congress all received exaggeratedly colorful and often inaccurate treatment. Moreover, there were fundamental shifts in emphasis in these later accounts. Many early versions of the legend had Kansas City's natural advantages determining the bridge decision; later writers hinged the outcome on the prewar contract. By the 1880's the doctrine of natural advantages, fundamental in Midwestern urban rationales in the ante-bellum period, had begun to pass out of fashion. The prior-contract story harmonized with the triumph of local enterprise, a theme consistently celebrated in local historiography of the late nineteenth century. Also important was the tendency for James Joy to disappear completely from later presentations. If a writer paid tribute to the "Kansas City spirit," he naturally found it inconvenient to have the future of the city dependent on the whim of an Eastern railroad builder.[7]

During the years after 1869, the story of the bridge victory was also absorbed into local folklore, and suffered the usual alterations of historical fact involved in community assimilation of the knowledge of significant events. This sort of material—available in quantity—adversely influenced any later writer's effort to reconstruct the events that led to the bridge victory. For example, one early Kansas Citian recalled a version of the episode that seemed to bear virtually no relation to the written accounts. "On wintry nights in 1867," he reminisced, "a few old chums would frequently meet in the back room of the little rented Postoffice to laugh and joke over the contest for the bridge in other cities. . . . As the pleasantries subsided, one of those present cried out: 'What about Kansas City's getting into the fight?' A guffaw laugh followed. Then an interchange of hospitality. Then the question was renewed. The fun in the question gradually abated. Kansas City's contempt for its northern rivals seemed to grow in the little gathering. No arguments followed. . . . 'We can get all the money needed; we are not poor. Our banks will back up their customers. Let us get going.' Checks were drawn out. Everyone present was a committee to arouse the bankers. Horses were mounted, and every man with money within a radius of ten miles was ordered out of bed. When the second morning cast its light, reports were nearly all handed in at the rendezvous. The bankers accepted the checks and drew up orders on their eastern correspondents. The amount demanded to insure the bridge was at hand. Before noon four of Kansas City's enterprising citizens had started for the nearest railroad, miles east. When they presented themselves in the general office of the railroad interest way off in Boston they handed their certified checks from Kansas City to the capitalists who owned the North Missouri Railroad, now the Wabash Railroad. Those checks were large enough to justify bringing the railroad from Cameron junction to what is now North Kansas City . . . and to meet the bonus for the bridge. . . ." [8] Every fact in the account is wrong. The year is wrong, the wrong railway company is involved, and the origin of the idea of trying to obtain a bridge is altogether fanciful. But the presentation is true to the spirit of the legend, for it emphasizes spontaneous community decision and inspired, vigorous local action. And these qualities are fundamental in all versions of the episode.

During the 1870's the legend of the bridge became part of the city's history. By this time, Kansas City was on its way to becoming the metropolis of the lower Missouri River valley. Railroad rivalry had been settled in her favor. The arguments that town promoters had used in prewar days, strategic location and natural advantages, had little utility in advancing the interests of an established city facing problems other than the attraction of outside attention and investment. The bridge victory offered a new basis for appeals to action: reassert the spirit of the Cameron railroad builders; continue the monumental work that they had started; show the same type of enterprise, aggressiveness and daring that they had shown. If this were done, all would be well, and Kansas City would continue on its path to greatness. In subsequent years, the bridge legend became, as Roberts made clear, the main buttress of a more comprehensive urban myth, "the Kansas City spirit," which emphasized the community's superior leadership, energy, and willingness to support projects to advance the city.

The bridge legend, at least in some of its presentations, supplies reasonably accurate history. Some facts are misinterpreted: the prior contract and Van Horn's Congressional coup did not have the importance that has been assigned to them. But the actual chronicling of events is sometimes reasonably close to the truth.

Nevertheless, there are serious weaknesses in all presentations of the legend. Even considered just as an account of one narrow aspect of community policy during the period—the building of the Cameron road and the winning of the bridge—it is far from adequate. In all the versions, time is compressed. By implication at least, events extending over several months are treated as if they had occurred in a day or two. Moreover, the legend is extremely selective. It ignores a complex of regional railroad developments during the period that affected the decision to bridge the Missouri River at Kansas City. The whole story hinges on one brilliant stroke of local effort—the successful persuasion of the Hannibal and St. Jo. railroad to support the Kansas City project. All that came before or after is ignored. The Boston journey may well have been a rather spectacular affair, but it was preceded by months of fruitless negotiations. Even after the Hannibal and St. Jo. decision, the local promoters experienced many trials before they were able to complete their railroad. The legend of the bridge isolates for consideration only one achievement in a succession of failures.

The early history of Kansas City does not sustain the view that local leaders through heroic action created a city. Nor does it reveal the unfolding of a design whereby a wilderness community steadily and surely emerges as railroad center and metropolis. It shows instead a pattern of false starts, obvious turning points, and fortuitous combinations of circumstance. The scope, character, and direction of community policy—conditioned by a complex framework of ideological, geographic, and economic influences—had profound effects on the rise of a leading American city and on the pattern of the American railroad system. But Roberts' proposition that "men, not chance did it" posed false opposites. In this case, as perhaps in all cases, the two were inseparable.

I

Prophets of Railroad Destiny

ON Christmas Eve, 1857, the business leaders of the small western trading town of Kansas City, Missouri, held a banquet to celebrate the year's progress. Perhaps they met in part to reassure themselves. This had been a year of severe panic in the land, yet there was no talk of depression on this occasion. Each of the speakers at the dinner foresaw a bright future and proclaimed that their town would soon become a magnificent metropolis. In the course of a long evening the assembled community leaders set forth the fundamental aspects of a rationale for building a city and indicated clearly that they had joined together in an enterprise designed to transform a river town into a great western metropolis. The dinner, in supplying formal recognition of this prospect, marked the beginning of a new stage in the history of a community.

The early years of settlement at the juncture of the Missouri and Kansas rivers were inauspicious and provided little evidence of future promise for the site. In 1821 François Chouteau, acting as an agent of the American Fur Company, established a wilderness fur-trading post a short distance from the eventual city. Noting that Santa Fe traders frequently used the river landing for the small

French settlement around the post, a group of Western merchants in 1838 organized a town-company to try to develop the location. During the 1830's and 1840's, as the depots for the overland trade moved up the Missouri River, a number of small trading towns including Independence, Weston, and Westport sprang up in the vicinity to serve the commerce of a vast Western empire. Like these other communities, the town of Kansas for the first fifteen years of its existence was little more than a collection of warehouses and general stores, an entrepôt of the river-caravan trade providing a convenient location where goods could easily be transferred from steamboat to wagon for shipment to a distant hinterland.

There is no evidence that the diverse group of traders and merchants who platted Kansas foresaw that it would ever be much more than this. Complicated legal battles among the town-company members prevented any serious attempt to build up the site; the town simply languished. But the rapid settlement of Kansas Territory after 1854 created a new opportunity—a regional city to serve this potentially rich trade area. By this date, Kansas City (as it was generally called after the opening of the territory) had begun to eclipse many of the rival towns in the area. Local leaders, with their court fights out of the way, showed signs of responding to the challenge of accommodating individual business ambitions to the broader design of building a city. They started to shift their investment from Western merchandising to fields such as banking and real estate, which were directly related to urban economic functions, and began to participate in an identifiable "urban enterprise" through the organization of joint business efforts and community projects necessary to foster city growth. The gains during 1857 indicated that this venture in city building might ultimately be successful. The local newspaper, in its frequently inflated annual review of trade, recorded over $6,000,000 in business transactions. The town had grown from 2,000 inhabitants in January to 3,224 in June; the review asserted that its population at the end of the year had reached 5,158. This kind of progress called for celebration.[1]

The banquet took place at the usual gathering place of local leaders, Colonel Henry C. Titus's Exchange Hotel. Titus had become a hero of the pro-slavery forces during the Border Troubles of the preceding two years; he was shortly to win more military fame for his part in minor filibustering expeditions in Mexico and Central America. As was customary when the town's elite gathered, Titus served an elaborate meal featuring various kinds of western game. During the early years of Kansas City, emphasis on the use of products of the plains and prairies provided symbolic recognition of the city's identification with the interests of the Great West. After the waiters cleared the tables, the toasts began. In response, local leaders delivered a series of lengthy speeches discussing the institutions and forces they considered instrumental in the town's progress.

The speakers were particularly appropriate to their subjects. Hiram M. Northrup spoke on the contributions of businessmen to community progress. Perhaps the town's wealthiest merchant, Northrup had come as an Indian trader to neighboring Westport in 1844 and with a number of partners soon owned a string of trading posts throughout the Southwest doing an annual business in excess of $300,000. Patrick Shannon, an Irish immigrant and operator of the town's largest clothing store, paid tribute to the Emerald Isle and the part her sons would play in building the city. Joseph C. Ranson, like Northrup, a long-time Western trader and commission merchant who spent most of his time working at his city addition, described the development of the local real-estate business. Edward C. McCarty, a Santa Fe trader since 1828, garrulously related the origins of the far Southwest trade, which had been a mainstay in the town's economy since its founding.

Charles C. Spalding, a twenty-four-year-old journalist, civil engineer, and professional town boomer, discussed the future of the city in grandiloquent terms. Spalding had come to Kansas City the year before and, with support from community authorities, was at work on a book to advertise the prospects of the aspiring town.

The region's perennial political candidate, Nathaniel C. Claiborne, who was to become a leader of the Secessionist forces in Missouri during the Civil War, supplied the evening's required tribute to flag, country, and constitution. Indicative perhaps of the character of the leadership structure that had been established in the town was the fact that no one arose to respond to the toast to the early French settlers who had founded the community.[2]

The most forceful address of the evening was delivered by a man who during his two-and-a-half years' residence in Kansas City had already become its leading spokesman: Robert Thompson Van Horn, editor of the *Western Journal of Commerce*. Van Horn responded to a toast, "Railroads and the Press—Twin Brothers in Progress and Development," but he touched only briefly, and seemingly as an afterthought, on the role of the latter. Although Van Horn was a newspaperman by profession, he primarily concerned himself with the economic affairs of Kansas City. It was natural that he should devote his time to examining the role railroads would play in making Kansas City the great metropolis of the West. From his arrival in 1855, he had insisted that the future of the young town depended on its doing something about attracting or building railroads. For the next twenty years, he was to be intimately associated with nearly every railroad effort evolved in the city.[3]

Born in Pennsylvania in 1824, Van Horn early in life had fitted himself for a career as a kind of journeyman-intellectual. Although he had received little formal education, schoolteaching, brief study of the law, and employment as printer or editor on numerous Ohio and Pennsylvania newspapers provided solid practical training for his later role as a city's spokesman. As a newspaperman, Van Horn was always a booster. "Standing around scratching heads," he editorialized in Ohio in 1850, "will never make Pomeroy the city nature intended it to be." Bad luck dogged his early years. On one occasion he attempted to establish a daily newspaper in Cincinnati, but his printing plant burned to the ground. "It has failed," he wrote to his parents, "and I am again a loser." He admitted he was heavily in debt, and had a wife and children to support. But he said, as always, he was optimistic and had taken a job as a clerk on a river steamboat. "If I can financier so as to be able to raise in a few years a few hundred dollars," he concluded, "I am going out West, probably to Nebraska, where I hope to retrieve my fortunes and kick up a dust generally among the natives." [4]

His chance came in July, 1855, in St. Louis where he met a lawyer from the Kansas City settlement. The lawyer represented a committee of businessmen who were seeking someone to manage an unsuccessful local newspaper and offered Van Horn the job. After a brief trip to the town, Van Horn accepted, agreeing to pay $250 as a first installment on the newspaper and a second $250 a year later. He was no longer to be a "loser." So satisfied were the local business leaders with his efforts that they waived the payment of the second installment. Their confidence was well merited. For the remainder of his career, he consistently supported their programs and unceasingly devoted himself to promoting the economic interests of the city. It is to his credit that he never exploited his position as community leader for personal gain. Unlike many of his fellow townsmen, he built no large fortune from the control and manipulation of community assets during the era of local promotion in Kansas City.

Van Horn had the cast of mind and held the attitudes necessary for the successful translation of local business ambitions into community ideology. Above all he loved the West. His continual fascination with its development bred the conviction that the destiny of the nation would be decided in the West. Back in Ohio he had predicted that in the Mississippi Valley would "concentrate the population, wealth, and civilization of America." His later experience reinforced this view. Inviting an Ohio friend to visit him in Kansas City, Van Horn wrote that he would "be led to wonder why God . . . first offered the continent to men at its eastern portals, and so long kept the great and glorious West a *Terra Incognita* to humanity. This is the masterpiece of creation and the perfection of topography." [5]

Van Horn had an abiding interest in the technological developments that were a part of the rise of an industrial nation. Machinery fascinated him. He could describe with clarity and with great love of detail how to lay a railroad track, construct a factory, build a bridge, or operate a meat-packing plant. He accepted wholeheart-edly the view of the late nineteenth century that the destiny of the nation lay with its businessmen and builders, not its politicians. His career, accordingly, revealed startlingly frequent party shifts and changes in fundamental political positions. The journalist and western traveler, Albert Richardson, who had been an associate of Van Horn's in Ohio, was surprised to find him a pro-slavery man in 1857. A few years earlier, the two had produced a newspaper that contained in almost every issue a pungent Van Horn editorial de-nouncing the "Nebraska infamy." Van Horn's Kansas City as-sociates, however, heartily approved of this kind of political op-portunism. An 1888 sketch of his career observed that before the Civil War, Van Horn had been a Democrat, "and, as Jackson County was largely of that faith he was respected and influential at home, and able to accomplish more than if he had been of other politics." By 1865 he had become a Radical Republican, "and again he was on the side where he could do the most good for the town." [6]

Many things important to Kansas City's welfare—army and mail contracts, railroad land grants, Indian treaties—involved govern-ment policy and thereby politics. Van Horn recognized this and be-came a successful candidate for office, serving in the state legisla-ture, as mayor, and as a U. S. Representative. Essential, however, to the opportunism of town building was a negative attitude to-ward the general issues of politics, for these might produce com-munity divisions. "Congress may wrangle," he wrote in one of his frequent attempts to quiet local controversy on the issues that led to the Civil War, "intervention or non-intervention, tariff or anti-tariff may prevail; this man or that man succeed, and yet neither the success of the one nor the failure of the other will build our railroads, regulate our banks, maintain our public institutions, or protect our growing internal interests. Let who will triumph, so far as Presidents, Senators and Congressmen are concerned, the busy world will plod on and nobody look after our own affairs if we do not do it for ourselves." [7]

Van Horn could write well. The numerous pamphlets and

memorials that he was commissioned to prepare are models of research, vividness, and clarity. Although on occasion he followed the
ornate literary style of mid-century, he generally wrote in a sim-
pler and more effective manner. He regularly spent months and
sometimes even years marshalling facts and figures for articles on
the woolen industry, narrow-gauge railroads, river transportation,
and similar subjects. Especially before the Civil War, when he was
able to avoid embroilment in local politics, Van Horn devoted his
newspaper, as its name accurately indicated, to chronicling the economic progress of the city. He often seemed fanatic in his continual, vigorous insistence on the city's need for railroads and public
improvements. Although sincerely believed, much of this was only
a necessary part of his role as a semi-official city propagandist.

Van Horn had time for the good life. His editorials revealed his
love for the lavish meals, the fine whiskey, and the holiday parties
that were a part of community leadership. On one occasion, he discussed the theft of his pipe collection. With great care he described
each pipe's appearance and smoking quality. To Van Horn, the
loss of a favorite meerschaum, brought half-way around the world
by an acquaintance and burnished gold-brown through years of
careful use, was truly equivalent to the loss of a friend.

Seen through Van Horn's eyes, ante-bellum Kansas City was a
good place to live. He wrote with enthusiasm of all its diversions:
the first Santa Fe wagons coming to town in the spring; summer
circuses; Swedish bell-ringers; winter ice-skating parties; traveling
Shakespearean companies; or conversations with Mexican traders,
western explorers, and mountain men. Van Horn enjoyed it all.
Aside from his single-mindedness concerning the interests of Kansas City, his attitude toward life was relaxed and tolerant.

In his Christmas Eve speech to the assembled merchants of
Kansas City, Van Horn was the only speaker to comment at any
length on the fine dinner that Colonel Claiborne had provided. He
professed to be too full to think clearly; many of the evening's
toasts had already been drunk. But he soon came round to his subject. He admitted initially that it might seem presumptuous to

speak of Kansas City railroads when not a mile of line had yet been built. But local leaders had done something concrete; they had obtained a number of charters, and after all railroads could not be built without charters. And, more importantly, they would be built —and here he stated the view that underlay the Kansas City railroad movement—because geographical considerations dictated that they must be. The great commercial cities, New York, Chicago, St. Louis, Cincinnati, and New Orleans, had grown in accordance with fundamental commercial laws determined by geography. Kansas City would become a railroad center and a metropolis for the same reasons. "God has marked out by topography the lines of commerce," he said, "and by the ranges of mountains and courses of rivers has fixed its centers and marts—and it is by studying these great tracings of the Almighty's finger that the pioneer of trade and the herald of civilization has selected the site of those gigantic cities of the Republic, and which has fixed upon the rock-bound bay of the Missouri and Kansas as the last great seat of wealth, trade and population in the westward march of commerce toward the mountain basins of the Mississippi and Pacific. If men will only study topography the problem is solved." [8]

Van Horn granted that there would be many obstacles to overcome before Kansas City realized its destiny as the mid–continent's railroad center. In spite of these, however, lines from Kansas City would soon reach the rich agricultural produce of the Kansas Valley; the cotton, sugar, and livestock of Texas; the robes and furs of the mountains; the manufactures of the East; and the copper of the Great Lakes region. Financing the construction of these railroads would not be difficult once the world was informed. To prove his point, Van Horn considered it necessary only to cite the example of Chicago. Because of the iron-clad laws determining the location of great commercial centers, the lake city had obtained a magnificent set of railroads built almost entirely with outside capital.

In expressing the idea that Kansas City had inherent natural advantages that predetermined the building of its railroad system,

Van Horn reflected general community sentiment. His view was contained in nearly every pronouncement official or private emerging from the city in the pre-Civil War years. As early as 1855, when the town's population was only a few hundred, John Johnson, an early mayor and businessman, wrote to his son-in-law describing the prospects of the ambitious village: "It is certainly geographically one of the best positions in the whole country of *America* a perfect Chicago or St. Louis in position. . . . In railroads nothing is doing but in a year or two we shall have railroads I doubt not and nothing but railroads. This must eventually become a great railroad centre. . . ." [9]

The natural advantages of the town emphasized constantly by local leaders were real enough. The town was located on the south bank of the Missouri River, just below its great elbow where it changed its course from south-southeast to flow eastwardly across the state to St. Louis and its confluence with the Mississippi. The swift current at this point kept the river free from obstructions to steamboat navigation. The rock river-bank eliminated the danger of washouts. The city's position on the elbow placed it on the path of the only natural north-south line of communication in the area between the Mississippi River and the Rocky Mountains. Moreover, the Kansas River, after making a loop southward in its flow across Kansas, turned north and emptied into the Missouri near the elbow, just above the site of the town. The Kansas provided a natural water route westward. Furthermore, the country directly west of Kansas City was easy of passage for wagons, and contemporary prophets generally assumed that railroads would tend to follow either wagon ridge-routes or the paths of river traffic. The town's location south of both the Missouri and Kansas rivers placed it in an excellent position to serve a vast region to the west and south. [10]

More important, however, than the actual character of these natural advantages was the fact that they could provide the basis for a popular kind of argument that could win the attention of outside investors, upon whom the city's future really depended. From the first days of settlement across the Allegheny Mountains, all aspiring communities probably incorporated in their boosting, semi-official pronouncements the view that city growth could best be accounted for by natural geographic advantages. In an 1826 work that circulated widely in Europe among potential immigrants, Benjamin Drake painted an attractive picture of rapidly growing Cincinnati, with a hinterland capable of sustaining 3,000,000 people. Citing a number of natural assets that Cincinnati enjoyed, Drake concluded that "reference to its geographical features" would indicate that the city possessed "greater local advantages than any site within this region." [11]

With more obvious justification than in many places, St. Louis writers worked out the doctrine of natural advantages in great detail. Their arguments were frequently incorporated in the gazeteers and traveler's accounts of the mid-nineteenth century. The British traveler, Alexander Mackay, stated their point emphatically:

The advantageous nature of its position . . . renders St. Louis a place of very great commercial importance. It occupies as it were the central point, from which the great natural highways of the Union diverge in different directions. The different radii which spring from it bring it into contact with a vast circumference. The Missouri connects it with the Rocky Mountains, the Ohio with the Alleganies [sic], the Upper Mississippi with the Great Lakes, the lower with the ocean. It is destined soon to become the great internal *entrepôt* of the country.[12]

New Orleans, Louisville, Nashville, Chicago—all the early cities of the New West—advanced comparable arguments and claims.

This kind of geographical justification of urban ambitions continued as settlement moved westward from the Mississippi Valley. During the period of Kansas City's initial development, Albert Richardson wrote of the New Babylons springing up along the Missouri River. Each of these had beautifully lithographed maps showing magnificent city development and railroads converging from all directions. In many cases, however, not a single habitation had been built at the site. Richardson warned immigrants and investors to turn "deaf ears to plausible theorists with elaborate

maps, who prove geographically, climatically, and statistically, that
the great city *must* spring up in some new locality." In Leavenworth, Kansas, Kansas City's greatest neighboring rival, Daniel R.
Anthony, later to become a prominent politician in the state, wrote
in 1858 of his city's advantages in terms virtually the same as those
being employed in Kansas City. Leavenworth, he concluded, "can't
help what seems to be its destiny, becoming the Metropolis of
Kansas and the west." The doctrine of natural advantages was a
necessary part of the ideological equipment of town boosters
throughout the Midwest in the pre-Civil War era. Probably no-
where, however, did it receive the formalized, elaborate, and continual statement that it did in the writings and speeches of Van
Horn and the other Kansas City propagandists.[13]

In his Christmas address, Van Horn tied natural advantages to a
broader concept of geographical determinism that emphasized the
significance of the mid-continent in the future of American development. This too was old doctrine in the Midwest, and was
closely related to the emergence of distinct sectional attitudes in the
region. In an 1849 address, for example, Governor William Bebb
of Ohio predicted that within a hundred years the Atlantic slope
would have a population of only 60,000,000 while 200,000,000
million people would live in the Mississippi Valley. For numerous
reasons, he ruled out much growth for other Western cities and
concluded quite naturally, considering his residence, that Cincinnati was destined to be the great metropolis of the populous center.
The same year a St. Louis writer asserted that within the lifetime of
his readers the Mississippi Valley would contain 150,000,000 people and would completely eclipse the Eastern seaboard in importance. As part of this growth, St. Louis would become the "great
commercial emporium of the continent," the central world distributing point for the commerce of Europe and Asia. Jesup W.
Scott, a Toledo editor and a frequent contributor to such national
journals as *Hunt's Merchants' Magazine* and *De Bow's Review*,
asserted in the 1850's that cities in the Midwest would inevitably
eclipse those of the seaboard. He won considerable attention for his

reflections on the location of the new national metropolis to succeed New York. "The centre of power, numerical, political and
social," he wrote, "is . . . indubitably, on its steady march from
the Atlantic border toward the interior of the continent. That it will
find a resting place somewhere, in its broad interior plain, seems as
inevitable as the continued movement of the earth on its axis." [14]

Kansas City's claim to mid-continental destiny gained particular
attention because it accorded with the visions of two prominent
spokesmen for the interests of the West: Thomas Hart Benton and
William Gilpin. The Missouri Senator's conception of Western empire fitted well with local promotional designs. Kansas Citians directed much of their agitational effort toward the realization of his
plan for a transcontinental railroad along the thirty-ninth parallel,
central route, which would pass through or near the site of the
town. Benton predicted that "a line of oriental and almost fabulous
cities . . . Tyres, Sidons, Palmyras, Balbecs," were destined to
spring up along the route of his road. His 1853 speaking tour
along the Missouri on behalf of his plan focussed considerable attention on the "Kawsmouth region." It is a persistent but unveri-
fiable legend of Kansas City that during the course of this trip, Benton predicted that the town would become the great metropolis of
the West.[15]

Because of his years of residence near Kansas City, of even more
influence in shaping the geographic theories of local promoters
was Benton's disciple and associate, William Gilpin. A minor military hero, and a noteworthy explorer who allegedly crossed the
continental divide fifty times, Gilpin was also a thoughtful intellectual who speculated in an original fashion on the meaning of the
American experiment. Although he often wrote semi-mystical
wanderings that approach nonsense and often distorted fact that
failed to square with theory, his writings had a significant influence
in shaping nineteenth century views of the nature of the West.
He inspired a generation of spokesmen for America's manifest destiny, directly influencing Benton and probably Walt Whitman. His
widely circulated arguments on the Great Plains as a pastoral gar-

den contributed to the breakdown of the prevailing Great American Desert image. And his insights into the future, particularly his anticipation of the rise of the United States, Russia, and China as world powers, were in many ways more meaningful than those of much better known American prophets. His ideas, many of which had direct local application, lent themselves well to the aims of Kansas City promoters. Historians of Kansas City have assigned him a high position in the pantheon of local heroes—as the major prophet of the city.[16]

Born October 4, 1813, into a cultivated Quaker merchant family of Brandywine, Pennsylvania, Gilpin received a thorough, classically oriented education from private tutors at home and during family trips abroad. Perhaps reflecting his adoption in his later career of the credo of practicality of the Gilded Age businessman, his authorized subscription biography remarked that he had been "educated almost to death by the brightest intellects in the world." After graduating from the University of Pennsylvania, spending a few months at West Point, and briefly studying law in Philadelphia, he came to Missouri as a young army recruiting officer during the Second Seminole War. The West captivated him. He wrote to his sister at the time that all he had read about the region was inaccurate and distorted. Words could not indicate the great natural wealth to be exploited. "The part of the Valley which lies on the Mississippi River and *West* of it," he continued, "must one day surpass aught now existing or which has existed . . . indeed, one who has not seen the valley of the Mississippi can hardly be said to have been in America—he knows not what a *Heart* and *Sinews* she has." [17]

Gilpin's military ambitions probably contributed to the chauvinistic tenor of his later writings. He had earlier tried unsuccessfully to enlist in a revolutionary army being recruited in England to fight against the Don Carlos regime in Spain. In Missouri, he came up with the idea of raising a military expedition under his command to take Oregon, and he attempted to get support for this venture among family friends in high positions in Washington.

Disappointed by his failure, he resigned from the army and returned to St. Louis, where he assumed the editorship of the Democratic *Missouri Argus* and allied himself with Benton's political machine. After holding a variety of minor political jobs, in 1841 he moved to Independence, Missouri, one of the small trading communities on the western edge of settlement. There he edited a newspaper, practiced law, and kept up his political ties. Although Independence was to be his home until 1861, the town often served only as a base of operations. He accompanied John C. Frémont's second expedition to the West and participated in the early efforts of Oregon settlers to organize the territory. As their informal delegate, he was on the scene in Washington in 1846 as a noisy advocate of America's manifest destiny. Through his family connections, he got a hearing for his views in the administration and in Congress, but his extreme stand alienated even ardent expansionists. According to his own later recollections, critics contemptuously dismissed him as the "Squatters' Delegate"; John C. Calhoun, he said, called him the "ambitious young man who wanted to throw aside his lieutenant's uniform for senatorial robes." When one of his long letters on the West was read to the Senate, both Senators and spectators in the galleries greeted his perfervid plea for manifest destiny with derision.[18]

During the Mexican War Gilpin served as a major with Stephen Kearny's Army of the West in the conquest of New Mexico. After spending several months in 1847–1848 in command of an expedition to subdue Indians along the Santa Fe trail, he returned to Independence, renewed his interest in politics, and became a leading spokesman for Benton's transcontinental railroad plan. He took part in efforts to organize the Kansas-Nebraska territory, and prepared the text of its first provisional constitution. Abandoning his long-time Democratic allegiance, he early supported the Republican Party in Missouri. As a reward for his services, Lincoln appointed him territorial governor of Colorado in 1861. Through quick military action, he helped to save Colorado and New Mexico for the Union, but financial irregularities in the conduct of his office caused his dismissal two years later. After the war, having realized a large fortune from a profitable land speculation, he settled in Denver, where he spent the remainder of his life. His biography enthusiastically commented that having once directed his talents toward accumulating money he "found no great difficulty in making a million or two of dollars." [19]

Although his reports and letters on the Oregon question had earlier attracted some attention, Gilpin began to win real recognition for his ideas with a series of widely reprinted essays on the West in the late 1850's. These he published along with some of his speeches in *The Central Gold Region* (1860). In an obvious effort to capitalize on the interest in Colorado stimulated by the gold discoveries there in the late 1850's, Gilpin gave the book an inaccurate title. In *Mission of the North American People* (1873), he presented a slightly expanded edition of the earlier work. In his last book, *The Cosmopolitan Railway* (1890), he attempted a more formally organized piece of writing, but it, too, relied on his earlier speeches and articles. Gilpin had formulated his ideas of the West by 1846. Although he traveled widely in the region throughout the rest of his life, he seldom corrected the frequently incorrect information sustaining his theoretical conceptions. [20]

Much of Gilpin's work consisted of topographical description, but running through all his writings was a consistent thread of geographical determinism derived from the optimistic eighteenth-century belief that there is an ascertainable and benevolent order in nature. He acknowledged his indebtedness to the German geographer, Alexander von Humboldt, and supposedly carried a copy of Humboldt's *Cosmos* in his saddlebags during his frequent trips to the West. Gilpin accepted the Humboldt thesis that nature controlled the development of society. He also adopted Humboldt's concept of the Isothermal Zodiac, an undulating belt of land approximately thirty-three degrees wide encircling the earth across the Northern Hemisphere. Through this zone, according to the theory, passed the Axis of Intensity, a line not straight but running approximately along the fortieth parallel where the mean temperature was fifty-two degrees. Within this region and there alone, Gilpin asserted, the civilizations of the world had flourished. Upon the Axis of Intensity had pressed the migratory movements of the human masses. Here men had constructed the world's primary cities, the "foci from which have radiated intellectual activity and power." His *Cosmopolitan Railway* presented an elaborate argument for a world railroad whose main branch would be built along the Axis of Intensity.[21]

Gilpin further asserted that North America was a vast bowl that focussed all forces to the center and led to a harmonious pattern of social development. The continent was a "symmetrical and sublime" geographic unit, the Mississippi Valley its dominant center. In words that recalled his earlier letters to his family, he declared in *The Central Gold Region* that the "Great Basin of the Mississippi is the ampitheatre of the world—here is supremely, indeed, the most magnificent dwelling marked out by God for man's abode." [22]

In contrast, the geography of Europe and to a lesser extent that of Africa and Asia was inherently divisive. This accounted for the conflicts that had plagued mankind in these regions. Such was not the case in North America; fundamental physical facts destined the success of the American experiment. "Our North America will rapidly attain," he wrote, "to a population equalling that of the rest of the world combined; forming a single people, identical in manners, language, customs, and impulses; preserving the same religion; imbued with the same opinions and having the same political liberties." [23] Throughout his works, Gilpin used these conceptions to formulate a weird but often impressive appeal for American expansion and a chauvinistic assertion of the rights of the West against the Eastern seaboard.

During the twentieth century, Gilpin, always a verbose and at times a chaotic writer, fell into obscurity. Lacking accurate information about many phases of his life, scholars who have revived interest in his ideas have to some extent misinterpreted his place in American thought. Considering Gilpin largely from his published works, they have tended to portray him as a mystical, eccentric prophet who speculated originally and dispassionately on the West and its relationship to the American and world future. Actually, though he set his views within a more elaborate theoretical framework, many of his themes were contained in the promotional writing that Western sectional and city boosters had been turning out for years. Moreover, Gilpin's practical concerns unquestionably influenced the development of his theories about the West. In many ways, he represented a promoter-intellectual type who played a leading role in the development of many Western cities. His activities in the Kansas City region clearly demonstrated the close relationship between practical promotion and exuberant prophecy.

During this period, as a political supporter of Benton, Gilpin spent much of his time developing the geographic rationale for the central route. In a series of speeches, pamphlets, and memoranda, dating from the late 1840's, he fitted the Benton proposal to mid-continental conceptions. He asserted that the route through central Missouri, passing through Independence and Kansas City, running along the Kansas River, and crossing the Rocky Mountains at South Pass conformed to the natural grades between the two oceans. It was "exactly central," thereby vindicating and exemplifying the "sublime order and fitness of nature." [24]

From the beginning of his residency in the area, Gilpin took part in town-promoting ventures in the Kawsmouth region. As a lawyer he represented the two St. Louis members of the Kansas City town-company and managed the settlement of its tangled affairs in the courts. In the 1840's he purchased a parcel of land just north of Independence along the Missouri in an area that came to be called Gilpintown. Through his persuasion, the Independence city council extended the limits of the city around his settlement. He organized a company to develop the addition, had a road built from Independence to the river, and hired an engineer to plat the area into town lots. [25]

As part of this venture, Gilpin prepared an elaborate map of "Centropolis" to circulate to potential investors. Although no copies of this map are known to have survived, it apparently showed the national capitol and national observatory located in the heart of Gilpintown, which served as the nucleus of a magnificent city embracing an area of over a hundred square miles. Gilpin went East to try to obtain financing for the ambitious project but was unsuccessful and delayed returning. Other members of the town-company sued and obtained a judgment against him. He eventually met his obligations, but the project failed completely and was the subject of considerable derision in the region. Temporary misfortune, however, seldom discouraged urban prophets. Asserting that he had merely put the site of the great central city ten miles too far east, in 1858 Gilpin prepared a second map of "Centropolis," which corresponded rather accurately to the present area of greater Kansas City.[26]

As part of these promotional ventures, Gilpin in 1853 had developed an explicit theory of city growth to justify Independence's claim to urban greatness. Independence, he asserted, was destined to become a magnificent metropolis because of its key location on the zodiac of the westward movement. Throughout history man had erected the world's cities along great navigable rivers—the Ganges, Nile, or Danube—which ran through broad fertile basins. By carefully selecting his examples, Gilpin attempted to demonstrate that the law locating emporiums a hundred leagues apart had operated along the rivers of North America. A slight inspection of a map of the river system of the world, such as Humboldt had prepared, would immediately draw the eye, he wrote, to the portion of the Missouri River running east from the mouth of the Kansas to St. Louis. Independence, because of its location at the western end of this natural throughway, would become the next great American emporium. St. Louis and Independence stood out on the continent "like eyes in the human head." The mere works of man could not alter the rise of Independence to metropolis. "The peculiar configuration of the continent, and its rivers and plains," he asserted, "make these *two* natural *focal* points. This will not be interfered with by any railroads or any other public works which may be constructed by arts, as these latter are successful and permanent *only* when they conform with the water grades of nature and the natural laws which condense society." [27]

In this article Gilpin developed the logic of a railroad from Independence to Galveston and the Gulf of Mexico. Prophets who speculated on city location in the West or on the future of the region generally included a great north-south railroad as part of their designs. Assuming that railroads would always be bound by geographic rules, they argued that such a line would be of vital importance because it conformed to natural physical channels of trade and communication. Furthermore, a railroad to the Gulf—and this view persisted into the latter part of the century—would enable the West to escape the exploitation of the East. As part of this essay in town-booming, Gilpin expounded the other themes that he repeated over and over again in his later writings: the rise of the Mississippi Valley to dominance in the nation; the federal government as an agent of the coastal, maritime power suppressing the interests of the West; and the Great Plains as pastoral garden not desert.

Gilpin's most famous prophecy concerning city location can be found in his *Mission of the North American People*. "As the *site* for the central city of the 'Basin of the Mississippi' to arise prospectively upon the developments now maturing this city, Kansas City, at the mouth of Kansas, has the start, the geographical position, and the existing elements with which any rival will contend in vain." All the developments affecting the West focused at this point—the settlement of the pastoral garden, the gold discoveries in the Rocky Mountains, and the transcontinental railroad. "There must be a great city here," he concluded, "such as antiquity built at the head of the Mediterranean and named Jerusaleum, Tyre, Alexandria, and Constantinople; such as our own people name New York, New Orleans, San Francisco, St. Louis." [28]

The evolution of this prophecy demonstrated the essential opportunism of appeals to nature in Western town-booming. In its initial version, as published in an article in the *National Intelligencer*, Gilpin obviously intended it to apply to Independence. He left "this city" unnamed in the text but submitted the article under an Independence dateline. When he included the article in *The Central Gold Region* three years later, he identified "this city" as "Kansas City, at the mouth of the Kansas," by an asterisked footnote. In *Mission of the North American People*, the identifying phrase finally found its way into the text. As in the case of "Centropolis," reality forced Gilpin to move his great central city westward, for by the late 1850's Kansas City had clearly eclipsed Independence as a potential site for a major regional city.[29]

Although Gilpin apparently had no close personal or economic ties to the inner circle of business leaders in Kansas City, he spoke frequently in the city. His ideas were thoroughly familiar to the leading spokesmen of the community, and they used them freely. Their polemics permitted no doubt that all railroads would have to converge on the geographic focal point of the mid-continent, the juncture of the Missouri and Kansas rivers. In his able boosting volume, *Annals of the City of Kansas*, Spalding directly acknowledged his indebtedness to Gilpin, "the master scholar of Interior Geography," and for the major portion of the first chapter of his book condensed Gilpin's famous article on the Great Plains as pastoral garden. Spalding argued that railroads had to be the paramount interest of the young community if it was to realize its continental destiny. Hard work and entrepreneurial aggressiveness would be necessary to bring them to Kansas City. But he left no doubt that geographical considerations would in the long run prove decisive in making the city the commercial center of a vast Western empire. It would then have a system of railroads more elaborate than that of Chicago. Kansas City enjoyed unparalleled natural advantages of soil, climate and rivers that came "stamped with the patent of the creator." Following Gilpin, he argued that nature created great cities approximately 350 miles apart. Because of its strategic location, Kansas City would be the next American metropolis. It was "her destiny," Spalding wrote, to become "the extreme western and central emporium of mountain, prairie and river commerce." [30]

During the winter of 1855–1856, while railroads were hardly past the projection stage from the Mississippi River, a prominent town builder and businessman translated the Gilpin vision into a master plan for western railroads radiating from Kansas City. This man was Johnston Lykins, next to Van Horn the most prominent of the early Kansas City railroad advocates. First president of the Chamber of Commerce, president of the Mechanics' Bank, commission merchant, real-estate developer, Dr. Lykins by the mid-fifties was eminently a man of affairs. But like many Western businessmen, he had spent a large part of his career in very different pursuits and had come to be a town-builder in somewhat accidental fashion. Born in Virginia on April 19, 1800, he had grown up in Indiana, where as a young man he had raised cattle and then taught school. In June of 1822 he was converted to the Baptist Church and decided on a career as an Indian missionary. He completed a medical education at Transylvania College, and in 1831, as regional director of Baptist missionary activities, located with a missionary group a short distance from the mouth of the Kansas River.[31]

At first this religious career fully occupied him. He established several missions among the Shawnee Indians, supplied the tribes with a written alphabet so that they could read his translations of the Bible and other religious material, and even edited a newspaper in Indian dialect. Lykins gradually shifted his interest from philanthropic to business pursuits. He was soon involved in a conflict with G. W. and W. G. Ewing, leading Westport Indian traders, who regarded him as an "old rascal" and a "hypocrite" more interested in promoting the fortunes of himself and his son than the welfare of the Indians. From a French settler he purchased sixteen acres of land near the landing at the future site of Kansas City, which years later became Lykins and Lykins Place additions to Kansas City. Because of this holding he was drawn into the business affairs of the young town so completely that he ultimately abandoned his missionary activity. His intellectual equipment made him an able town propagandist. A student of geography and geology, Lykins, like Gilpin, was considered an authority on the nature and resources of the West. Because of his regional reputation, local leaders usually picked him to head their promotional enterprises.[32]

Lykins presented his plan for a regional system of railroads in a series of letters to Van Horn's *Enterprise,* the predecessor of the *Western Journal.* Van Horn reprinted these as a pamphlet along with his own editorials commenting on the letters. In his first article describing a railroad to run from Kansas City up the Kansas Valley to Fort Riley, Lykins supplied a theory of economic history that could well have been taken directly from either Benton or Gilpin. "Commerce," he wrote, "like the star of empire wends its way to the West; and commerce creates at given distances commercial centers." The location of great American cities—New York, Baltimore, Pittsburgh, Cincinnati, Chicago, and St. Louis—provided evidence that the laws of progress always created major emporiums three or four hundred miles apart. The stage of continental development dictated the appearance of a new one: the logic of geography—of river courses and distances—pointed clearly to Kansas City. Because of its location midway between the Mississippi delta and the source of the Missouri River, Kansas City would become the "great barter city for the central continent." All railroads would inevitably have to converge there. Turning to his specific proposal, Lykins argued that the Kansas Valley railroad would be a vital part of the Kansas City system. It would provide the natural extension of the Pacific Railroad of Missouri and would reach one of the most fertile regions of the West, capable of sustaining a dense population. It would bring to Kansas City, salt, minerals, and an enormous surplus of grain to be sent to foreign markets.[33]

Lykins' second letter dealt with the Great Pacific Road. The Pacific Railroad of Missouri, which was then being built west from St. Louis, would soon reach Kansas City, he said, and would in a short time be extended onto the beautiful prairies of the West, the "modern Egypt." Writers trying to destroy the Great American Desert assertion frequently employed this kind of image: Benton had spoken of Kansas as "rich like Egypt" and Gilpin's pastoral garden concept was an enlargement of the idea. The Pacific road would connect two vast oceans, Lykins went on, and would pour into Kansas City the production of half a world, seeking exchange there with the regional staples of grain, hemp, cotton, tobacco, and meats. Two years later, Lykins was even more expansive in again commenting on the Pacific road. The discovery of gold in Colorado and the consequent settlement of the mountain region would make "Kansas City the San Francisco of the Eastern slope of the mountains, to the wealth of which both Asia and Europe will contribute, making it the great dispenser of both gold and grain to these nations." [34]

Second only to the Pacific Road, in Lykins' view, was a railroad to Galveston. His design projected a road down the Osage and Neosho river valleys. The line would pass first through a region of extensive coal and lead deposits; would next reach the cotton, sugar, and rice-growing areas of the South; and then would be extended to the Gulf of Mexico. Once this road was completed, goods requiring twenty days to reach the city by water could be received in forty-eight hours. And as the area to the west and northwest was settled, these products would be in enormous demand. The construction of this railroad, Lykins concluded, would be "the crowning glory of our great city, and stamp upon it the indelible impression of greatness—the grand emporium of the West."

The fourth of Lykins' proposals envisaged a road to the north eventually to reach the Great Lakes, uniting at Kansas City with the line to Galveston Bay. He asserted that the road would provide an easy access to Eastern markets for the Kansas Valley and northwestern Missouri, areas of unsurpassed fertility. The filling of the region through which the road passed with agricultural emigrants would make Kansas City the emporium of from eight to ten states, each of them wealthier than Ohio or Illinois. In summarizing his proposals, Lykins admitted that the design was ambitious. Nevertheless, it was bound to be realized, for the laws of nature determined that Kansas City was to be a great metropolis. The trade of sixteen hundred miles converging on the city would complete its destiny. "No other city," he concluded, "has such a background—no other such promise of magnificent greatness." [35]

A year later, when the prewar Kansas City railroad boom was well under way, Lykins moved even closer to the tones of Gilpin and Benton in writing about a Galveston to Great Lakes road. The road, he wrote, "in its extent, in the fertility of the country through which it passes transcends anything of the kind to be found in the known world." Contemplating the future of the mid-continent, he conjured up the line of magic cities, so common in geographical prophecies of the period. "Cities at some day," he declared in a flight of visionary rhetoric, "greater than Babylon, Nineveh, or Thebes will tower above its green hills and become the wonder and glory of the world;—when the passage from Galveston to Lake Superior will be as through an enchanted Eden." [36]

In commenting on the original Lykins' series, Robert T. Van Horn got out maps, ruler, and pencil and gave his readers one of their many lessons in mid-continental geography. A great commercial city, he argued, by iron-clad laws of nature had to develop somewhere within three or four hundred miles of St. Louis. A line drawn from Fort Riley, Kansas, which he assumed would be a point on the transcontinental railroad, to Baltimore, Maryland, which he picked as a mid–point between North and South on the Atlantic coast would nearly cut Kansas City, St. Louis, Cincinnati, and five other cities varying but a few miles from the same parallel of latitude. Van Horn's selection of Baltimore was significant; both Gilpin and Benton had considered it the key city on the seaboard. Any railroads built, Van Horn asserted, would tend to follow productive river valleys and would hew as closely to straight lines as possible. The line that he had drawn, because of its central position, would become the great central trunk crossing of North America, along which would pass the trade of Europe and Asia. Then Kansas City, astride this central trunk and with railroads running to the Great Lakes and to the Gulf of Mexico, would begin to complete its destiny as the great metropolis of the mid-continent. [37]

Van Horn was continually bemused by Kansas City's strategic location. In an 1858 editorial he told his readers to take a map, sketch in the railroads proposed by the Kansas City promoters, and look at the completed roads of the country. They would then observe a vital fact: all railroads, in spite of the rival interests and competing forces involved in their location, pointed "with the certainty of the magnetic needle" in the direction of the mouth of the Kansas River.[38]

Doctrines of strategic location, natural advantages, and mid-continental destiny won wide endorsement in Kansas City. Letters to editors and public addresses echoed the arguments of Lykins, Spalding, and Van Horn. But this general acceptance was a mixed blessing. Acceptance contributed to community unity, but the pre-deterministic aspects of these doctrines could encourage an unwholesome community complacency. Their presentation, therefore, had to be qualified with the reservation that to realize the benefits of nature, initiative was still vital. Van Horn in 1860 summed up his four years of experience in using these boosters' tools. From his first days of knowledge of the West, he said that he had known that there could be but one grand commercial emporium in the Missouri Valley. He had recognized that Kansas City was destined to be that point; he had continually asserted this as fixed fact. But the people of the city had acquired such an abiding faith in their natural advantages that they had failed to recognize that these might be overcome through the money and enterprise of rivals. Had the citizens of Kansas City not aroused themselves from this lethargy and "put their shoulders to the wheel" in the nick of time they would have found that their natural advantages were "just so many monumental mockeries of their folly." [39]

Mayor G. M. B. Maughs expressed similar sentiments in addressing the City Council in 1860. Although Kansas City's natural advantages were greater than those of any city in the Missouri Valley, he emphasized that they were not completely self-generating. On the contrary, they merely provided a stimulus to human effort to obtain the improvements so important to the growth of the city. On another occasion, Van Horn bluntly stated that he approved wholeheartedly a "remark made by one of our most prominent citizens that 'the man who first used the expression 'natural advantages' ought to have been hung.' " [40]

In the years 1855–1860, the prophets of railroad progress did not really direct their argument toward the community itself. Their primary aim had to be the attraction of attention outside the city in the hope of stimulating investments of capital. The view that the city in obtaining railroads was only carrying out a compact with destiny was a forceful one. The promoters hoped that men of power could be made to believe it. Although geographic arguments were generally a part of Midwestern community ideologies in the ante-bellum period, Van Horn and his fellow propagandists gave them particularly systematic and frequent statement. In so doing, they gained recognition for the myth of Kansas City's geographic destiny. This myth proved serviceable. It helped to bring railroads to Kansas City, and this in turn affected the pattern of the nation's eventual railroad network. Even though it may have been totally illusory, it was so zealously advocated that men came to accept and to act on it.

A Town And Its Railroad Plans

I NSPIRED by doctrines of mid-continental destiny, Kansas City
prophets prepared elaborate maps, wrote memorials, talked of
isothermal zones, and dreamed of their city's greatness. But they
knew that realization of their vision of metropolis lay far in the
future; for the present it could serve to sustain prosaic objectives.
The Kansas City railroad boom, which started in the mid-eighteen-
fifties and continued virtually unabated down to the Civil War, developed in relation to plans being made elsewhere for a state and
regional system of railroads. It was one thing for local promoters to
project roads in every direction; it was quite another to build them.
Construction of even the shortest connections with major lines
required large amounts of capital, and this capital was never available in the city. The fundamental problem of local promoters was
to persuade outside investors to project contemplated lines to Kansas City. Their first efforts centered on the railroads being built in
Missouri from points on the Mississippi River.

Shortly before the panic of 1837, Missouri had undergone a minor railroad boom. The legislature chartered eighteen projects designed to connect interior areas with the routes of river travel. Be-

cause of the subsequent depression and the unwillingness of the state to extend aid, none of these was ever built. During the late forties and early fifties, Missouri capitalists planned a system of trunk lines converging on St. Louis. These were intended to open new economic hinterlands in Missouri to the state's commercial metropolis. From the beginning of the era of railroads, St. Louis businessmen had been interested in the lines building westward and had assumed that the city would become the terminus of the principal railroads from Boston, New York, Philadelphia, and Baltimore. This belief rested on the doctrine of natural advantages: laws of geography and commerce dictated that great cities developed at vital points along major rivers; St. Louis occupied the strategic position of the continent at the heart of the Mississippi Valley; since natural forces would determine railroad routes, all main lines would inevitably come to St. Louis. The belief was false. The rapid rise of Chicago demonstrated that railroads did not have to follow the lines of trade marked out by the national system of rivers. As early as 1851, Chicago had already surpassed St. Louis in many items of trade. By the time St. Louis leaders began to recognize the economic significance of the developing Eastern railroad pattern, a large share of the city's commerce had been permanently lost to Chicago.[1]

St. Louis' preoccupation with a transcontinental railroad also hampered the city's attempts to gain eastern connections. Reflecting the view that the future of St. Louis lay in its continuing to be the metropolis of a vast Western empire, local spokesmen emphasized the necessity of building a line to the West Coast from the city. A number of developments—the acquisition of Oregon in 1846, the Mexican cession in 1848, the gold discoveries of 1849—contributed to the popular demand that the federal government assist in the building of a transcontinental line. Support developed for three principal routes: (1) the northern route to connect Lake Michigan with Puget Sound; (2) the southern route from Memphis to San Diego; (3) the central route, sponsored by Thomas Hart Benton, to join St. Louis and San Francisco. Despite efforts to harmonize the variety of conflicting local and sectional interests represented in these proposals, controversy continued into the 1850's. In 1853, Congress authorized the War Department to survey five possible routes; the reports from this undertaking released two years later made a strong case for the practicality and comparative inexpensiveness of a thirty-second parallel, southern route. In part, it was fear of the possible adoption of a southern route, which would curtail Missouri's rich trade with the Southwest, that led to the flurry of railroad activity in the state in the early 1850's. Although for years the majority of Congress favored some type of federal support for the transcontinental project, intensification of the north-south sectional controversy prevented any further Congressional action before the Civil War.[2]

The state project of first importance to Kansas City, the Pacific Railroad of Missouri, bore a close relationship to plans for a transcontinental railroad. The name of the company reflected its origins. Organized by a group of St. Louis capitalists who received a charter from the Missouri legislature on March 12, 1849, the railroad was intended to supply a vital first link in a road to the Far West. Many communities during this period laid plans for western railroads in the hope that the prize of Congressional support would go to the first project that succeeded in constructing a line some distance out onto the plains. The Pacific's charter authorized a route from St. Louis to the western border of Missouri at some point in Van Buren (now Cass) County and advanced the optimistic expectation "that the same may be hereafter continued westwardly to the Pacific Ocean." The *American Railroad Journal* viewed the chartering of the Pacific as the most important step taken up to that time in relation to a transcontinental railroad.[3]

Although the Pacific succeeded in gaining considerable support from St. Louis businessmen, it soon became clear that private capital would not be sufficient to finance the building of the road. As in most sections of the West, investment capital was scarce in Missouri; local investors put their funds into established lines of enterprise, not into anything as speculative as railroads. The Pacific appealed successfully to St. Louis city and county authorities for governmental subscriptions to the capital stock of the company, and, on February 22, 1851, the Missouri legislature authorized state assistance. With security to be provided by a first lien on the assets of the road, the state was to loan $2,000,000 in bonds to the company to be issued as construction progressed. This law served to initiate a monumental program of state loans to railroads that by 1860 had pledged Missouri's credit to the sum of $23,701,000.[4]

Despite outpourings of publicity concerning the progress and prospects of the railroad, actual construction was tortuously slow. In 1852 the state granted the company the loan of another $1,000,-000 in bonds, but completion of the first segment of the road extending thirty-seven miles to the town of Pacific exhausted the resources of the company. Although this section opened for business on July 25, 1853, it was obvious that more state and local aid would have to be forthcoming if the work was to continue. Through the years down to the Civil War, construction moved fitfully. By 1861, twelve years after the chartering of the company, only 181 miles of the line was in operation, and it was still 93 miles from the western border of Missouri.[5]

The road faced a number of problems. People living along the route offered to buy large amounts of stock but subsequently failed to honor their pledges. The officers of the company were unable to attract outside capital; Eastern moneyed interests had already invested heavily in Chicago railroads and were not disposed to put their money into competing lines. Although the Pacific's charter placed virtually no restriction on the company's solicitation of subscriptions from counties, municipalities, and townships, the bonds provided to pay these subscriptions could only be sold at a large discount, owing to Missouri's poor financial standing in the Eastern market.[6]

The dismal record of the Pacific before the Civil War affected the character of the Kansas City railroad movement. Promises made and broken, optimistic forecasts that went unrealized, years of impatient waiting all contributed to the intensity with which the community sought alternative railroad connections. The ill feeling engendered by the company through its vacillation and poor management before the war persisted for many years after the railroad finally reached the city.

The second major state project of importance to Kansas City, the Hannibal and St. Joseph Railroad, was also initially conceived of as a possible first link in a transcontinental railroad. The charter of the railroad, granted on February 16, 1847, authorized the construction of a line between the Mississippi and Missouri rivers connecting the two named cities, a route that passed through the most fertile part of the state. Under the leadership of Robert M. Stewart of St. Joseph, who later became Governor of Missouri, the company was efficiently run. In February, 1851 the state loaned the railroad $1,500,000 in bonds under the same terms as in the grant to the Pacific. The next year the railroad received 611,323 acres of public land as its portion of a Congressional grant to Missouri to aid in the building of roads across the state. The company attracted the interest of John Murray Forbes and a group of New England capitalists, who had already invested heavily in the Michigan Central and Illinois Central railroads. After 1855 these investors controlled the Hannibal and St. Jo.; the company obtained another loan of $1,500,000 in state bonds; and the road was placed on a sound financial footing. Forbes insisted that profits should come from the earnings of a completed road, and construction proceeded on a scale commensurate with capital invested. For this reason, and because the land grant, which contained some of the best farm land in Missouri, proved particularly profitable, the Hannibal and St. Jo. became the most prosperous railroad company in the state. The line was completed and opened for business in February, 1859.[7]

Clinging to the notion that trade patterns would be determined by the paths of river commerce, the original Missouri investors in the Hannibal and St. Jo. had assumed that the railroad, like the other contemplated trunk lines, would benefit St. Louis by bringing the rich trade of northern Missouri to the great central highway, the Mississippi River. Instead the railroad became for all practical purposes an extension of the Chicago, Burlington, and Quincy Railroad, run by the same financial interests who were trying to divert trade to Chicago from its river passage to St. Louis.[8]

Although Kansas City leaders had shown interest in the state-supported building program from the early fifties, not until 1855 did the local boom really get under way. That year the foundering Pacific petitioned the state for further assistance, and the legislature voted over the governor's veto to loan an additional $2,000,000 in bonds to complete the line between Jefferson City and the western border. At this time, the route to be followed west of Jefferson City was still uncertain. The laws providing aid had specified only that the road terminate somewhere in Jackson County. However, Kansas City, which was located at the northwestern edge of the county, had been considered a likely terminus, since it was rapidly becoming the headquarters for much of the Southwestern trade. Local leaders hailed the passage of the aid bill with great enthusiasm. "Clear the Track . . . Look Out for the Locomotive," headlined Robert Van Horn's *Enterprise* on December 15, 1855. "Bring out the big guns! Hats off! One thousand cheers for the People's Representatives, the Railroad, and the City of Kansas." [9]

A committee of Kansas Citians visited Pacific officials in St. Louis to urge that Kansas City be definitely fixed as the western terminus. Company officers told them, however, that steamboats could handle freight for much less than railroads. Therefore, it might well be necessary for the railroad to build through the interior, away from the Missouri River towns, in order to avoid steamboat competition.[10]

The unwillingness of the Pacific to decide on its terminus set off the Kansas City railroad boom. Down to the Civil War, city leaders organized, abandoned, and revived—in sometimes bewildering succession—a multitude of railroad companies whose only assets were their charters. In a state seeking to encourage the growth of business enterprise, it was an easy matter to obtain a charter from the legislature, which until the adoption of a new constitution in 1865 could grant charters of incorporation by special act. The many local companies organized had little of the importance assigned to them in the city at the time. Kansas City leaders used them not to build railroads but to advance promotional ends.

From the beginning, local businessmen recognized that Kansas City, a town of a few thousand, did not have the resources to finance railroads itself or to control the pattern of a state or regional network of railroads. The paper railroad company provided a device to advertise the city and possibly to attract outside support. If investors or railroad officials could be interested in one of the paper companies, then the local promoters could set out to raise governmental bond issues to the company. The state placed little restriction on railroad companies in soliciting city and county subscriptions. The possibility of a substantial subscription might provide an inducement to make a local line part of a larger railroad plan.

Out of the array of local railroad projects organized in the period 1855–1860 emerged the design of a practical community policy. First, local leaders recognized that an eastern connection was essential to realize their aspirations and two eastern connections, which would reach alternative markets, highly desirable. Their initial efforts centered on an attempt to persuade the Pacific Railroad of Missouri to make Kansas City its terminus and to get the road completed as quickly as possible. If this failed, it was vital for the city's prospects that a connection be obtained to the Hannibal and St. Jo., some forty-odd miles to the north. At first, local leaders considered this proposition only as an alternative. Once the Pacific decided on Kansas City as its western terminus, they recognized that the northern line offered an attractive additional connection, which would open the city to Chicago, St. Louis' great trade rival. As another goal, they sought through constant agitation to ensure that Kansas City would be a point on any transcontinental railroad to the west. Finally, they projected a number of roads in different directions that would, if built, open new hinterlands to the town and ensure the continuance of trade patterns already established. An elaborate set of paper roads could also be used to reinforce their central promotional theme of Kansas City's mid-continental destiny.

Although the community had no capital with which to build railroads, it did have certain assets important to the accomplishment of its objectives. It had able propagandists who presented a reasonable argument that accorded with prevailing conceptions: strategic location and natural advantages. Of course, railroads did not have to build along established lines of river or wagon trade; eventually it was conclusively demonstrated that railroads could create cities anywhere. But at the time, the arguments of geographical determinists were still accepted and were still reasonably persuasive. St. Louis' experience in this period demonstrated that arguments derived from doctrines of natural advantages could have a significant effect on a city's railroad policies.

Moreover, Kansas City was an economically unified community. A coterie of about twenty leaders, who themselves were entirely united on the question of obtaining railroads, made the decisions for the town. Nearly every bond issue or any other measure concerning railroads that they proposed received overwhelming approval at the polls. In contrast, other communities in the region faced the problem of internal economic divisions over railroads. Much larger St. Joseph, located to the north of Kansas City, had the first railroad connection with the east through the Hannibal and St. Jo., and before the Civil War seemed a likely site for a Missouri Valley metropolis. But this earlier settled town had developed influential groups opposed to the coming of railroads because their profits were closely tied to the wagon trade. Cattle dealers and pork packers, who sold cattle and meat to overland emigrants and western traders, fought the coming of railroads, for they feared that railroads would bring cheap Texas cattle and the products of eastern packers into their market. They had sufficient power to check many aspects of the St. Joseph railroad program. Another of Kansas City's rivals, Independence, the seat of Jackson County, had also developed significant interest groups, such as wagon makers, who opposed any local support for railroad projects.[11]

The lack of opposition to railroad proposals in Kansas City reflected fundamental differences in the stages of economic development of the river communities. Merchants and real-estate speculators, the same groups who pushed railroad programs elsewhere, organized and led the Kansas City railroad movement. But largely owing to the fact that Kansas City was a newer town than either Independence or St. Joseph, Kansas City promoters did not encounter resistance from well-established, specialized economic interests. Not until after the Kansas-Nebraska Act did an organized program of community action coalesce in Kansas City. By this time the opportunities in an essentially "urban enterprise"—the creation of a city that would serve an immediate trade hinterland and that would offer large profits in real-estate, banking, and other essentially urban economic functions—appeared so great that a narrow concern with particular aspects of the river-overland trade by members of the Kansas City business community was unlikely.

There were commission and warehousemen who for years had been using Kansas City as their base for western trading operations. These men had reason to oppose railroads, for they made their profits in the transhipment, storage, and handling of wagon-trade goods, especially to and from the Far Southwest and the northern Mexican provinces. This caravan business, still known generally as the Santa Fe trade, constituted a vital element in Kansas City's economy before the war. Many of the leading commission men found their businesses ruined with the coming of railroads. Still, in the prewar period, they supported the policy of extending full support to local railroad projects.

Economic reasons partly accounted for this seeming stand against self-interest. Members of the Kansas City business community who were primarily western traders—such as the William Miles Chick family, Hiram M. Northrup, and Charles E. Kearney—generally held extensive and diversified western investments. At an early date, they had acquired land at or near the Kansas City site or else purchased property there when the town began to show signs of growth. If railroads came to Kansas City, they stood to gain more from the rise in value of real-estate holdings than they stood to lose from the destruction of the riverboat-wagon trade. By the time of the Civil War, many of the early Kansas City commission men had sold their stores and warehouses in order to devote full effort to local real-estate development.[12]

Moreover, local propagandists carefully shaped their geographic appeals to overcome possible resistance from those with heavy investments in the existing western trade. Ordinarily, people such as Van Horn, Lykins, and Spalding took their text from Gilpin: the region to the west was the pastoral garden, the New Eden. The assertion that the plains would rapidly fill with settlers was an essential part of the argument that Kansas City was destined to become a great mid-continental metropolis. Nevertheless, in trying to quiet the fears of western traders, they took the opposite tack and incorporated desert conceptions in their polemics. A *Western Journal* editorial of 1860, for example, asserted that the existing business arrangements in the Southwestern trade would not be disturbed by the building of railroads. Because of the character of the country between the western limits of civilization and New Mexico, only one railroad would ever be built onto the plains. The country between, "eight hundred miles of waste," could not justify competing lines. The railroad would follow the best and shortest route: the Santa Fe trail from Kansas City to New Mexico. These "facts," the writer said, proved "that Kansas City can and *will* always retain the trade of New Mexico, no matter whether it comes all the way by wagon, or comes part of the way by railroad." Good propagandist that he was, Van Horn was seldom bothered by a regard for consistency where he thought the future of the community at stake. Because of the amorphous nature of prevailing ideas of the nature of the West, this kind of reversal probably did not appear as striking as it might have at another time, for during this period readers of newspapers and magazines were constantly exposed to elaborate arguments on both sides of the question.[13]

An unusual degree of political unity in the community constituted another of Kansas City's advantages in realizing local promotional plans. The town was located in an area of Missouri, where because of the concentration on hemp and tobacco culture, the percentage of slaves in the population was substantially higher than in the state as a whole. Kansas City leaders in the 1850's came from the South; of thirty-nine pre-Civil War businessmen who were at least prominent enough to have left records, thirty-one came from below the Ohio River. Slaves represented a substantial part of local property holdings; culturally, Kansas City was a Southern city. In national and state elections, it consistently returned an overwhelming Democratic vote. More fundamental than these considerations, however, was the fact that community leaders almost to a man developed the view that partisan politics was a luxury they could not afford, that concern with the ordinary issues of politics was a disruptive force that could only interfere with the orderly growth of a city.

The attitude had its origins in the town's experiences during the fighting between free and slave-state settlers in Kansas Territory after the passage of the Kansas-Nebraska Act. The Border Troubles almost paralyzed business activity in Kansas City during periods in 1856 and 1857. Diversion of trade to the better protected Kansas town of Leavenworth, a few miles up the Missouri River, constituted a real threat to the plans of the local promoters. Some prominent Kansas Citians joined proslavery bands on raids into the territory, and on the whole the community sympathized with their cause. But the town leaders, because of the threat to local business, soon came to stand determinedly for the protection of property and lines of trade and to express themselves publicly in terms of a moderate, law-and-order approach to the events in Kansas. In neighboring Missouri towns, such as Independence and Westport, secret societies organized and outfitted companies of Border Ruffians. The business leaders of Kansas City organized armed groups to stand guard over incoming merchandise and to protect free-state migrants who might pass through the city. An Osawatomie settler, writing during the winter of 1856, got to the heart of the matter in explaining why conditions there would soon improve. "The merchants of Kansas City are very tired of the past state of things," he wrote to his father, "and will do what they can undoubtedly for quiet. They were getting a great trade from the Territory but war of course cut it off." Milton J. Payne, mayor of Kansas City, summed up the neutralist official view of the business community when he told the Howard Congressional Committee investigating the events in Kansas that in his "reasoning" concerning the Border Troubles "two wrongs make a right. . . ." [14]

During the subsequent years as the nation drifted toward the Civil War, the character of national events intensified the local conviction that politics was dangerous. The Border Troubles had demonstrated conclusively, the leaders argued, that politicians in their concern with ideological principles could set off conflicts that would interfere with business and the task of city building. It might well happen again. In almost every issue of his newspaper, Van Horn warned his readers of the evils of partisan politics. Charles Spalding in his *Annals* expressed similar feelings in the starkest terms. Conditions along the border, he wrote, might still overthrow rapid commercial and agricultural growth in the region. But he professed to be optimistic, for "the great idea of progress and money making so peculiarly characteristic of the American mind" was causing people to lose interest in the activities of politicians. Soon, he said, commerce, farming, railroad building, and stock raising would occupy the thoughts and labors of the people. Then, fortunately, political negotiations would be looked upon "as a matter of profit and convenience only on the part of those engaged in such negotiations." [15]

Owing to the success of Kansas City leaders in imposing this moratorium on politics, local elections aroused little controversy. Never did railroad questions or any of the economic policies of the business community become issues in city campaigns. The members of the City Council were selected almost by consensus of the business leadership and were chosen from its ranks. Government functioned informally: policy was made in the Chamber of Commerce, through the columns of Van Horn's newspaper, or at meetings of the business leaders. Carefully controlled public meetings gave popular approval to these programs, and the City Council quickly and almost automatically ratified the decisions that had really already been made.

In contrast, political factionalism plagued neighboring Leavenworth, which emerged in the late 1850's as Kansas City's most formidable urban rival. Proslavery settlers from across the Missouri
River in Weston, Missouri, had founded Leavenworth in 1854 as a
base for slave-state operations. As time went on, the town gradually filled with free-state migrants causing intense political conflict
between the two groups. Daniel R. Anthony, a Leavenworth businessman and a dedicated free-stater, wrote in 1858 that political
passions had been high in the municipal elections of that year. The
Whiskey-Ruffian, Irish-Catholic crowd had banded together
against those of sincere free-state persuasion; the opposition had
singled him out "as the embodiment of all that was horrible in
the way of *Niggerdom*." As a result of these divisions, community
economic programs became entangled in national political issues.[16]

Moreover, Leavenworth grew rapidly after 1856 and quickly
outdistanced Kansas City in population. This made it difficult for
one group, no matter how ably they might advance their program,
to win community consensus on a particular railroad policy. Subscriptions were issued, cancelled, and reinstated depending on
which groups controlled the municipal offices. In the late fifties,
Thomas Ewing, Jr., a Leavenworth lawyer and speculator who
was later to become one of the most powerful men in the state, supported projects to build railroads into the interior of Kansas and to
establish a connection with the Platte County, a state-aided Missouri road authorized to build between St. Joseph and the western
terminus of the Pacific. He vigorously opposed a rival group of
promoters who had solicited a bond issue for a Leavenworth railroad to connect with the Hannibal and St. Jo., but he wrote that he
feared that they might succeed, since they had gained the support
of the "greedy laboring men" of the town. This kind of division
never developed in the prewar Kansas City business community.[17]

That it did not was in part a result of the way in which the
local railroad movement had developed. Well before Leavenworth had begun to grow, a small group of pioneer Indian and
Santa Fe traders who had acquired land around the site of Kansas
City as a result of a diffusion of entrepreneurial activity common in

the West organized a program for local railroads as part of a broader program to promote the growth of the town. Johnston Lykins, who built a fortune through sixteen well-located acres that he had purchased long before the town was platted, was a representative of this group. In the wake of the rapid settlement of Kansas Territory in the mid-fifties, a number of more deliberate speculators came west with money looking for ripe investment opportunities in land and town real estate. Many of them went on to the territory, but many also joined the pioneer promoters of Kansas City. An advantage these late arrivals found in Kansas City was that a program of town development had been agreed on and the instruments to achieve it already established. Lykins had fixed the design to support a system of local railroads. Speculators who chose Leavenworth or the other new towns in Kansas found that promotion there had to start from scratch; it was natural that conflict should arise in formulating specific railroad plans.

The new Kansas City leaders contributed to the ultimate success of the city. They recognized more clearly than the pioneer promoters the importance of obtaining favorable governmental policies and the support of outside capital if plans for railroads and other community programs were to be realized. They brought astute promotional techniques to the development of local real estate that they purchased. They were part of a new stage in the community's development, for they reinforced and intensified the conviction of the early leaders that financial success lay in tying individual business ambitions to the broader ambition of building a city and provided much of the means to achieve this goal.

Two leading representatives of the landed group of leaders in the city were Kersey L. Coates and John W. Reid. In background and outlook, they were little alike, and they represented extremes of the local business leadership. But it was a measure of the character of the community that they were both at home in booming Kansas City. Their concern with building a town, which in turn would increase the value of their property, made their actions and attitudes similar when it counted. Neither was a railroad polemicist; they left agitation to the Van Horns and Lykinses. Coates particularly preferred to stay deep in the background of events. But for the next twenty years, if there was business to conduct with Eastern capitalists, legislation to influence in the capitals of Missouri and Kansas, or lobbying to do in Washington, they were almost invariably among those chosen for the assignment.

Born in Lancaster on September 15, 1823, Kersey L. Coates was the scion of an influential family of Pennsylvania Quakers, and through his family ties he was able to become an ambassador of the Kansas City business community to Eastern financial circles. A lawyer, a close associate of Thaddeus Stevens, and an outspoken antislavery man, Coates came west in 1855 as an agent of a group of Philadelphia capitalists who wanted to make investments and to promote the influx of free-state settlers into Kansas.[18]

After looking over several sites in Kansas, Coates decided to purchase a tract of land in Missouri on the immediate outskirts of Kansas City. Because of the Border Troubles, his syndicate became concerned over the security of its investment and ordered Coates to sell the property. Instead, using loans from his friends, he purchased the tract himself, and it eventually provided the means by which he built a considerable fortune in Kansas City. He took an active part in the border fighting, aiding in the escape to Illinois of Andrew H. Reeder, the antislavery governor of Kansas Territory. Because of his important part in promoting the free-state cause, a group of Border Ruffians determined to kidnap him when he returned. He was met in St. Louis and warned not to return by "pro-slavery men" from Kansas City, "who though opposed to him in politics admired his influence in commercial affairs." Because of the danger, Coates spent the winter in Wisconsin, and when fighting quieted, returned the next spring to assume an active role in the town. Daniel R. Anthony, whose political persuasions were those of Coates, had similar experiences in Leavenworth. When he arrived there in 1857, he thought it necessary to carry a knife and a revolver because he feared assassination by Border Ruffians who might drift into the town. But, he said, his slave-state neighbors in Leavenworth were a "better class of men," who deplored the violence in the territory. Later, he continued to be attacked viciously in public for his political stand, but he implied that this was unimportant, for, as he put it, "after all in business I have the *full confidence of the people*." Although Anthony prospered, Leavenworth leaders, unlike the Kansas City town builders, were unable to make respect for entrepreneurship an official community position.[19]

As a citizen of Kansas City, Coates modified his politics to conform to the cultural consensus of the community. Although he vigorously supported Lincoln in 1860, his moderate position during the war aroused the ire of Radicals in the region. As a colonel in the Missouri Militia, he tried to protect the property of his pro-Southern townsmen, and because of these efforts was attacked as a Secessionist sympathizer. Coates' wartime experience with the Franklin Conant store indicated that he did not permit his anti-slavery views to influence his business dealings. In 1863 Conant, who had operated one of the largest prewar dry-goods houses in the town, defaulted on a note to Coates, and he began to run the business. He took as a partner an ardent, avowed pro-Southerner, William Gillis. He eventually had to replace Gillis, not because of any ideological differences—the two men were close friends—but because federal authorities threatened to close the store unless Gillis was removed. In the postwar period, Coates set about building a large fortune from his real-estate investments and became perhaps the city's most influential promoter of railroads and other community projects.[20]

John W. Reid in his early career was politically at the opposite pole from Coates, but he too came to accept the fundamental position of the Kansas City business community. A Virginian by birth, Reid had grown up in Indiana, and before the Mexican War practiced law in Saline County, Missouri. After serving as member of Doniphan's Expedition during the Mexican War, he began to farm on a section of land in Jackson County. In 1856 he joined a Border Ruffian band in the attack on Osawatomie, where the Abolitionist John Brown had his headquarters. The same year he purchased land in Kansas City, which he began developing as Reid's Addition. He joined the newly formed Chamber of Commerce, became active in city affairs, and as a member of the state legislature adopted the "plague-on-both-your-houses" attitude characteristic of the Kansas City leaders. In an 1858 speech, he sharply attacked those who agitated the slavery question: "I denounce it as pestiferous, come from what source it may, calculated, if not intended by the political jugglers who use it to undermine the peace and the safety of the very institutions they pretend so zealously to protect." He pointed out that he had been born in a slave state, had lived in slave-holding communities all his life, and would not feel at home without his Negro servant in sight. But the time for agitation of the question on either side had passed. On the eve of the war, he joined Van Horn in urging a policy of disengagement through the formation of a great western republic with Missouri at its center.[21]

Reid was elected to the House of Representatives in 1860, but he resigned with other Southern Congressmen the next year. When war came, the Confederate government offered him a general's commission, but he refused it to serve as a Federal commissioner negotiating claims in Missouri against the Union. After considerable harassment on his Jackson County farm by Kansas free-staters, he joined General Sterling Price's Confederate army on its raid into Missouri, and fought in the battle of Lexington. Shortly thereafter, Union forces captured him. After a year in a St. Louis prison, he was released on parole through the influence of his Kansas City friends, Coates and Van Horn. He immediately returned to Kansas City to live and took an active part in the involved railroad negotiations that occurred after the war. A florid-faced, huge man of 250 pounds, quick to anger, he was very unlike the precise, polished Coates. But, as his son wrote, Reid was a "very thorough man of business," and this provided the bond between the two men. Until 1881, when he dropped dead running to catch a train—it was perhaps an appropriate way for him to die—"General" Reid played some part and usually a significant one in almost every railroad project affecting the city.

Other railroad promoters were important: Milton J. Payne, five-term mayor of Kansas City; Thomas H. Swope, probably the most single-mindedly avaricious of the local landowners who was later the victim in a celebrated Kansas City murder case; and Joseph C. Ranson, one-time Santa Fe commission merchant, who after 1857 devoted most of his efforts to his city addition and railroad activities. Several years later, in this connection, Van Horn recalled the names of Johnston Lykins, Joseph Ranson, M. J. Payne, J. W. Reid, William A. Hopkins, as particularly important. "These, with the writer," he wrote, "constituted the 'crazy club'—as they talked only of railroads." The events of subsequent years proved, according to Van Horn, that the club "was not so crazy after all." [22]

Van Horn often treated the struggle among the small towns along the Missouri River as an exciting game. During the nineteenth century, it was fashionable to portray urban rivalries in almost Manichean terms, and this contributed to the intensity of local sentiment. In these small relatively homogeneous river communities, a disinterested identification with a town's future was possible: any citizen could feel elation at winning a railroad from a rival or depression at its loss. Obviously, however, the drive for urban supremacy had an economic base, and Coates and Reid, who had acquired large stakes in local real estate, were representative of the power group that organized the program to make Kansas City a metropolis. Town leaders who were primarily western traders and merchants—such as Hiram M. Northrup and Washington H. Chick—took part in the local railroad movement, but their roles were subordinate ones. The movement achieved its force from the real-estate dealers, who had the most to gain from realization of the program. The lists of incorporators, directors, and officers of local railroad companies nearly always contained the names of the same group of men—the owners of city additions. Carefully marking off their properties into town lots and business properties, these land promoters ardently worked for railroads and awaited the influx of settlers and the attendant enterprise that they knew would follow.

In the long run, they realized their hopes. Twenty-five-foot lots in Reid's Addition sold for $50 to $100 each right after the war. By the 1880's these same lots had reached a minimum value of $250 a front foot. Strategic holdings brought from $600 to $700 a front foot. At his death in 1881, Reid left an estate of $500,000. Other early promoters, such as Coates and Swope, fared even better.[23]

The harmony of Kansas City on railroad issues before the Civil War was in part the result of the efficacy of local propaganda, particularly that advanced in Van Horn's newspaper. Even today, his editorials urging citizens to be up and doing in the cause of railroads are persuasive. His influence in producing unity behind the policies that he advocated can hardly be exaggerated. A guide to better railroad promotion that he included in his newspaper demonstrated the zeal of community efforts. The writer—probably Charles Spalding—observed initially that the success of the city depended *"entirely* upon her *Railroad system."* Since it was useless even to try to build up a city without railroads, the paramount object of businessmen and property holders should be to obtain *"all* the Railroads we can get."* He asserted that every businessman in the city could exert considerable influence if his actions were properly directed; it was his duty to study the railroad problem as diligently as he attended to price or commercial reports. Even simple things might prove effective: "telling a visitor at our City what we are doing in Railroads *may help us get more done."*

With humorless intensity, he presented his most important direction: a way to overcome the natural resistance of farmers to railroads. "Make it a *business rule,"* he wrote, "to never let a farmer go out of your store until you have said more or less to him about Railroads. By constantly keeping up this rule, you soon have all our farmers in the habit of thinking about our Railroads, and then, and not till then will they see their worth and help us to build them. For myself, I never knew a farmer yet, if he once got fairly to thinking for himself on this subject but what he soon convinced himself that the Railroad was exactly what he needed in order to farm to advantage and with profit. As soon as he thinks for himself, he reasons this way—my crop of wheat, my crop of corn, my hemp, my crop of hogs, are worth so much here; but if I have a railroad to take them to market, I see by the papers that I could realize several hundred more." [24]

Van Horn even presented his business advertising in terms of the railroad boom. In January, 1860, for example, the *Journal* announced that Joseph Guinotte, developer of Guinotte's Addition, was offering all his livestock and implements for sale. Since a recent state-aid bill for railroads had been defeated, Guinotte, the paper declared in heavy-handed but still amusing fashion, "has become a little desperate about railroads and is selling everything about his farm calculated to divert his thoughts and attentions from the grand and stupendous railway system that years ago he marked out for Kansas City." [25]

The Kansas City Chamber of Commerce provided an institutional framework for the direction of this intense local effort. Organized unofficially on October 21, 1856, as the Kansas City Association for Public Improvement, the Chamber received a charter of incorporation from the legislature the next year. The decisions about projected lines to support, land grants to solicit, and capitalists to consult were made at the Chamber's meetings. The City Council, because of the absence of any substantial interest group opposing railroad policy, ratified these programs virtually without debate. The Chamber initiated most of the city's promotional actions. It sponsored the preparation of an elaborate map of Kansas City's railroad system showing thirteen potential railroads radiating from the city; this was lithographed in the East and circulated widely among investors. The body commissioned Van Horn to write a memorial to Congress urging the adoption of the central route for a transcontinental railroad. The document, which provided a detailed, analysis of the West based on Van Horn's extensive study of Gilpin and other geographers, was distributed to members of Congress in 1858. [26]

The Chamber advanced other aspects of a general community promotional program. It initiated efforts to persuade the federal government to make Kansas City the starting point for mail service to California; to improve navigation facilities on the Kansas River; to obtain state charters for local insurance and banking companies; to import goods directly from Europe by way of the Gulf of Mexico; and to remove the Indians from Kansas Territory. But above all the Chamber concentrated on railroad planning, for the city leaders clearly recognized that railroads provided the key to realizing their ambitions to build a great city. Writing at a time when the unity of the local business community had begun to break down, William H. Miller perceptively analyzed the earlier influence of the Chamber. The Chamber, he asserted, had been the "center of thought and opinion" and had united the people in commercial efforts. "Under its potent influence," he wrote, "the people all worked together for common ends, and whatever public movement or enterprise it decided upon, received the support of all, and the strength and intelligence of all were united in giving it shape and carrying it forward. It thus inaugurated a system of railroads for Kansas City. . . . It thus projected nearly every line of railroad now coming to Kansas City and proposed for them substantially the routes now indicated." [27]

As part of their constant agitation, Kansas City leaders organized a plethora of local paper railroad companies. Since these were promotional devices, often they did not even bother to obtain a charter authorizing a formal organization. The Kansas Valley Railroad provided an example of the ordinary function of a paper railroad company. The road was part of the Lykins plan; before he wrote his letter to the *Enterprise* about it, he and a group of promoters in 1855 obtained a charter from the Kansas territorial legislature authorizing the project. The charter set the capital stock of the company at $5,000,000 to be divided into $100 shares, and permitted the company to build a railroad from the western terminus of the Pacific Railroad of Missouri—the act assumed this to be Kansas City—up the southern bank of the Kansas River to a point near Fort Riley. The charter generously allowed the company seven years to start the road and ten years to complete it.[28]

Not until January, 1857, did the incorporators actually organize the company. Lykins served as president, Coates as treasurer, and the usual group of city-addition owners as directors. The officers closed the books of the company after 300 shares of stock had been subscribed. Stock subscriptions to these paper companies meant little. As in this instance, company directors, according to most pre-Civil War Missouri and Kansas charters, determined the method of payment on the stock and the amount and times of the calls on the pledged subscriptions. Usually charters required only an initial payment of five per cent on the purchase price of the stock, and the company could accept private notes. If nothing came of the proposed road, and this was normally the case, the company never demanded payment of the notes, or else nominal services by the subscribers were credited in the books of the company to the amount of the note.[29]

In a letter to a General Van Antwerp of Keokuk, Iowa, Lykins revealed rather honestly, for a statement made public, the reason for the organization of the company. He pointed out that neighboring towns had been organizing companies to build along rival routes and that it was therefore necessary that Kansas Citians move quickly to forestall these plans. "We organize, thus early," he declared, "in order to place ourselves in position for negotiations. Our wish is to get some good and reliable company to take the road and build it." [30]

During the late 1850's, this "grand enterprise of the present time," as Van Horn termed it in 1859, was considered a part of the Kansas City railroad network. It was helpful to have a charter and a company organized to prepare for any eventuality; someone, some day, might be interested in building such a road. In this case, local promoters hoped particularly that the project might form a link in a transcontinental railroad to the West. Never, however, did the company take any action toward construction. Yet, in any summary of the status of the Kansas City railroad program, the promoters always listed the project as being only a step away from completion.[31]

The most significant paper project of the Kansas City promoters was the magnificently named Kansas City, Galveston, and Lake Superior Railroad, chartered by the Missouri legislature in 1857 as part of the grand design proposed by Lykins a year earlier. The road acquired its importance at a later date when its charter provided the means for the construction of a short connection to the Hannibal and St. Jo. The sweeping, vague charter authorized the company to construct a railroad from Kansas City "by the most direct and practicable route" to Galveston and Lake Superior. It also permitted the company to construct branches to the southern border of Missouri to connect with any roads leading to Memphis, Tennessee, or Napoleon, Arkansas.[32]

The provision for a branch road to Napoleon undoubtedly came at the instigation of F. A. Rice, a druggist who had bought land in Kansas City in the early fifties before returning to his home in Kentucky. He became interested in a road projected from Napoleon on the Mississippi River to run up the Arkansas and Neosho River valleys to Kansas City. He wrote letters to local leaders extolling the merits of this road, and for a time the project was the subject of considerable agitation. The ultimate fate of the project may be indicated merely by noting that Napoleon, once a fairly prosperous town at the juncture of the Arkansas and Mississippi rivers, fell into the Mississippi shortly after the Civil War and no longer exists.[33]

At the time of its chartering, Van Horn argued that the ambitious Kansas City, Galveston, and Lake Superior Railroad was far more than another paper road. He said that the new company had combined the interests of two roads already being built, the Galveston and Red River, and the Fort Smith, and that sixty miles of these lines were already in operation in Texas. He predicted that the whole road would quickly be completed.[34]

At an organizational meeting of the new company in February, 1857, Van Horn, Lykins, Ranson, Robert J. Lawrence, and Sands W. Bouton constituted themselves the directory. Lykins became president. Van Horn was even more exuberant than usual in discussing his friend's high qualifications for the post. His many years in the West had given him an intimate knowledge of the country to be developed by the road. His scientific training and habits had made him an expert on its topography. He understood thoroughly the significance of the mid-continent, particularly its capacity to sustain a dense population. For these reasons, Lykins was particularly fitted to present the case for the road to Congress and to acquaint the nation with the importance of a project that would be a "great commercial magnet through the heart of the continent, that will bind us together in bands indissoluble as the continent itself." [35]

The project became even more ambitious two months later when the Louisiana legislature chartered the New Orleans, Shreveport, and Kansas City Railroad, with Coates and Lykins as two of the incorporators. For two-thirds of its route, this road was to be identical with the Galveston, joining the latter somewhere along the border of Arkansas and the Indian Territory. The chartering of the railroad proved, as did all such developments in Van Horn's analyses, that the "eyes of the country are now fixed upon the great centre of trade in the Missouri Valley, and the iron arms of commerce are being projected from all points East, North, and South to reach us, and thus secure the immense trade of the Egyptian region. . . . It is a most gigantic, important and magnificent enterprise." [36]

For a time Kansas City promoters tried to tie their project to the railroad enthusiasm that developed in Kansas in 1858. Many public meetings were held and many resolutions adopted in its support, but before the war the company did nothing to build the ambitious project. [37]

From 1855 to 1860 Kansas City was in the throes of an almost continual railroad boom. The panic of 1857 checked for a brief time any concrete railroad planning, but the agitation continued. At times the community reached a state of near frenzy in its desire to obtain railroads. Speeches, public meetings, rallies, parades, barbecues, all designed to stir up enthusiasm for one railroad proposal or another, were frequent affairs. The test of a good political candidate, or of a man for that matter, was whether or not he was sound on railroads. The symbol of the city became the iron horse, and it must have taxed the imaginations of editors and orators to think of new versions of the metaphor. The iron horse taking his first drink at the juncture of the Missouri and the Kaw; the iron horse, steam snorting from his nostrils, galloping into the city on iron feet; the shrill neigh of the iron horse echoing along the Blue; the iron horse, serenely surveying the majestic Kansas Valley; the iron horse finally slaking his enormous thirst in the waters of the Pacific merely suggest the many variations on the theme.

In 1857 Van Horn wrote of the "awful agony of sundry one horse towns" that wanted railroads. He referred to the fact that all small towns in the region had organized railroad programs without the means necessary even to begin to support these schemes. This could only mean frustration. Van Horn obviously did not intend the analysis to apply to Kansas City, but before realizing any part of its grandiose railroad plan, his own community experienced much of the "agony" that he found Kansas City's rivals enduring.[38]

Huckstering ... Honeyed Promises
The Prewar Program

ROBERT T. Van Horn attended the 1856–1857 session of the Missouri General Assembly to look after railroad legislation of interest to Kansas City. While in Jefferson City, he turned his attention to a bill to extend further state aid to the Pacific Railroad of Missouri. In a letter to his newspaper signed with his customary traveling pseudonym, "Crosstie," he discussed the attitudes prevailing in the capital toward the railroad. He said that almost every legislator with whom he had talked was disposed to extend more assistance. This was right and in accordance with the wishes of the people and the needs of the state. At the same time, he found a clear inclination on the part of the legislators to check the "huckstering policy" that the company had been following in locating its line. By "holding out bids like an auctioneer, and peddling depots and connections between county seats and interior towns, holding out baits here and expectations there," the Pacific was demeaning its own dignity and that of the state. The legislature should therefore insist that the railroad fix its route once and for all before any more aid was extended. Van Horn's criticisms were harsh, but he said that he wrote "in no unkind spirit but as a friend and a devoted friend of the Pacific Road." His explanation for this attitude epitomized the position of his community: "It could not be otherwise, as no point has a more vital interest than Kansas City as its western terminus." The community's future depended on the Pacific's being built to the city. The policies of the railroad aroused resentment in Kansas City, as well as throughout western Missouri, but grievances had to be suppressed, at least until the road was built. As Van Horn said, it could not be otherwise, if the town promoters were to realize their design of building a metropolis.[1]

Owing to the fact that substantial public contributions helped to finance the building of American railroads in the nineteenth century, many Midwestern communities in their negotiations with railroads shared the problems faced by Kansas City during this period. Governmental aid was particularly significant in the antebellum period, when up to 1861 it probably comprised some 30 per cent of the entire investment in American railroad building. Cities and towns provided a substantial share of this investment, and in so doing many of them accumulated sizable debts. In 1853, for example, the railroad indebtedness of Wheeling amounted to $55 per capita; Baltimore $43; Pittsburgh $34; St. Louis $30; New Orleans $23, and Philadelphia $20. Mixed enterprise was probably an efficient way to promote economic growth in an "underdeveloped" nation, but the system created considerable hardship for individual communities. More often than not, the future of a Midwestern town depended on whether or not it obtained a railroad. Recognizing this, local leaders were willing to extend whatever assistance was demanded. A public meeting in North Liberty, Iowa, in adopting a resolution, "That Johnson County donate half a million dollars rather than this Railroad should be made twenty miles east or west of us," expressed the common attitude. As a part of this system, both railroad leaders and community spokesmen accepted relationships involved in intricate bargaining. Towns and counties

tried to protect their investments and subsidies with complicated restrictions and qualifications in order to assure that they actually realized some gains from their assistance. Railroad representatives
were equally calculating. John W. Brooks of the Chicago, Burlington, and Quincy system cautioned his fellow executive, James F.
Joy, that local aid had to be obtained before a route was announced.
"Nothing can be realized from any locality after they are sure of
the road." [2]

Because of the willingness of Missouri in the early 1850's to
encourage enterprise, the charter of the Pacific Railroad placed virtually no restrictions on the company's solicitation of stock subscriptions from counties, townships, and municipalities. As Van Horn indicated, the railroad in making plans to build west of Jefferson City
followed a policy of leaving the route in doubt as a means of gaining favorable terms from localities along the line. This policy,
which went back to the early years of the company, accounted for
much of the animosity that developed toward the Pacific in Kansas
City and other parts of western Missouri.

As a result of the initial surveys made to the western border of the
state, the Chief Engineer of the road had made a strong case in
1851 for the advantages of a route by way of the Missouri River
west of Jefferson City. His report asserted that touching the Missouri River in the vicinity of the Kansas City settlement would
tap the flourishing western business beginning to center there. Once
the railroad was completed, this trade would rapidly expand. Although the Pacific would face the problem of river competition, it
would be able to operate profitably because of the enormous potential growth of trade with the Far West. On the basis of this report,
the Board of Directors of the Pacific tentatively recommended ter-
mination in Jackson County at the juncture of the Missouri and
Kansas rivers. A new set of directors took over the company in 1852.
Communities in western Missouri proposed changes in the route.
A newspaper in Liberty, located north of the Missouri, reported
that a plan to divert the road northward had gained support among
the St. Louis officers of the company. [3]

Late in 1852, however, the new officers declared that in view of the earlier decision they believed themselves bound to terminate the road in Jackson County. They stated though that the railroad should be allowed to determine its own route through the county leaving it free to bargain for subscriptions. The law granting an additional state loan of $1,000,000, passed in December of that year, recognized the railroad's demand. It provided that the road should pass west of Jefferson City "along the best and most practicable inland route" by way of Johnson County, which lay to the east and south of Jackson County, and should terminate somewhere in Jackson County. The law required that the counties west of Jefferson City subscribe a sum of $400,000 to the capital stock of the railroad in addition to any amounts already granted. If these subscriptions were not authorized within a year, then the railroad was free to select any route to the western border of Missouri that it wished. Consistently during the early 1850's the legislature, reflecting the state's desire to get railroads built, yielded to the demands of the state-supported trunk railroads.[4]

This law presented grave dangers to the interests of the river towns of Kansas City and Independence, located on the northern edge of Jackson County. Since the Pacific had been permitted to build outside the state, they faced the possibility that the railroad in following an "inland" route straight west of Jefferson City would be built northward only far enough to touch the southern end of Jackson County and then would be continued straight westward to hit the Santa Fe trail somewhere in Kansas Territory. A route to the two river towns represented a northward diversion of about thirty miles from the direct "inland" route. This possibility of a "southern cutoff," which would funnel the trade of the Southwest in a more direct fashion to St. Louis, continued to be a problem of Kansas City promoters well into the post–Civil War period.

For several years, however, this concern was academic, for the Pacific exhausted all its initial resources in completing its first thirty-seven miles of line west of St. Louis. The passage in 1855 of an additional aid bill of $2,000,000 to complete the railroad to the western border revived the danger. Unlike the earlier law, the measure made no provision for any specified grants to ensure the line's location. The failure of local leaders early the next year to get assurance that Kansas City would be the western terminus set off the local railroad boom. The promoters launched their program of advertising the town's natural advantages, organizing paper railroad companies and, more concretely, trying to obtain some connection northward to the Hannibal and St. Jo., which unlike the Pacific was rapidly being constructed across the state.[5]

Again early in 1857, while the Missouri legislature was considering a new aid bill, local leaders with the backing of the city council met with Pacific officials to offer a $50,000 city subscription. The passage of a law in April granting an additional state loan of $1,-000,000 brought the president of the company, William McPherson, to Kansas City. Tentatively, he offered to complete the line through Jackson County to Kansas City by way of Independence provided the county raise a $150,000 subscription. If this were done, he assured local leaders that the road could be finished in eighteen months. In commenting on this visit, Van Horn said that Kansas City was willing to take $50,000 of this amount and that Independence, still the larger and wealthier of the two communities, could easily take the remaining $100,000. As a result of this proposal, Kansas City and Independence each voted to subscribe $50,-000 to the capital stock of the railroad. Van Horn asserted that the rest of the amount demanded had been pledged in private subscriptions.[6]

The railroad took no immediate action on these subscriptions. Consequently, a Kansas City correspondent signing himself "Jackson" bitterly attacked the dilatory policies of the Pacific in a letter to the *Missouri Democrat* of St. Louis. Jackson, although not clearly identifiable, was unquestionably one of the leading Kansas City promoters, and he frequently served as the spokesman for their views. His arguments were typical of those employed in the community. Personifying cities in a fashion common in this era of urban rivalry, he accused St. Louis of being jealous of a possible rival in the West and charged her with not making a major effort to com-

plete the Pacific. If she did not start co-operating, she would force
Kansas City to seek an eastern connection through the Hannibal
and St. Jo. At the very moment, he said, negotiations were in progress in Washington and New York to construct a line to the north.
When the road was completed, New York and Chicago would be
competitors of St. Louis for the rich Western trade.

Jackson accused the Pacific of trying to bargain for larger subscriptions by making conflicting promises to localities along alternate routes. The latest report circulating in the region was that the
railroad planned to run just far enough into Jackson County to obtain a county subscription and then to dash off westward to some
point in Kansas Territory. This kind of policy had disgusted the
whole community with the management of the railroad. He offered them another chance, however. If the directors would decide
on a definite route through the county, the $150,000 would be
paid; otherwise it would not.[7]

As Jackson's letter indicated, during this period the rumor was
current that the railroad planned to bypass Kansas City. The *Jefferson Inquirer* reported that the main trunk of the Pacific would pass
through Pleasant Hill, about thirty miles south of Kansas City. In
order to satisfy the legal requirement of a terminus in Jackson
County, the railroad would build a branch from Pleasant Hill to
Kansas City. As a result, the *Inquirer* argued, Jefferson City would
become the headquarters for all western trade. Regardless of the
company's plans, it was wise not to deny these kinds of rumors, for
they provided a convenient weapon in bargaining with Jackson
County.[8]

McPherson, the Pacific's president, answered Jackson's charges
in a letter to the *Missouri Democrat*. He argued that only the pov-
erty of the railroad had forced the many long delays in its construction. In no case should St. Louis, which had already contributed so much to the Pacific, be held responsible for the policies of
the company directors. The $100,000 in subscriptions from Kansas
City and Independence were short of the sum requested. Moreover, no provision had been made for right of way through the

county. A county subscription of $150,000 would ensure that the railroad would pass through Jackson County by way of the two towns.[9]

The Kansas City leaders took immediate action on McPherson's proposal. Speaking for the local railroad leadership, Van Horn suggested that Kansas City and Independence each immediately subscribe $75,000. After quick approval by the City Council, Kansas City voters ratified the subscription without a single dissenting voice—a characteristic outcome for railroad proposals during the period. But Independence again delayed.[10]

This result pointed up a major problem faced by Kansas City promoters in dealing with the Pacific. They enjoyed nearly absolute control over their own community, but they were not able to impose their authority on the whole county. In Missouri, railroads were anxious to obtain county rather than municipal bonds in payment of subscriptions, since the latter were difficult to market owing to the uncertain financial status of new Western towns.

Considerable opposition to railroads existed in the county seat of Independence. Interests there with close ties to the Western riverboat-wagon trade had made their influence felt in the county court, the general governmental agency of the county in Missouri. Moreover, the earlier-settled town, closer to the South in its traditions, had developed conservative attitudes—reflected politically and socially as well as economically—in part, simply because of its longer history. A traveler to the region in 1863 summed up the general prevailing impression of the character of Independence. Before the war, he wrote, it had been "one of the most beautiful and flourishing towns in Missouri." Here had retired wealthy and influential businessmen who devoted themselves to improving and enjoying their homes. It was one of the few places in Missouri, he declared, "where society was fixed and permanent, where retired merchant princes would desire to pass their declining years." But in the eyes of the Kansas City leadership, Independence suffered from "Old Fogeyism," a dread disease to prophets of material progress.

In their view—and they presented it often during this period—there was no hope once a community was infected. The town was doomed to wither and die, while neighboring towns that had avoided the contagion would grow into vigorous, healthy cities.[11]

After much prodding from Kansas City leaders on this occasion, Independence did once again vote a subscription of $50,000, but payment was dependent on the railroad following a specified route through the city. The Pacific rejected the proposal on the grounds that the route would be too expensive. However, the annual report of the directors of the company to the stockholders, issued in March of 1858, stated that negotiations would be continued and that it should be possible to fix a definite route within a year.[12]

Because of the delays and rumors, in April, 1858, the Kansas City Chamber of Commerce, the instrument of the local railroad leaders, adopted a set of resolutions vigorously denouncing the Pacific. This manifesto charged that the Pacific for years had been preventing the city from realizing its vital need for an eastern connection. The community could no longer delay acquiring the facilities its rapidly expanding commerce demanded. Unless the company gave definite guarantees that it would immediately begin to finish the road to Kansas City, the city would initiate vigorous measures to build a connection to the Hannibal and St. Jo. This action would mean that St. Louis would soon see the Western trade, which rightfully belonged to her and to the state of Missouri, passing to the commercial centers of the Middle and Northern states.[13]

Throughout the course of these fruitless negotiations with the Pacific, Kansas City leaders had been working on plans to obtain a connection northward to the Hannibal and St. Jo. As the Chamber of Commerce protest indicated, the threat of this line provided a weapon to use in bargaining with the Pacific. The effort had begun in the fall of 1855 with the preliminary informal organization of the Kansas City, Hannibal and St. Joseph Railroad Company. During the legislative session of 1855–1856, the Kansas Citians obtained a charter authorizing their company to build a line by the shortest and most practicable route to the Hannibal and St. Jo.

They launched their project in a spirit of professed optimism with the obvious hope that the enterprise would attract eastern investors in the same fashion as had the Hannibal and St. Jo. To win the support of outside capital was usually the purpose of the paper railroad company. In December, 1855, Van Horn wrote that the incorporators had assurance from men of wealth that if the project was conducted in the proper spirit the city would not be wanting in the "sinews of war" to finish it. The Kansas correspondent of the *St. Louis Intelligencer* reported, however, that a Kansas City group had tried to sell the stock of the company in the East but had been unable to dispose of a single share. Van Horn admitted that this report was substantially true. But, in his usual fashion, he put the best face on the matter. "Even if not a dollar of our stock is taken East, it will be taken at home—the Road is bound to be built." [14]

On December 28, 1855, the incorporators offered 1,500 shares in the company to local subscription. The company's failure to interest outside investors was not a total loss. With his knack for turning adversity to advantage, Van Horn now had a convenient appeal to garner support. This was to be the "people's road," financed by local citizens who had no desire or need for state aid and led by men who were concerned only with getting a railroad built, not with making profits from inflating the costs of railroad construction. Locally owned and operated, unhampered by a horde of speculators, the "people's road" would be responsible directly to the community it served. Through this argument, invidious comparisons could be made with the foundering, state-aided trunk lines. The Pacific, in particular, came under attack as an enterprise operated only for the benefit of a handful of St. Louis capitalists without regard to the interests of the state. "It is true that we ask for no State aid," Van Horn wrote, "for the road is intended for a business thoroughfare and not for plunder. We are of those who believe that 'State Aid' is only another name for swindling. There are railroads in Missouri which have had 'State Aid' until their directors, contractors, etc. have become rich and the State almost hopelessly in debt. These roads will be finished when no more money can be ground out of the burdened tax payers and not before." [15]

The "people's-road" argument was completely opportunistic. From the beginning of the project, officials of the company tried to attract outside investors. Van Horn himself was a consistent and ardent advocate of the necessity of attracting capital if the young town was to become a major city. Furthermore, once the Pacific had decided on Kansas City as its terminus, the company had no more faithful friend than he in its efforts to wrest additional money from the state. The local promoters, because of their continual efforts to get outside support for the project, eventually had to tone down the "people's-road" theme, for it became so patently false that it could not be accepted by even the most naive supporters.

Throughout this period, the promoters consistently advanced a second line—a warning to the St. Louis investors who controlled the Pacific that if more money was not forthcoming to finish this road, Kansas City would throw all its financial support to its northern connection. The danger to St. Louis interests was real. If a road to the Hannibal and St. Jo. were actually completed before the Pacific reached the edge of the plains, the lucrative wagon trade with the Southwest, which by 1856 had its headquarters at Kansas City, could be diverted to Chicago. Moreover, the rapid settlement of Kansas Territory had created a potentially rich new trade area.

During the course of the year 1856, the incorporators of the Kansas City company made brave efforts to obtain support for their northern project in communities along the route. In January a public meeting in Clay County, immediately to the north of Jackson County, pledged half the necessary funds for a preliminary survey of the line. During the summer business leaders in Keokuk, in southeastern Iowa, expressed interest in the project. As a result, the incorporators hired an engineer, Robert J. Lawrence, to begin a survey on the most direct possible line toward Keokuk. They dispatched Lykins to solicit funds for the completion of the survey north of the Hannibal and St. Jo. to the Iowa city. Out in the field, Lawrence filed regular exuberant reports with Van Horn.

Buoyant optimism was a prerequisite for employment in such a venture. Lawrence found the region unsurpassed in fertility; it was truly the "garden of the world!" He wrote to Edward M. Samuel, an incorporator and the leader of the Clay County forces, that every day citizens had begged him for a chance to invest in the company. Just the day before, he said, he could easily have raised $40,000 or $50,000.[16]

Lawrence's final report, published in November, 1856, estimated that the road could be completed to Keokuk for a little over $5,-000,000. Once in operation, he predicted that the railroad would provide an immediate profit of 9 per cent on the cost of construction. This percentage would increase rapidly as the area filled with settlers and land values rose. In the meantime Lykins had returned from Keokuk and had reported optimistically to the incorporators that he too had found widespread support for the project. Everything was going well, Van Horn wrote. No longer would the citizens of the region have to be deceived by the Pacific Railroad; no longer would they have to be the "victims of the honied tales of interested contractors and a huckstering Directory." [17]

In late September a public meeting organized by the Kansas City railroad leaders adopted a resolution petitioning the city council to authorize a special election to allow the city to purchase $150,000 in stock in the local company. In advancing their programs, the promoters consistently tried, with considerable success, to establish the illusion that all local railroad proposals originated in unified community demand. The council promptly called for the election. The voters approved the subscription with only five ballots cast against it. At about the same time, Lee County, Iowa, in which Keokuk was located, voted a county subscription of $450,000. Van Horn asserted that in view of the reports of Lawrence and Lykins, it would be easy to obtain additional subscriptions of $900,000 from other counties and towns through which the road would pass, making a grand total of $1,500,000 in governmental subscriptions alone. "This is what can be done," he declared, "by individual enterprise." [18]

At this point the Kansas City Chamber of Commerce entered the negotiations. Organized in the fall of 1856, the Chamber was apparently established to co-ordinate local railroad efforts. During the next few years this voluntary association became the most important agency of community policy and action. It assumed many of the functions ordinarily performed by formal instruments of government. One of the Chamber's first actions was to appoint Kersey Coates, Van Horn, and H. B. Bouton, a lawyer and developer of Bouton's Addition, to draw up articles of association for a new railroad company to expand the scope of the Kansas City, Hannibal, and St. Joseph in order to permit the Keokuk extension. The company's charter allowed the building of a line only as far as the Hannibal and St. Jo. The Chamber appointed Coates a "confidential delegate" to work out an agreement with the Keokuk leaders before the opening of a railroad convention scheduled to be held the following month at Linneus, Missouri. The Chamber insisted that Kansas City interests should maintain control in any new company and worked out a number of provisions to ensure that this would be the case. Coates obtained this approval from the Keokuk group.[19]

On November 26 and 27 the Linneus convention, composed of representatives from the counties through which the railroad would pass, ratified the necessary decisions. In all the maneuverings involving the "people's road," the promoters placed great stress on popular participation in the making of decisions. But well before each convention or rally, they had carefully worked out the necessary programs to be agreed to. The convention also approved the route from Kansas City to Keokuk and named Coates, Van Horn, and Samuel as a committee to obtain the charter change from the legislature and to petition Congress for a land grant for the railroad. Van Horn displayed his usual enthusiasm. He thought after talking with delegates that he had been too cautious in his earlier estimates; now he represented that $2,000,000 could be raised from the counties through which the road would pass. Financially the new Kansas and Keokuk would be the soundest railroad west of the Mississippi River he concluded.[20]

In two editorials written at the time, Van Horn put the Kansas City–Keokuk project in the context of the over-all Kansas City railroad plans. His argument demonstrated how the geographic rationale of the local promoters could be shaped to apply to a specific railroad proposal. Van Horn pointed out that ice in winter and low water in summer often stopped navigation along the Mississippi and Missouri rivers for several months out of the year. Because of the enormous growth of the Western trade, a railroad between Kansas City, Keokuk, and Chicago had become a matter of commercial necessity. Once it was built all the trade of New Mexico, Utah, California, and Oregon would flow through Kansas City on its way to the trade marts of the East. The great seaboard cities should be vitally interested in completion of this project, for the Western trade had been fundamental in their development and would remain for all time the highest prize within their reach.

The topography of the continent, he asserted, dictated that a northern transcontinental railroad would have to follow the route selected for the Kansas City and Keokuk. The line would cross the Mississippi and Missouri rivers at the only two points where there were narrow, rock-bound channels and at Kansas City would strike the great natural road to Santa Fe. The Santa Fe trail, the best track in the world for a railroad, provided the only route upon which a railroad could or would be built west of Kansas City. As the line was extended into the rich Kansas Valley, the region would quickly be filled with settlers. There would then be ample trade for three transcontinental offshoots from Kansas City to the East. The Keokuk road would provide the northern route; the Pacific of Missouri the central; and a line to Memphis, connecting with roads to New Orleans, Mobile, Savannah, Charleston, and Richmond, the southern route.[21]

Van Horn again had involved himself in the inconsistency, which appeared frequently in Kansas City railroad polemics, of attempting to use desert and garden conceptions of the West simultaneously. If the area beyond Kansas City was one of unsurpassed fertility, into which would quickly pour vast numbers of settlers, then it was illogical to assume that only one railroad would ever be built into the region. This view was consistent only with the argument that the purpose of a Western railroad should be to reach areas on the other side of a great wasteland. But because of the fluid nature of mid-nineteenth century conceptions of the West, the Kansas Citians in attempting to gain support for their plans often found it expedient to shape their appeals in a fashion that would accommodate itself to varying stands on this question.

The *Jefferson Inquirer,* published in the Missouri capital, considered the Keokuk road a serious threat to Missouri's interests, and its analysis echoed that expressed in Kansas City. The *Inquirer* asserted that it was just as likely that this railroad would be constructed as that the Pacific would complete its line to the western border of the state. Since the Kansas City and Keokuk had the support of substantial interests in Iowa, it could not be considered a visionary project. The completion of the line would be a grave blow to St. Louis and to Missouri, for the railroad would funnel the rich trade of Kansas Territory and the West to other markets. The time had come, the writer said, for St. Louis to stop denouncing Black Republicans and to get to work on the state projects. If not, northern interests would build the railroads that would eventually destroy St. Louis and seriously undermine the state's economy and institutions. To establish this threat and thereby force the completion of the Pacific was, of course, one of the main goals of the Kansas City promoters.[22]

After the Linneus convention, the local railroad leadership went to work. The Chamber of Commerce, in co-operation with the executive committee of the Linneus convention, drew up a new charter for the company and charged Van Horn with submitting it to the legislature. Coates went to Washington to present the request for a congressional land grant. The new charter proved no problem. On January 6, 1857, the legislature passed a law amending the charter of the original company to allow it to change its name and to extend its line to Keokuk. Reflecting the increasing importance of the sentiment that railroads to the east and north posed a threat to Missouri's Southern institutions, a legislator had argued that no railroad ought to be chartered to run outside the state since Negroes might escape on them. But this opposition had proved inconsequential.[23]

Raising the money was another matter. Coates failed to get the congressional land grant. Although several counties along the proposed route of the Kansas City and Keokuk held meetings to initiate subscriptions, Clay County, whose support was crucial, failed to act. Van Horn, however, remained optimistic. He reported that an agent's tour of the involved counties had demonstrated that a subscription of $2,000,000 could be raised by May. Eastern capital of which there had been so much talk by "certain interested croakers" would soon be proved what it really was, a "miserable humbug." Easterners, he said, would always be ready to build western roads but only when they could "skin" local citizens. It was to the credit of the Kansas City and Keokuk that "charter tinkerers, and mousers about eastern capital" had been excluded from this great people's enterprise.[24]

Van Horn's assertion that western railroads could best be built with local resources was totally inaccurate, and he probably knew it. But before local promoters could begin to negotiate seriously with Eastern railroad companies, they had to obtain bond issues, for these offered some concrete inducement to investors. The "people's road" theme provided a convenient argument to win the necessary local popular support.

Although the city council of Kansas City revised its earlier subscription so as to make it payable to the new company once construction commenced, other towns and counties took no further action. During July, 1857, Coates, who had been elected president of the company, went to New York to try to raise support, again without success. By this time, the Keokuk leaders had lost interest and the initial enthusiasm in the region had evaporated. With the advent of national financial panic in the fall of 1857, the Kansas City and Keokuk was quietly forgotten.[25]

The main reason for the declining support of the road during the

early months of 1857 had been the organization of competing projects. A company proposing to build to the Hannibal and St. Jo.
from Brunswick, on the north bank of the Missouri in the west-
central part of the state, attracted the attention of Clay County
leaders. Promoters organized projects to build lines from Weston,
up the river from Kansas City, to Canton on the Mississippi, and
from St. Joseph to Burlington, Iowa. As early as January, Van
Horn had begun to rail against these competitors: "There was not a
word heard of Railroads in all this upper country until Kansas City
started her system of Roads and now every little town has its meetings, Presidents, Secretaries, and Committees on Resolutions to
build Railroads in a night, and they all run *parallel to a Kansas City
road.* The poor devils have not even the energy to make out a new
route. Take them all together they have not even the means to
print their proceedings. . . ." From this time until the actual
completion of a system of major roads into the city, Kansas City
promoters were plagued by the existence of a myriad of paper railroad companies organized in the towns along the Missouri River.[26]

The panic of 1857 halted further construction by national railroads. For a year the state of Missouri was unable to extend additional aid to the state trunk lines. Consequently, for Kansas City
promoters even to propose bond issues or to approach Eastern investors at this time was unfeasible. But agitation continued. Kansas
City probably felt the effects of the panic less seriously than towns
in other parts of the country. The presence of a relatively stable
amount of hard money in the region resulting from public expenditures—Indian annuities, government mail contracts, and military
freighting payments—and from the gold and silver purchases of
Mexican merchants, who by this time conducted the caravan trade
to the Southwest, insulated the community from the worst aspects
of paper panics. In any case national depression did not dampen the
optimistic expectations of the Kansas City business leaders. It was
during the years 1857 and 1858 that they prepared their elaborate
maps and wrote their exuberant memorials. They held their famous
Christmas dinner celebrating the advancement of the town at a time
when panic gripped the country.[27]

With their northern project dead and with the country beginning to show signs of recovery from the depression, the Kansas Citians revived their negotiations with the Pacific. In April, 1858, the Chamber of Commerce appointed Lykins, Coates, and Reid to consult with company officials and with leaders in Independence in order to try to work out a satisfactory program of local aid. By this time Reid had become the chief intermediary between Kansas City and the Pacific. As a representative in the Missouri General Assembly from Jackson County, he had been a consistent spokesman for the interests of the company and had sponsored bills to extend further aid and to release the state's first lien on the road. Late in 1858, the Pacific appointed him its agent in Jackson County to negotiate subscriptions and right-of-way.[28]

As a result of these negotiations, the railroad apparently offered some favorable assurances to the Kansas City promoters. Van Horn reported early in May that word had been received that the company had definitely fixed Kansas City as the terminus of the road. A survey of the complete line would be undertaken immediately. He asserted that this outcome had never really been in doubt. The system of bargaining, however, had hurt the town by allowing rival communities a pretext for the argument that Kansas City would never get the road. In August the Pacific's transit party reached Kansas City and selected a route through the town.[29]

The report of the Chief Engineer of the Pacific on December 24, 1858, recommended immediate completion of the road and provided another restatement of the geographic arguments employed by Kansas City promoters. When the railroad was finished, the vast trade of Kansas would reach St. Louis by this route, and Kansas City would become the "new metropolis." Anyone who understood the topography of the region realized that central Kansas would soon be opened by a railroad built up the Kansas River valley. The Pacific would therefore be a profitable highway over which would pass the "crowds" seeking the rich agricultural plains. If the completion of the Pacific was delayed, the inevitable result would be to build up formidable rivals to St. Louis in other states.[30]

With the terminus now fixed at Kansas City, Van Horn could

abandon his early attitude of critical hostility to become a vigorous partisan of the Pacific. The promise of quick completion of the line had been predicated on another state loan. Van Horn attended the 1858–1859 session of the legislature to lobby for a bill to extend an additional $3,250,000 state loan to the road. The measure did not pass, and he warned St. Louis interests that they would have to do better at the next session. The threat was familiar: if more aid was not forthcoming, Kansas City would devote all her resources to obtaining a Chicago connection through the Hannibal and St. Jo.[31]

In January, 1859, while the aid bill was pending in the legislature, the Jackson County Court, as a result of considerable pressure from Kansas City, called for an election to approve a $100,000 county subscription to the Pacific. But the County Court, which represented anti-railroad interests in the area, went along with the local aid program only when it was forced to do so. When the legislature failed to vote the additional loan, the County Court seized on this as a pretext to abandon the test vote. Controversy immediately developed as to whether or not this subscription was still payable, for Missouri law did not require popular approval of county subscriptions even though county courts might seek such a mandate if they wished.[32]

During the summer of 1859 the Pacific again made plans to resume construction. In August a committee appointed by the company's directors came to Kansas City to try to realize payment on the municipal subscriptions from Independence and Kansas City and to attempt to obtain some agreement on a county subscription. The committee, after consultation in Kansas City and Independence, won agreement for a program to pay one general county subscription. Accordingly, on August 16, the County Court voted to consolidate the $100,000 from the county, the $75,000 from Kansas City, and the $50,000 from Independence into one county subscription of $225,000 to purchase capital stock of the Pacific. The court required that the entire sum be expended on construction in Jackson County and fixed September 3 as the voting day on the proposal.[33]

This election presented Kansas City leaders with a major challenge to their program, for many citizens in outlying parts of the county regarded the bond issue as merely a scheme to enrich Kansas City real-estate speculators. Opposition of this kind hampered local promotional efforts for years to come. In Jackson County the slavery controversy exacerbated normal rural-urban conflict. Because of its studied neutrality on the issue during the Border Troubles and after, Kansas City had gained a reputation in decidedly pro-Southern Jackson County as a hotbed of antislavery sentiment.

In defending the bond issue, Van Horn asserted that the view that railroads would only benefit city landholders was wrong. The increase in property values in Kansas City would be but a "drop in the bucket" compared to the rise in value of agricultural lands. Once the railroad was completed, every owner of a hundred acres would have a fortune. The Kansas City promoters conducted a series of rallies throughout the county, addressed by Van Horn, Reid, Payne, and other leading figures in the town. In Independence, however, opponents of aid vigorously organized against the measure. "The vote to be taken on the railroad question is equivalent to the life of the city," Van Horn asserted. Not one vote could be lost, he warned, because of the sizable opposition in the rest of the county.[34]

That the measure would carry decisively in Kansas City was never in doubt, but an overwhelming turnout of favorable voters was needed to override the rural opposition. Van Horn therefore appealed to all classes in his newspaper campaign. A manifesto entitled "Whom the Railroads Will Benefit" contained almost every demagogic appeal to self-interest that it was possible to make in the small community. The city would double its size in two years, supplying more work than brickmakers, carpenters, and other mechanics could take care of. Thousands of laborers would obtain work at good wages. Farmers and gardeners would have a market for their products. Appealing to the belief in urban growth, a fundamental aspect of the American doctrine of material progress, he concluded that railroads "make cities and contribute a hundred fold to the extent and profits of every kind of business. There is no interest that does not feel the influence of the Railway, and no great city can be built without them." It was ironic in view of the actual support of the Kansas City railroad program that Van Horn could cite only one group in the city who might not really benefit from the proposal. These were "the few, the property holders, the owners of corner lots and Additions," for they would have to pay the taxes necessary to bring the railroad to the city.[35]

The arguments employed by the opponents of the bond measure were reflected in a pamphlet reprinted by Van Horn, who occasionally let the opposition be heard at some length as a means of disseminating an impression of fair dealing without at the same time actually stating the full case. The technique, common enough in American politics, required that the most extreme and the most intemperate expression of the opposite view be selected. In reprinting this item, Van Horn observed only that the pamphlet was an example of the foolish, ill-natured type of criticism that the moderate leaders of Kansas City had to contend with in dealing with Independence.[36]

The pamphlet argued that the Pacific Railroad was insolvent beyond redemption. If the subscription was voted, it would be lost, for the company would soon pass into new hands. The Pacific had made conflicting promises and estimates of the cost to the county. Originally, the railroad had argued that it would require $5,000,-000 to finish the line to the western border. Already $10,000,000 had been expended, and the company still wanted $6,000,000 more. Further county aid would prevent any expenditures for turnpikes, which farmers so desperately needed to get their goods to market. The pamphlet concluded: "We object to the proposition now before us, because concocted at a Wine supper in Kansas City— it inures only to the benefit of a few land holders in that City, and to the injury of a great portion of Jackson County." [37]

The night before the election, the local promoters sponsored a huge rally, just one of many railroad celebrations that were to be held into the next year. A parade of demonstrators from McGee's Addition in the south end of town, complete with two bands, met in the heart of town with a delegation from neighboring Westport, which had marched in with its own band. In front of the newspaper office, a huge model railroad car had been set up with a "poor old fogy" impaled on the car of progress. There, with Van Horn presiding, railroad orators delivered rabble-rousing speeches throughout the evening. Van Horn, as was his custom on most such occasions, termed it the largest gathering ever held in the city.[38]

The election resulted in a decisive vote for the measure: 2,132 to 870. In the face of general opposition in the rural townships and in Independence, a tremendous majority in Kansas City carried the proposal.[39]

Immediately, opponents raised the cry of fraud. The small number of votes, only eight, against the measure in the city might have been expected to have attracted attention, but it did not, for almost every railroad election in Kansas City had shown the same lack of dissent. In one instance only five votes had been cast against a proposal, and on another occasion a subscription had carried unanimously. But the 1,667 favorable votes did cause concern. The *Independence Messenger*, which had led the opposition against the measure, charged that Kansas City did not have anywhere near the legal number of voters that had supposedly cast ballots in the election. In 1858, only 893 voters had been listed on the poll-tax register, and this was the approximate vote recorded in the general election that year. The paper doubted that Kansas City had more voters than that in 1859. If the result was allowed to stand, Jackson County would be at the mercy of a small clique in Kansas City.[40]

At first Van Horn merely advised the anti-railroad men to take a "vegetable diet and a gentle purgative for a few days." Later he countered their charge in detail. He stated that on the first of June, 1859, 1,313 names had been reported on the poll-tax register, and added that everyone knew that the number on this list was never equal to the actual number of voters. He said that the election of 1858 had not been a fair test of Kansas City's voting strength; with only one polling place and with oral voting, only some 800 voters could be accommodated in a single day. He had stood in line for several hours waiting to vote on that occasion and had seen many would-be voters leave in disgust. With his usual technique of turning argument into some inapplicable channel, he charged that the real basis for the opposition of Independence was political: Kansas City was overwhelmingly Democratic and that meant the end of the Know-Nothing group of office hunters in the county seat.[41]

It is impossible to determine the truth of the charge of fraud, for Van Horn himself supplied about the only available source of population data for the town. The Federal Census of 1860, however, listed the population of Kansas City at 4,418, and the city had supposedly grown from the preceding year. A total vote of 1,675, considering the exclusion of women and children, would seem on the face of it rather high, even accepting the 1860 figure as representative of the total population in 1859. Furthermore, railroad elections in the city usually attracted a much smaller number of voters. The *Westport Border Star* said that election day had been cold and a good many eligible voters had not gone to the polls. Considering this drawback, Kansas City "had done pretty well," the paper wryly observed. The *Border Star* accepted the calculation of 800 to 900 eligible voters as about correct. It would not be long, the paper observed in the same ironic vein, before Kansas City would be entitled to elect a Representative to Congress.[42]

The debate over whether the Kansas City promoters did stuff the ballot box (and the available evidence suggests that they did) or whether they were able to stir up enough support to get an extraordinary turnout at the polls proved inconsequential. The promoters had obtained the overwhelming vote that they needed to override the wishes of the county, and there was no way that county leaders could overturn the result. Because of Kansas City's unity on the railroad program, no dissident faction within the city could be called upon to support such an effort.

With the election won, Kansas City leaders launched a program to get more state assistance to complete the Pacific. Van Horn filled his paper with editorials and letters to the editor that stressed the urgency of passing an aid bill at the next legislative session. The City Council appointed a committee of five to support this measure and other railroad legislation at Jefferson City. Vigorous campaigning was necessary, for by this time considerable opposition had developed to the policy of extending loans to railroads. In neighboring Liberty, the editor of the local newspaper continually attacked what he termed a wasteful and extravagant policy. Because of the financial chaos into which all the state-aided lines, with the exception of the Hannibal and St. Jo., had fallen, there were good grounds for such charges. In general, local interest not theoretical positions about the role of government determined the attitudes assumed on this question. Once the pattern had been set as to what railroads were to be aided and their routes fixed, many areas felt they no longer had reason to continue to support the state program.[43]

Critics of state aid often tried to justify their stand with the contention that railroads controlled by Eastern financial interests represented a threat to slavery and to Missouri's Southern institutions. An anonymous pamphleteer charged in 1859 that the principal beneficiary of years of state assistance to railroads was the "Black republican party." The investors in, and the officers of the main Missouri railroads, who had been robbing the state for eight years, were to a man rank Abolitionists. Chiefly they had been concerned with "preying upon fellow citizens in Kansas." This kind of attack on Eastern capital as an agent of Abolition could also be directed against individual local railroad projects. The Kansas City and Keokuk had been attacked on these grounds. Even Van Horn, when it suited his purposes, appealed to proslavery sympathies in opposing railroad plans that did not appear to accord with the interests of Kansas City. For example, he accused John Duff and Company, a financial group that held temporary control of the Hannibal and St. Jo. during 1858, with using a Missouri railroad to promote the interests of the Massachusetts Aid Society in Kansas.[44]

This defense of Missouri institutions, which was often merely a mask for special local interests, was never expressed in Kansas City during the effort to drum up support for more state aid to the Pacific. By late 1859, owing to the promoters' agitation, sentiment on the issue had become intense in the city. A local representative in the legislature, George W. Tate, had expressed some opposition to extending more loans to the Pacific unless proper controls were initiated over the railroad's policies, a position quite in accord with that of the local promoters just a year before. Now, however, they called a huge protest meeting, which adopted a series of resolutions denouncing Tate and calling for his immediate resignation on the grounds that he was misrepresenting his constituency.[45]

In spite of the presence of Van Horn and the other promoters on the scene, the aid bill failed to pass. Van Horn wrote that the defeat had left him outraged and desperate. He wished, he said, that Kansas City had a road to Galveston and none to St. Louis, for the bill's failure could he attributed to the jealousy of St. Louis of a possible rival in the West. He confessed deep disappointment: for months he had been waiting with mouth open "to give a whoop of victory. . . ." But the aid had not come; God only knew when it would come. Still, in his indignation, he saw hope for the future: "Why this hesitating, servile policy of clinging to the knees of the Pacific Railroad and worshipping the power of St. Louis?" Let the city build its own railroad, a connection to the Hannibal and St. Jo.[46]

Upon his return Van Horn was considerably less distraught and assured his fellow citizens that all might yet be well. He had apparently received word that Governor Robert Stewart would call the legislature back to reconsider the aid question. If the *Journal* account was to be believed, the joy of the city at the passage of the aid bill at the special session knew virtually no bounds. The long day of agony was at last over. "Kansas City is now the great city of the West. . . . Let every body rejoice for a new day of prosperity has dawned." A flag unfurled from the *Journal* office an-

nounced the passage. Immediately, bonfires were kindled in down-
town streets; all the bands that could be gotten together played;
cannons were fired; fireworks set off. "Never have we witnessed
so happy a scene—and such universal rejoicing. It beggars all
description." Townsmen pulled a model railroad car up and down
Main Street during the festivities. "Several of our *high*—we mean
prominent citizens were favored with a ride on the pioneer railroad cart." "The jollification of Tuesday night," concluded the
editor's account, "will long be remembered. . . . It was an appropriate recognition of the inauguration of a new and glorious
era. . . ." [47]

If Kansas Citians long remembered the celebration, it must have
been regretfully. Stewart's veto of the aid bill shattered the glee
of the town. Although Stewart had been a consistent and vigorous
supporter of railroads, he argued that the bill as passed did not
adequately protect the interests of the state. It had released the
state's first lien, he stated in his veto message, without establishing
proper controls over the railroad's construction procedures. But
the Kansas City railroad partisans were in no mood for legal
subleties. "Stewart the great champion of internal improvements
in the State of Missouri has proved recreant to his vows, false to
his pretensions," the *Journal* angrily asserted on its first page,
"treacherous to his friends and a traitor to Missouri. . . . He has
outraged the confidence and forfeited the respect of the people and
we leave him to their mercy." On page two of the same issue, Van
Horn denounced him at even greater length for "his wicked be-
trayal of life long friends." "No man can defend him without
taint and no man desires to extend a hand to raise him from the
deep into which he has precipitated an honorable and distinguished
name." In concluding his diatribe, Van Horn reminded his readers
that "Lucifer, too, was once the son of morning." [48]

The Kansas City leaders immediately set out to salvage something from this disaster. At the suggestion of Lykins, they appointed a committee to formulate a program for the city to find
ways to extend further aid to the Pacific on a local basis and to

complete a connection with the Hannibal and St. Jo. A public meeting held a few days later produced a series of resolutions denouncing Stewart in terms as vitriolic as those employed by Van Horn. The meeting also supplied a keynote for future efforts: until the railroad question was finally disposed of, the city would "know no Democrat, nor opposition, but only Railroad and Anti-Railroad men." This was a concrete expression of the general doctrine so long advocated by the community leaders—that politics should serve as an instrument of material acquisition. In the region at least, Kansas City was ahead of its time in publicly adopting a view that became so generally accepted in the years after the Civil War.[49]

The public meeting also approved the key feature of the committee's plan, a city subscription in bonds of $200,000 to the Kansas City, Galveston, and Lake Superior Railroad to build a connection with the Hannibal and St. Jo.[50]

In the two years following the decline of the Kansas City–Keokuk project, local leaders had continued to maintain an interest in some kind of northern connection. During the summer of 1858, there had been a brief flurry of excitement about the state-aided Platte County Railroad, which had been authorized to build between the terminus of the Pacific in Jackson County and St. Joseph. John Duff and a group of Eastern investors who controlled the Hannibal and St. Jo. had made plans to construct this potential auxiliary road, but the effort had not been carried through. During the summer and fall of 1859, a project to build to the Hannibal and St. Jo. by way of Gallitan, Missouri, in co-operation with an Iowa company had aroused considerable interest in Kansas City.[51]

As a result of these proposals, surveys had been made of possible routes to the Hannibal and St. Jo. By mid-1859 the local leaders had decided that the best route would be provided by running the road to Cameron, Missouri, thirty-five miles east of St. Joseph and about fifty-four miles from Kansas City. The Chamber of Commerce had written to John T. K. Hayward, superintendent of the Hannibal and St. Jo., suggesting that his company assist in building this line. Hayward apparently believed that its prospects were good, for he recommended in his annual report for 1859 that the Hannibal and St. Jo. support the project. He estimated that a stock subscription of at least $400,000 could be obtained from cities and counties along the route. The railroad would pass through one of the most fertile parts of Missouri and could be cheaply constructed. Once built, it would command the immense business developing in the Kansas Valley, New Mexico, and the Southwest.[52]

In a letter to John W. Brooks, a director of the Chicago, Burlington, and Quincy and a leader in the Burlington system, Hayward wrote at greater length of the project. His letter offered an authoritative echoing of the arguments of the Kansas City promoters and provided a prophetic analysis of the future of regional trade patterns. He pointed out that the Kansas City–Cameron line would pass through a fertile corn and stock-growing region that would provide an excellent local market for the road. The cattle business with Texas and the Southwest was growing rapidly, but it was becoming increasingly difficult to drive livestock through Missouri. Here Hayward had in mind the fact that Missouri farmers had begun vigorously to resist the passage of cattle from the South because of the presence of Texas cattle-fever in the herds. Therefore, if the Kansas City–Cameron were built, nearly all cattle would be driven into Kansas Territory and would be brought to the railhead at Kansas City by way of the Kansas Valley. Moreover, the Valley was the best part of Kansas and would become a rich agricultural area; Kansas City provided its natural outlet. Even if the Pacific should finally struggle through to the western border of Missouri, Hayward went on, the Hannibal and St. Jo. would have a head start in dominating the Western trade. Financial prospects were good. He estimated that $400,000 could be obtained in subscriptions along the route of the road. If Brooks could raise $200,000 in the East during the year, the project could be completed. The Hannibal and St. Jo. would then be in a secure position for years to come.[53]

At long last some real use had developed for the Kansas Citians' grandiose Kansas City, Galveston, and Lake Superior charter, which because of its vagueness could be used to authorize any northward project. Stirred by the Stewart veto, they made plans to build a local railroad. On April 17, 1860, after the City Council had quickly ratified the town meeting's proposal, the community voted overwhelmingly to issue $200,000 in city bonds to purchase stock in the company. Only nine votes were recorded against the measure. The law authorized the mayor of the city, G. M. B. Maughs, to issue the twenty-year bonds to the railroad as he saw fit. On June 11, Clay County voted 1,200 to 832 to approve a subscription of $125,000 and in August increased this amount by $25,000.[54]

The overwhelming support for the bond issue in Kansas City and the contrasting sizable opposition in Clay County indicated how successful the Kansas City leaders had been in imposing their views on the community. The critics of the measure in Clay County voiced similar objections to those raised against the policy of state aid: corporations were inherently dangerous economic institutions and Eastern capital was trying to destroy slavery in Missouri. "Fishing River," in a letter to the *Liberty Tribune*, wrote that no faith could be put in the commitments made by an Eastern railroad; "corporations have no souls, and Railroad corporations least of any." Another opponent wrote that to turn down the bond issue would save Liberty, the county seat, "from the greedy grip of Boston capitalists, who would ruin a great market city, and who will ultimately abolitionize the northern half of the state." [55]

The pervasiveness of this kind of sentiment in the region and in much of Missouri accounted for the vigor with which Kansas City leaders advanced their central argument—that the political divisions arising out of the slavery controversy could not be permitted to divide the town on issues involving city progress. That the local business community was so successful in imposing this attitude was related to its own unity on railroad questions, the propagandistic abilities of its leaders, and the newness of the town. For popular opposition to railroad policies to have developed, some influential interest group would have had to give it direction. Kansas City had grown too quickly for this to have taken place. The ambitious settlers pouring into the town were easily swept up into the boom; and enthusiasm was kept high through Van Horn's stirring manifestoes, the continual public meetings, and the near-evangelistic railroad rallies.

While the local bond issue was being considered, several Kansas City addition owners, all of whom had been active in most stages of the local railroad movement, set up an informal organization for the Kansas City, Galveston, and Lake Superior Railroad Company. On August 2, after the city subscription had been approved, they officially established the company according to the terms of the charter. In the meantime, a local contractor, William Qualey, had worked on the costs of the project and came up with an optimistic estimate. He offered to complete the fifty-some-odd miles of roadbed for $300,000. The directors agreed to pay him $275,000 in cash and the rest in shares of stock in the company. Van Horn estimated that the $200,000 in Kansas City bonds should yield $150,000 and the $125,000 in Clay County bonds, of which a major portion had been immediately issued to the company, $100,000. These amounts when supplemented by private subscriptions would more than provide for the cost of construction. Constantly through 1860 Van Horn emphasized the large individual purchases of stock in the company. When the company was organized, he said for example that $25,000 had been subscribed in Kansas City and $15,000 elsewhere. These sums may have been pledged at the time, but actually the company never collected more than a few hundred dollars from private subscribers. As was the case with all the local Kansas City projects, the Cameron Railroad was financed to all intents and purposes exclusively through public funds.[56]

Almost immediately a serious problem developed. G. M. B. Maughs, the new mayor of Kansas City who was elected president of the company, went East to market the Kansas City bonds but was unable to sell them at anything even approaching favorable terms. Consequently, Qualey had to agree to a new contract on September 17. The company was to pay him $140,000 in cash, to be realized from the sale of Clay County bonds some of which had been marketed regionally, and $200,000 in Kansas City bonds. The cash and bonds would be released to Qualey in accordance with this seven-to-ten ratio as construction progressed. On October 10, Qualey went to work.[57]

Meanwhile, during the summer, further negotiations had been conducted with the Hannibal and St. Jo. The directors had again interested Hayward in their project. He stirred up support for the bond issue in Clay County, and once the company was organized the Kansas Citians hired him as chief agent of the road and put him in charge of overseeing Qualey's construction. Through his assistance, on October 29, 1860, they signed a contract with the Hannibal and St. Jo., which agreed to equip the road between Kansas City and Cameron with rails, to furnish rolling stock, and to run regular trains over the line in return for the first-mortgage bonds to be issued on the completed roadbed. This was the famous pre-Civil War contract, which has played a critical part in presentations of the Kansas City bridge legend.[58]

During the summer of 1860, a year of continual, frantic railroad activity in Kansas City, the local promoters again encountered problems in their relations with the Pacific. Shortly after Stewart's veto of the aid bill, the Jackson County Court, reflecting rural sentiment, ruled that the $225,000 consolidated county subscription voted the year before was not payable since additional aid had not been voted to the Pacific by the state. The Kansas City railroad executive committee established at the mass meeting after Stewart's veto immediately began to circulate a petition calling for the immediate payment to the company of the $100,000 subscription which had earlier been authorized by the county. The court refused to act, and Van Horn launched a series of broadsides against the judges. "Such a tyrannical outrage upon the people by a couple of brief-authority old fogies," he wrote, "was never before witnessed."[59]

In June, however, after consultation between Mayor Maughs

and company officials, the Pacific agreed to begin work outside of Kansas City on the line's roadbed, apparently with the understanding that some type of satisfactory county subscription would ultimately be paid. Again came the huge celebration as groundbreaking ceremonies took place the next month. The *Journal* termed it the great carnival day in Kansas City's history. The day's events—cannons at sunrise; the parade led by the band of the local music teacher, the ubiquitous "Professor" Bantie; speeches on the town's early history; the hauling off of the first wheelbarrow full of dirt by the president of the Pacific; a mammoth barbecue in the late afternoon—culminated in two evening balls in Concert and Metropolitan halls. Appropriately, William Gilpin, the prophet of Kansas City railroads and its mid-continental destiny, was a major speaker of the day. "We are ready at last," he observed, "to debouch out upon the great plains to the once far West. . . . We start out under the shadow of names of great and intrepid men, and should there be any trepidation on our part?" [60]

In August, 1860, after months of legalistic controversy over which of the many county and municipal subscriptions were actually payable and after one more election was held, the Pacific agreed to a new subscription arrangement. All earlier subscriptions still deemed payable—$100,000 from Jackson County, $50,000 from Independence, and $75,000 from Kansas City—were canceled. A general county subscription of $200,000 was substituted to be payable in county bonds over a ten-year period. [61]

In spite of these arrangements, the summer's celebration again proved premature. Although the Pacific let the contract for grading the roadbed of the uncompleted section of the line, by January of 1861 the company was once again in difficulty. During the legislative session, the railroad tried unsuccessfully to obtain a release of the state's lien on the part of the roadbed already completed so that first-mortgage bonds could be sold to raise more funds. The outbreak of the Civil War checked any attempt to complete the ninety-three remaining miles of the railroad.

The Kansas Citians' attempt to build the road to Cameron fared no better. Local accounts have generally asserted that the war caused the abandonment of the construction of the road. Well before the outbreak of the fighting, however, the company was in severe financial distress. Through the early months of 1861 Qualey continued to work, but not enough Clay County bonds could be marketed to meet the required cash payments. Van Horn continued to make optimistic forecasts. "Mark the prediction," he told his readers in January, "that in less time than has been taken to talk about the Pacific Railroad, the K. C. G. & L. S. Railroad will be running from the sunny bay of Galveston to frigid Lake Superior and exchanging the commodities of the Antipodes at our wharf . . . ." He could not have been a worse prophet. In April construction ceased. The payments due Qualey for his work amounted to $62,333.05 in cash and $89,050 in Kansas City bonds. But he actually had received only $48,688.63 in cash and $45,000 in bonds.[62]

What were the results of the prewar efforts of Kansas City leaders to obtain railroads? After several years of negotiation, the Pacific was still ninety-three miles away. In May, 1861, on the orders of the pro-Southern Missouri governor, Claiborne F. Jackson, troops destroyed several bridges on the part of the road already built, and the railroad suffered other damage as the war went on. Through their agitation, the Kansas Citians had won some recognition in Congress for their claim to be a point on any transcontinental railroad that might be built to the west, but there was no assurance in 1861 that this hope would be realized. As a result of their effort actually to build a railroad with local resources, they had a roadbed not more than two-thirds finished. During the war, this was nearly ruined by the elements and neglect. They had a contract with the Hannibal and St. Jo. to equip the road. The contract expired in 1862. For this enterprise the city, considering its size, had accumulated a significantly large debt. And through the next years, the debt became even greater as the interest on the unpaid cash settlement due to the contractor and on the city bond issue steadily mounted. The eventual effort to settle these claims became so complicated that a city investigating committee a few years later decided that the arrangements would never be fully understood. But through twists of circumstance, the road to Cameron, which in 1861 could not be assessed as anything but a complete disaster, proved to be the means by which Kansas City realized its predicted destiny as the metropolis of the Missouri Valley.

Town Rivalry: The First
Railroad

BEFORE the Civil War, the rise of towns along the Missouri
River and in Kansas Territory, each with its own ambitions
for the future, had plagued Kansas City promoters in their efforts
to build a metropolis. Measured solely in terms of growth, the
criterion ordinarily employed by contemporary boosters, the progress of Kansas City had not been striking. In 1860 its population
was only about 4,500. This made it substantially larger than the
older towns in the immediate vicinity: Westport, just to the south,
contained 1,200 people; Independence, a few miles east, 3,200.
But upriver to the north, St. Joseph, the outfitting point for much
of the emigration westward, had experienced a boom after the
completion of the Hannibal and St. Joseph Railroad in 1859; with
over 8,900 residents, it was nearly twice as large as Kansas City.
Leavenworth, Kansas City's great rival in the territory, had grown
more rapidly than any town in the region and contained nearly
7,500 people.

Other important towns had sprung up in Kansas. Atchison, on the Missouri River midway between Leavenworth and St. Joseph, could point to the geographical advantage of location on the westernmost bend of the Missouri River in Kansas. Like Leavenworth, Atchison had been founded as a base for slave-state operations in the territory. The free-state leaders who migrated into the town were able to work in harmony with the older Border-Ruffian faction; in its degree of internal unity, Atchison resembled Kansas City rather than Leavenworth. Built up initially through trade with Utah, Atchison's business expanded with the rush to the Colorado gold regions in 1859. In 1860, the town obtained a railroad connection. The Platte County Railroad, a state-aided Missouri company authorized to build a railroad from St. Joseph to the terminus of the Pacific, gained control of a local paper company, the Atchison and St. Joseph, and completed the line to the Missouri River opposite Atchison. During the war, guerrillas stopped the railroad's operation, and it did not prove a satisfactory connection once the war ended. But in 1860 Atchison seemed to have bright prospects for the future; its population stood at over 2,600. Just across the state line from Kansas City on the north bank of the Kansas River, the new town of Wyandotte had 2,000 residents. Forty miles westward, below the Kansas River, Lawrence had obtained comparable growth. Founded in 1854 by the early wave of settlers sent to the territory by the New England Emigrant Aid Company, Lawrence won national attention during the Border Troubles as the Free State Fortress. It continued to be the residence of many of the important leaders of the territory's economic and political life.[1]

Travelers, who visited the border region and played the nineteenth century game of predicting where great western cities would grow, were often unimpressed by Kansas City's claim to future greatness. Henry Villard, who came to the town in 1859, found Leavenworth much more imposing than Kansas City. He recalled later that he could hardly imagine a more unfavorable site for a future city than the forbidding bluffs upon which the Missouri town had been located. Horace Greeley, who traveled through the

West during the same year, thought that St. Joseph had the finest location of any of the Missouri River towns. Wyandotte also impressed him: it had, he said, "decided natural advantages over Kansas City." He wrote that one set of his friends thought that New York, St. Louis, and Leavenworth would be the three great cities of America; another group assured him that New York, St. Louis, and Atchison would be. After visiting the two towns Greeley was unwilling to advance an opinion on the question: Atchison had the better location, but Leavenworth had the head start.[2]

Although few observers accepted the thesis of Kansas City's predetermined greatness, the town's prewar progress had been steady. Two major elements in the western economy—the Southwest trade and military freighting—had centered there. The town's location south of St. Joseph, Atchison, and Leavenworth gave it important advantages in serving the trade area beginning to develop below the Kansas River. Moreover, in 1860 local leaders had high hopes that the Pacific would soon be completed, giving the city its much desired eastern outlet. They anticipated also that the railroad might eventually be extended westward as the main line of the transcontinental.

The early years of war shattered these favorable prospects. The community's carefully imposed neutrality on the slavery question broke down; many pro-Southern businessmen departed voluntarily or were forced to leave the city. The federal government transferred the headquarters for military freighting to Leavenworth. Because of the absence of sufficient military forces in the West, Indians put the Santa Fe trail under attack; the colorful caravans of the New Mexican traders arrived only intermittently in the city. Landholdings—optimistically platted into city additions—were sold for nonpayment of taxes. Van Horn went off to war. Payne, the Irish immigrant, and Coates, the Pennsylvania Quaker, both sound on the slavery issue, maintained the community as best they could, vigorously asserting the town's loyalty and at the same time trying to protect the interests of their pro-Southern townsmen.[3]

They were not particularly successful. Southern guerrillas sur-
rounded Kansas City on three sides and harassed Union soldiers
and merchants alike. For long periods of time it was unsafe to leave
the city limits. The trade of Kansas settlements went elsewhere, to
better protected Leavenworth or Atchison. Apparently, not a single
Kansas City prewar merchandising, wholesale, or commission business survived into the postwar era under the same management.
Only a few of the more intrepid city-addition owners attempted
to maintain their stake in the town. And they had to concentrate
on surviving, not on building railroads or on planning community
growth.

Leavenworth, on the other hand, seemed fortune's favorite. Built
near Fort Leavenworth and supported by a politically oriented
military policy, the Cottonwood City continued its rapid growth
and prospered from the adversities of war. According to a local
newspaper, during a single year, 1864, its wholesalers sold goods
in the interior of the state worth nearly $19,000,000 and its freight-
ers shipped westward over 40,000 pounds of supplies. New businesses opened and the old ones expanded. The streets of the city
teemed with soldiers from the fort and emigrants going west. There
were over 200 saloons, a dozen brothels, and several theaters.
Albert D. Richardson, the Ohio journalist, visited the river towns
at the end of the war and like many postwar observers thought
Leavenworth the likely winner in the struggle among the towns
to gain regional supremacy. He came west from Chicago in September of 1866 and found that the region had recovered quickly
from the havoc of war. Leavenworth, he said, looked more like a
"great city than any other point between St. Louis and San Francisco." Five newspapers (three in English and two in German),
gaslights, well-built brick buildings, all gave it the "air of a metropolis." His explanation for this gain was simple: St. Joseph,
Leavenworth, and Kansas City had started even before the war.
St. Joseph had age and a rich surrounding countryside; Kansas
City had the Santa Fe trade and a good rock river landing; Leavenworth a fine prairie site and a military post. "But," Richardson

concluded, "the two Missouri towns were Border Ruffian; with the great war, the whirligig of time brought in his revenges. Their business went to Leavenworth, while Kansas troops swept Missouri with fire and sword." [4]

In the region, however, Leavenworth had gained the reputation of being internally disunited. Other towns used its political troubles to point up the value of concerted community action. "While Leavenworth quarrels, Atchison works . . . ," commented the *Daily Champion* of Atchison. "Those who fight Atchison have to fight her as a whole, for *her* people are one in sentiment and resolve, wherever her welfare is at stake." This point, frequently expressed in regional newspapers, was even echoed in Leavenworth itself. The editor of the *Daily Times* wrote that the city had lost many opportunities in the past because unlike Lawrence, St. Joseph, or Kansas City its citizens had not gotten behind necessary home policies. The community had permitted itself "to be torn by party divisions and really to be governed by tricksters and demagogues who led these divisions." This seemingly inconsequential matter of contrasting internal community unity proved of considerable significance in shaping decisions that ultimately determined the outcome of urban rivalry in the border region. [5]

Some observers favored Atchison as the site for the regional metropolis. It too had grown rapidly, with a population at the end of the war estimated at 8,000. During 1865, according to local estimates, the town sent over 21,500,000 pounds of freight westward. Local leaders were optimistic about the future. "The interior location of our city," said Mayor John A. Martine, "full twenty miles further on the Overland highway to Utah, California, and the Gold Mines of the West than any other point on the Missouri River, gives us unparalleled advantages as a shipping point. Let us improve them." Most of the travelers into the region at the end of the war, who predicted greatness for the bustling Kansas towns, were northern journalists, still under the sway of wartime passions. Their denigration of the former slave-holding Missouri towns was to be expected. Still, in view of the growth and progress of both

Leavenworth and Atchison, and the decline of Kansas City, judgments against the latter's claims to being the city of the future were altogether reasonable.[6]

An unusually perspicacious analysis of the future of towns in the region was supplied by Charles M. Chase, one of the few journalists to tour the area systematically before the war was over. He came to the region in August, 1863, to record his impressions for a Syracuse, Illinois, newspaper. Unlike many travelers, he seemed to be little affected by the prejudices of war: his observations had a surprising tone of objectivity. He reached St. Joseph first and found that the city had suffered greatly from having a large population of Secessionist sympathizers. Hundreds of citizens had fled because of the severe military discipline imposed on the community. Property had depreciated by two-thirds; business was disorganized. Nevertheless, Chase wrote, St. Joseph still supplied the only satisfactory rail point for Kansas. Before any other railroads reached the western border of Kansas, the city would once again regain wealth and influence. Its future importance appeared to be secure.

Traveling south, Chase found Kansas City a town virtually under siege. The thickets of Jackson County, he observed, provided the best haven in the state for the Secessionist guerrillas known as Bushwhackers. The operations of these "infernal devils," he wrote, made it unsafe to travel on any road leading into the city. Every man carried a revolver and slept with it loaded at night. These conditions had caused a drastic decline in Kansas City's business. Property in town had declined by nearly a half in value, and surrounding farm property by nearly as much. Leavenworth on the other hand was booming with business from the fort and from other government transactions; the city was "leading everything west of St. Louis." Still, Chase was optimistic about Kansas City's chances in the future rivalry. The city's location at the great bend of the river impressed him, for this made it a natural depot for the great Southwest and for southern and western Kansas. But more important in determining the outcome would be the pattern of future railroad connections. In this regard, Chase found Kansas City to be

ahead in potential lines, and he implied therefore that the two communities would have to be considered about even in the race. Both
cities were sanguine about their chances. "They are now balancing,"
he wrote, "but a few years more will settle the question and do
away with all rivalry. The world will soon speak of one of these
places as one of the thriving cities of the country—and the other,
the world won't speak of at all." Chase was quite right in his evaluation: it was the pattern of railroad connections that was ultimately
responsible for the fact that Kansas City, a candidate favored by
few observers, ultimately became the regional metropolis.[7]

Before the Civil War, the Kansas City railroad movement had
been tied to the Missouri system of roads. By 1860 local leaders
had clearly formulated the program to be followed in relation to
these lines. Eastern connections were indispensable, but the city
looked westward for trade hinterlands. During the midst of the
war, while Kansas City leaders concentrated on protecting their
stake in the shattered community, railroad developments occurred
in Kansas and in the councils of the nation that were critical in
Kansas City's rise as regional railroad center.

During the late 1850's, as towns grew in the territory, Kansas
underwent a railroad boom as intense as that in Missouri. In the
years before and immediately after the Civil War, the state chartered over 1,100 railroad companies; 200 of these actually built
some line. Although each community had its own local concerns,
the broad aspects of a regional strategy were discernible. In part,
businessmen in the new Kansas towns wished to design a plan that
would circumvent the efforts of Kansas City promoters to make
their city the major regional railroad and trade center. The prewar
boom culminated in a large railroad convention held in Topeka on
October 17, 1860, through which Kansas promoters hoped to
harmonize conflicting town interests and to propose a system of
land grants to be petitioned for at the next session of Congress.
Nineteen Kansas counties sent delegates. After much debate the
convention agreed on resolutions recommending requests for
public lands for the following railroads:

1. A railroad to be built diagonally in a northwesterly direction across southeast Kansas from the border of Missouri through Emporia, Fremont, and Council Grove to Fort Riley.

2. A railroad from Wyandotte to run up the Kansas Valley on the south side of the river by way of Lawrence, Lecompton, Tecumseh, Topeka, and Manhattan. At Wyandotte this road would connect with the Missouri Pacific and a line to the Hannibal and St. Jo.

3. A railroad running from Lawrence to the southern boundary of Kansas in the direction of Fort Gibson and Galveston Bay.

4. A railroad from Atchison to Topeka and westward from there in the general direction of Santa Fe.

5. A railroad from Atchison to be built straight westward to the boundary of the territory.[8]

These proposed railroads competed with those contemplated by the Kansas City promoters. A railroad to Galveston Bay, a road north to the Hannibal and St. Jo., a road up the Kansas Valley, a road to Santa Fe would all operate to destroy the trade patterns that Kansas City interests had built before the war and those that they hoped to establish in the future. Some of these lines would also supply new potential first links for a transcontinental road to the coast.

As a result of the Border Troubles, the sectional tension of the late fifties, and the war itself, polemicists of the period often portrayed the railroad rivalry between Kansas and Missouri in terms of ideological conflict between a free and a slave state. Each Kansas town, however, had its eager land speculators anticipating growth and profits just as did Kansas City promoters. The support-loyal-Kansas theme employed to build up trade and to promote railroads did not prove to be very persuasive. When it was in the economic interest of Kansas businessmen to buy in Kansas City or to support its railroad plans, they did so.[9]

Certain characteristics of regional geography, especially the location of rivers, bore a significant relationship to Kansas railroad plans. It was demonstrated in the 1860's that operation of a major railroad across a river required bridging, particularly in areas where winter conditions hampered ferries. The existing level of engineering knowledge made the building of a railroad bridge a formidable and costly undertaking. In fact, the first bridges across the Missouri and Mississippi rivers represented outstanding technological accomplishments.

Two major rivers, the Missouri and the Kansas, cut through the area in which railroad planning centered. The former in its flow across Missouri formed a reversed capital "S" pattern. From Kansas City it passed northeastward for the width of three counties, then southeastward to Jefferson City, located over fifty miles south of the most northern point of the river in the state. From Jefferson City it flowed in a general northeastward direction to a point above St. Louis, where it turned sharply in joining the Mississippi.[10]

The Kansas River between Fort Riley and Kansas City formed a similar pattern. Eastward from Fort Riley to Lawrence, the greatest north-south variation was about eighteen miles. Outside of Lawrence the river turned northward and emptied above Kansas City northeastward into the Missouri. Lawrence, located at the southernmost bend of the Kansas, was about eleven miles south of both Topeka and Kansas City.

These geographical considerations meant that it was possible to build straight-line railroads that would strike established commercial centers on the rivers and yet not make it necessary to follow a river route. Sedalia, Warrensburg, and Pleasant Hill, points on the route of the Pacific Railroad of Missouri, were from twenty-five to thirty miles south of Kansas City. A direct line from Lawrence passing through these towns would miss Kansas City by about twenty-five miles and would provide a short cut by which Western trade could be channeled to St. Louis. Earlier the Kansas City promoters had faced the possibility that the Pacific might decide to locate its line in this fashion. Similarly, a line from Kansas City directly to Topeka on the north side of the Kansas River would miss Lawrence by about ten miles.

The river pattern also affected potential north-south connections.

Any railroad from southern Kansas north to Leavenworth or Atchison would have to bridge the Kansas River somewhere west of Kansas City. Although the Kansas could be bridged with reasonable ease, it would still involve considerable expense. A road into south or south-central Kansas could be built from Kansas City without a railroad bridge. And it was the region below the Kansas River that constituted the greatest opportunity for the development of a rich immediate trade area. A section embracing the south-central quarter of the state (east-west from Chase to Rush counties and south to the Oklahoma line) grew in population by 465 per cent during the sixties in contrast to 240 per cent for Kansas as a whole. During the seventies, this section gained 1,794 per cent in population, in contrast to 173 per cent for the state. This growth was largely the result of the enormous expansion in wheat raising in Kansas after the Civil War. In the early 1860's, railroad planners and promoters recognized the potential of this region, for its fertility had been well advertised in presentations of the garden-of-the-world view of the West.[11]

A Kansas railroad—the Union Pacific, Eastern Division—gave Kansas City its first railroad connection. The planning and building of this line—accompanied by bribery, corruption, intrigue, and violence—demonstrated the part played by circumstance, individual decision, political maneuvering, local promotion, and the force of sheer human greed in the growth of a major railroad center.[12]

Fundamental in this development was an early obscure Kansas paper railroad. Leavenworth interests as part of their prewar promotional campaign had organized a local company, the Leavenworth, Pawnee, and Western Railroad, and in 1855 had obtained a charter from the territorial legislature authorizing them to build from Leavenworth to Pawnee (near Fort Riley) and to extend their line to the western boundary of the territory, then at the summit of the Rocky Mountains in what is now Colorado. In 1857 the legislature supplemented the original act of incorporation to permit a southern branch; this could be built to the border of Kansas to connect with any railroad constructed through Indian Territory and Texas to the Gulf of Mexico. The charter allowed the company an original capitalization of $5,000,000 and added another $5,000,000 for the branch. This project competed directly with the roads of the Kansas City promoters, who had planned lines both to Fort Riley and south to the Gulf.[13]

The Leavenworth businessmen organized their company in January, 1857, with a supposed initial pledged subscription of $156,700 and, after preliminary surveys, fixed a route from Leavenworth to Fort Riley. But like Kansas City companies, the Leavenworth, Pawnee, and Western had no real assets, and no further work was done for the next three years. It would probably have remained just another of the hundreds of regional paper railroads had it not fallen into the control of an "Executive Committee" composed of Thomas Ewing, Jr., A. J. Isaacs, James C. Stone, and James H. McDowell. These men had important political connections and sufficient cleverness to use them to advantage. Ewing in particular was one of the more influential men in the territory. His relationship with Isaacs paralleled that of Coates and Reid in Kansas City. During the Border Troubles, he had been an anti-Lecompton leader at the same time Isaacs held office in the pro-Lecompton administration. Among railroad and town promoters, ideology was seldom permitted to interfere with the search for profits.[14]

The Leavenworth committee was one of the first of many groups to hit on the idea of trying to gain control of land held by Kansas Indian tribes. These holdings comprised a fifth of the total amount of land in Kansas including some of the most fertile. The promoters also understood clearly the methods that would have to be employed to achieve this. We must, Ewing wrote at this time, "secure aid from the rapacious lobby," which would not let any favorable measure through "until their hunger is appeased." But, said Ewing, among this lobby were "gentlemen of character & influence." For a reasonable fee in property they would get to work and provide substantial service. Through negotiations with the Interior Department, the Leavenworth leaders obtained a federal treaty in 1860 that permitted the company to purchase nearly 224,000 acres of Kansas Valley land from the Delawares, at a price to be set at no lower than $1.25 an acre. With little difficulty they got the treaty through the Senate. When government appraisers subsequently fixed a near minimum figure—$1.28 an acre—for the entire holding, the dissatisfied Delawares initiated legal action. To assist them, they hired a specialist in land claims, an Indiana lawyer named John Palmer Usher. Usher felt that he was supporting a just cause; he denounced the "gross heartless and nefarious fraud" being perpetrated against the tribe. But when the Senate refused to order a reappraisal and other actions against the company failed, Usher went to work for the Leavenworth promoters in their efforts to try to obtain control of additional Indian holdings.[15]

The Leavenworth, Pawnee, and Western now had the right to buy the Delaware land at a most favorable price. But the treaty stipulated that the land had to be paid for in gold within a year after the appraisal, and the company could not raise the money. To solve this problem, they again turned to the federal government. A new Republican administration was now in office; Kansas politicians had power in the party. Ewing saw Lincoln and got him to extend by executive order the time allowed in the treaty for the company to pay for the land. Then with the assistance of the Office of Indian Affairs, the promoters obtained a highly favorable supplemental treaty, which the Senate approved in mid-1861. This revision authorized the company to pay for the Delaware lands with a bond issue to be secured by a mortgage on 100,000 acres of the holding and meant in effect that the company could use less than half the lands to pay for all the lands. The government recognized the bonds issued by the company secured by only 100,000 acres as having a value at least equivalent to the total appraised price of the 240,000 acres. The supplemental treaty represented an admission, of course, that the Indians had not been allowed anywhere near a fair market value for their lands. Best of all for the promoters, in view of the financial status of their company, this transaction required no immediate capital investment. This was a most dubious arrangement, but the nation had committed itself to a policy of "pre-emption and exploitation." Such transactions became commonplace in Kansas in the 1860's and 1870's as speculators moved to acquire the rest of the valuable Indian holdings.[16]

Through Usher's assistance in Washington, the Leavenworth promoters next obtained a treaty negotiated on November 5, 1861, and approved by the Senate on April 15, 1862, which authorized the Leavenworth, Pawnee, and Western to purchase the Pottawatomie Reserve, located northwest of Topeka, the Kansas capital. The company subsequently was unable to take advantage of this opportunity, and the right to purchase the tract passed to a later railroad, the Atchison, Topeka, and Santa Fe. With a party in power pledged to provide federal support for the building of a transcontinental railroad, the promoters went to work to get their railroad named as the beneficiary of any governmental largesse that might be forthcoming from Congress for this great national undertaking.[17]

Obtaining these various concessions necessitated a good deal of maneuvering within the administration. Usher was a close friend of Caleb Smith, Lincoln's Secretary of the Interior; he later became Smith's assistant and succeeded him as Secretary in 1863. During the early months of the new administration, he continually advised Smith and was also in close touch with Smith's subordinates including the Commissioner of Lands and the Indian Commissioner. For his services on behalf of the company, Usher obtained options on substantial portions of the Indian holdings, but he apparently purchased only a small amount of the land. Several years later, he denied vigorously that he had ever received gifts of stock or land from the company; but in one fashion or another he apparently realized considerable benefit from his association with the Leavenworth promoters. When he became Secretary, his close involvement with their company led to the frequent charge that he was using his office for the benefit of a business in which he had a personal stake.[18]

During Congressional consideration of the transcontinental bill, Isaacs and Stone set up headquarters in Washington. Usher worked to get administration support for the claims of the Leavenworth, Pawnee, and Western to be included in any federal benefits. He persuaded the company to hire Henry C. Bennett, a former congressman, to draft a suitable Pacific Railway bill, and added portions to it himself. Bennett also directed the company's lobbying activities at the Capitol.

In 1861 the Leavenworth, Pawnee, and Western was still a paper company; its only real asset was the right to purchase Indian holdings. The "Executive Committee" had originally intended, as soon as all the land was in hand, to sell the whole enterprise to Eastern capitalists. Leavenworth businessmen had promised to buy stocks, of course, but as was usually the case these pledges had not been collected. Stone, a man of considerable wealth, had met some of the expenses of the company in return for shares of stock, but the whole operation was informal. From 1860 on, the "Executive Committee" manipulated the affairs of the company as they saw fit. Their task was to persuade sufficient people in Washington that they were operating a going concern quite capable of building a major western railroad.[19]

To further this effort, the Leavenworth promoters floated a rather mysterious bogus stock issue. On the books of the company, Stone subscribed to $5,000,000 worth of shares. The directorate then issued these to him as trustee for the company with full power of attorney to transfer them. Stone, Isaacs, and Ewing then freely distributed the certificates around Washington and in Kansas.

Years later when Congress was investigating the Pacific railroads, a memorandum summarizing these transactions came to light. Stone had hurriedly prepared it at a time when the Leavenworth promoters were selling out their interest in the company. The memorandum listed large amounts of the certificates to be distributed to professional lobbyists, newspapermen, lawyers, government officials in Washington and in Kansas, and to members of Congress, who were to receive theirs by way of relatives and friends. It also enumerated the amounts of Indian land to be distributed, including substantial amounts for the Commissioner of Indian Affairs, the chief clerk of the Indian office, and various Indian agents and officials in Kansas. The memorandum contained a number of interesting notations after share listings: "supposed to be for S. C. Pomeroy," the Kansas Senator; "supposed to be for T.[haddeus] Stevens and others;" "Hold over them in terror;" "mostly blackmail." Stone perhaps understated the case when he commented, "A careless memorandum, that was." During the course of his often frank testimony, Stone denied that he himself had ever directly offered shares to members of Congress, who were considering the Pacific Railway bill. He had warned his associates of the dangers in this kind of action. But he admitted that they might have done so anyway. At least, he had heard rumors to this effect. How much of the stock actually reached the intended parties was never ascertained. Usher, who was down for a substantial amount, denied in his testimony that he had ever received any of the certificates. He asserted that his later connection with the railroad came entirely from a $10,000 cash investment.[20]

In large part because of these lobbying efforts, the Leavenworth, Pawnee, and Western Railroad did emerge from the months of deliberation over the transcontinental railroad as a major beneficiary of federal action. The principle of government assistance for a transcontinental had won wide endorsement before the Civil War, but North-South conflict had made agreement on a route impossible. The Republican platform of 1860 had pledged federal support; Secession had taken all the supporters of the thirty-second parallel, southern route out of Congress. With the Republican Party having majorities in both houses, the program could go ahead.

Although Congress spent little time in debating the necessity of federal aid, it was necessary to compromise and harmonize a variety of conflicting local and sectional interests before a bill could be passed. This of course permitted a good deal of behind-the-scenes maneuvering of the kind engaged in by the Leavenworth promoters. St. Louis and the Missouri representatives stood firm for the old Benton route—to run westward from the terminus of the Pacific Railroad of Missouri at Kansas City. Interests representing Cincinnati, Baltimore, and Philadelphia supported their plan. An Iowa–Chicago–Great Lakes belt of interests favored a more northern route. But there were many significant divisions within these broad groupings.

The Kansas representatives, who stood to benefit directly from land and railroad stock if they succeeded, fought tenaciously for the rights of the Leavenworth, Pawnee, and Western and in general supported the plan for the central route. But they struggled with the Missourians over the location of the line. The initial House bill based on Bennett's draft contained the proviso that the Kansas company could build in accordance with its Kansas charter: this would mean that Leavenworth would definitely be on the line. Fearing that passage in this form might mean that the road would not be joined with the Pacific Railroad of Missouri, the Missourians managed to get this clause struck out. Against the wishes of the Kansans, they also obtained a statement in the bill specifying that the terminus of the railroad should be below the Kansas River at its juncture with the Missouri and that the railroad should connect with the Pacific. Conflicts of this sort occurred over all sections of the bill: the Pacific Railway Act of 1862, as finally passed, was the product of compromise. Instead of providing for a single transcontinental, as had always been the intention of those who proposed the program, the law set up an elaborate system of branches, which had the effect, as one contemporary critic put it, of turning an "artery into a sprinkler." [21]

The law first chartered a new company, the Union Pacific, and authorized it to build a trunk line from a point on the hundredth meridian about midway across Nebraska near Fort Kearney toward the Pacific Coast. The Central Pacific Railroad of California, a company of substance that had actually constructed some line, could build eastward toward the point on the hundredth meridian until it effected a connection with the Union Pacific. The presumed meeting place was the border of California, although either line could be continued if it reached the border before the other. The act required the Union Pacific to build a branch from the hundredth meridian to the eastern border of Nebraska (Presidential action later fixed the terminus at Omaha) and to construct a line from this latter point to Sioux City. This much of the law represented a substantial victory for the northern belt of interests.

In providing support for other branches, the act recognized the supporters of the central route. It authorized the Leavenworth, Pawnee, and Western to build from its required eastern terminus below the juncture of the Missouri and Kansas rivers to the "initial point" on the hundredth meridian. The Hannibal and St. Jo. was authorized to build westward from St. Joseph, by way of Atchison, to connect with the line through Kansas, or provided it could obtain the consent of the Kansas legislature to build northwestward to connect with the line across Nebraska.

The act provided federal subsidies for the construction of these lines: five full sections of land on each side of the track for each mile of construction and the loan of government bonds at the rate of $16,000 per mile. Higher payments were specified for construction in the western mountains. The Hannibal and St. Jo. could collect subsidies for only 100 miles of construction. The railroads were to repay the federal loans by annual payments of 5 percent of their earnings after the roads were in operation. In order to facilitate the building of the lines, the act permitted the Kansas company to consolidate either with the Pacific Railroad of Missouri or with the Hannibal and St. Jo. Moreover, all the beneficiaries of the act could consolidate with the Union Pacific.

Because of the necessity of compromise between Kansas and Missouri interests, the law left the route to be followed by the Leavenworth, Pawnee, and Western indefinite. From the required eastern terminus, the company was unrestricted in locating its line as far west as Fort Riley; from there to the "initial point" on the hundredth meridian, the President would have to approve the route. The act, in rather ambiguous fashion, partially recognized the claims of Leavenworth in stating that the Kansas company "may construct their road from Leavenworth to unite with the road through Kansas." [22]

Because of the law's complexities, it was subject to varying interpretations. The *Western Journal* hailed it as a momentous victory for the interests of Kansas City. The federal government, the newspaper argued, had at long last recognized Kansas City's strategic location and natural advantages. "Providence has done much for us, Congress has aided . . . as much as the most sanguine of us could ask," it declared when the amendment fixing the Kansas City terminus passed. Now it was time for the city to see that the railroad was rapidly constructed. People who had expected a "modern Thebes to spring from the site . . . occupied by a few frame structures and paper maiche [sic] edifices" at Leavenworth were doomed to disappointment. The paper argued that the privilege of Leavenworth to unite with the main line through Kansas was entirely barren, for this would not provide the city with a necessary eastern connection. Natural position had settled the matter of regional supremacy once and for all. [23]

As was so often the case, Kansas City leaders were unduly optimistic. The Pacific Railway Act contained a number of ambiguities and few considered it the final settlement. Within the framework of the law, a route by way of Leavenworth could have become the main line across Kansas: the pattern of subsequent events demonstrated clearly that this was a possibility.

After the passage of the law, most national attention centered on the organization and activities of the company created by Congress, the Union Pacific. But the Leavenworth, Pawnee, and Western, in the hope of winning support as the main line of the transcontinental system, immediately made plans to begin building. On September 19, 1862, the company let construction contracts to a Montreal firm, Ross, Steele, and Co. A fundamental concern of the Leavenworth promoters was to get a line built from their city; this would enable them to profit from their town property speculations. Accordingly, they initiated grading operations both at Leavenworth and at the required eastern terminus near Kansas City. In order to begin collecting federal subsidies, the company had to complete forty miles of railroad. Lacking any substantial capital of their own, the Leavenworth promoters realized very early that they would have to solicit outside support.

Owing to the potential value of the congressional subsidy, this did not prove too difficult. Two ambitious promoters, John C. Frémont, the famed explorer and adventurer, and Samuel Hallett, a young New York investment broker who had raised money abroad for the Atlantic and Great Western Railroad, purchased for $200,000 the stock held by Isaacs, Stone, Ewing and McDowell, amounting to about 114,500 shares. Acting for the company, the directorate also conveyed to Frémont and Hallett the rights to the rest of any stock issued, subject to any legal claims that might be made against it. Stone held the bulk of the stock in the hands of the four men. The committee had assigned it to him, apparently without payment, in much the same fashion they had assigned the pool of certificates to influence legislation. The history of the Leavenworth, Pawnee, and Western demonstrated how an inner group of town leaders could manipulate a local paper railroad company. In this case, the manipulation resulted in substantial personal profit for a small group of Leavenworth promoters.[24]

In order to better publicize the company and to give it a greater degree of prestige, Hallett and Frémont immediately changed its name to the Union Pacific, Eastern Division. The "Executive Committee's" handling of stock presented the new owners with a number of problems that they sought to solve by a series of legal and financial maneuvers. First, they imposed a heavy assessment on any shares that had earlier been distributed to outside parties. Next, under the terms of their agreement with the Leavenworth promoters, they transferred all the assets of the company on deeds of trust to an Eastern investment firm as security for a loan of $5,500,000 to be paid through a company bond issue. In addition to being a step to raise capital, this transaction represented an effort to freeze out any outside shareholders. Also involved was an attempt to avoid payment on the earlier construction contract. Ross, Steele had not been paid for any of its work; the action by Hallett and Frémont disposed of the assets on which the construction company had given credit. Hallett, who assumed active direction of the company, probably recognized that the quickest way to realize profits from the congressional subsidy was through use of the construction company device, whereby exorbitant construction costs could be paid to a separate company controlled by the same investors who owned the railroad company. Later, of course, the Union Pacific's use of this method led to the infamous Credit Mobilier scandal; the owners of the Central Pacific also resorted to the device in building their line. As soon as the new owners took over the Leavenworth railroad, Hallett canceled Ross, Steele's contracts and ordered them to stop work. They refused and continued grading near Leavenworth.[25]

In initiating these moves, Hallett encountered sharp resistance from rival promoters. Stone had distributed over $4,000,000 of the bogus stock issue, and some of the certificates that had been passed out contained his notation that the shares represented were not assessable. Moreover, some Leavenworth businessmen had invested small sums in the company during its early days. C. A. Trowbridge, a member of the law office of James Joy of Detroit, took up the cause of a group of these stockholders and began to prosecute the legal claims of Ross, Steele against the railroad company. Trowbridge had lobbied for the original Leavenworth company in Washington; Stone had given him a large block of stock for his services. He therefore had a personal stake in the venture to undermine Hallett, but in addition he was working closely with Joy in an apparent effort to gain control of the Kansas company for other major railroad interests. Joy, a leading American railroad entrepreneur of the period, was at this time one of the chief figures in the Hannibal and St. Jo.—Chicago, Burlington, and Quincy system. The Pacific Railway Act had suggested the possibility of consolidation of the Leavenworth, Pawnee, and Western with the Hannibal and St. Jo.; the Kansas railroad could logically be integrated into the Western system of roads being developed by the Burlington. Trowbridge obtained a temporary injunction to stop the sale of the Union Pacific, Eastern Division's bond issue and initiated other legal action against Hallett. While he was engaged in these matters in Topeka, the state capital, Hallett went to Fort Leavenworth, and in some fashion obtained command of a company of cavalry from the post commandant. At the head of these troops, Hallet stormed the construction camp.[26]

Hallett telegraphed his eastern associates: "I had an awful row with Carter, a battle on the works and a pitch in to get possession. We drove them back until they cried enough. And my foreman S. S. Sharp led Carter to the bank by the collar and but for his begging would have ducked him. I expect Steele and Carter back with reinforcements. Let them come. We are ready. We have all their ties, houses and works and shall hold them." [27]

Trowbridge described a much more prosaic encounter. "Hallett," he wrote to Joy, "swore and tore around considerably, and finally (he and his troops) they all went off—we had some cool fellows as foremen." Hallett, armed with two revolvers and a bowie knife, had threatened to kill an engineer working for Trowbridge if he dared to go to work for Ross, Steele. But the engineer had told Hallett "to go to H—ll" and had gone on with his business. By telegram, Trowbridge protested to Ewing, now a general in command of the Kansas military district. Ewing denied that he had authorized Hallett to use the troops and ordered them back to the fort. But Hallett retained control of the construction camp.[28]

The Trowbridge group continued their legal efforts but hardly in terms of prosecuting points of law. "Hallett will leave no stone unturned to buy & bribe & what not, all to defeat us—," Trowbridge wrote to Joy, "so we want to play as sharp as he can." Initially they concerned themselves chiefly with trying to influence the appointment of a new district judge sympathetic to their interests. Finally after several months of maneuvering, Trowbridge and his group were defeated in a case decided in Keokuk, Iowa. However, the

Union Pacific, Eastern Division, continued to be plagued with law-suits from holders of stock in the original Kansas company and from those entitled to benefits from the Ross, Steele construction con-tract.[29]

Meanwhile, Hallett had set up his company offices in Leaven-worth. At the time of the purchase, he and Frémont had promised that the city would definitely be on the line of the road. In August, 1863, Leavenworth interests assured the Illinois editor, Charles M. Chase, that though the line might begin at Kansas City, the road would swing northward by way of Leavenworth before cutting back to the Kansas Valley to reach Lawrence. This would mean that all Western trade would reach Leavenworth before it passed on to Kansas City. If this development actually took place, Chase predicted, "Kansas City is blasted and Leavenworth is to be the town of the West." The *Journal* of Kansas City in its comments pointed to the congressional authorization as binding. Kansas City was the required eastern terminus, and the road was compelled to connect with the Pacific of Missouri. In lighter vein than usual in the ordinarily heavy-handed railroad polemicizing, the editor of the *Journal* had earlier satirized the efforts of the rival city: "The Leavenworth newspapers are perpetrating a huge joak [sic] about the Great Pacific Railroad. The entire editorial force of the city has turned out with pick and shovel and gone to work on the road, and expect to have it completed through to California in a couple of weeks. They are going to have it run three times around Leaven-worth, so as to be sure it will stop there. But the great difficulty for them to determine is whether they will build most of it by tele-graph, stage or newspaper puffs—probably the latter. They are go-ing to commence it—tomorrow or yesterday—and they are also discussing the propriety, after a few miles of it is built, of 'break-ing it off' and running it into the ground for fear it may go to some other town besides Leavenworth." [30]

Shortly after setting up operations in Leavenworth, Hallett abruptly moved his company offices and the construction equipment to Wyandotte, located just above the Kansas River opposite Kansas

City. Several developments probably dictated this move. As part of his negotiations with Leavenworth interests, Hallett had obtained assurances of a $100,000 city subscription to the company. Because of conflict among rival railroad groups, he was unable, however, to work out satisfactory terms with city authorities. Moreover, Trowbridge and his group stirred up opposition to Hallett in Leavenworth. On one occasion, for example, Trowbridge proposed that Joy frame a letter to him, saying that Joy had talked to John W. Brooks, the head of the Boston investment group controlling the Hannibal and St. Jo.–C. B. Q. lines. Joy should write that Ross, Steele, and Company had submitted a proposition to the Eastern investors to ask for their support in building the Kansas road. He should then go on to say that "from what Mr. Brooks said, and what you know of these gentlemen you have no doubt but that they will accept Ross, Steele, & Co.'s proposition as soon as Hallett & Co. are got rid of." Trowbridge would show this letter around to Leavenworth people who had invested in the original Leavenworth company. Probably, he said, they would then "unite with us in driving Hallett off." [31]

Apparently, Joy could not obtain the support of the Boston group in his efforts to gain control of the road. Brooks told him that the Hannibal and St. Jo.–C. B. Q. owners were not interested because of the entanglements in the company. Later they might be willing to become involved in Joy's plans, but for the time being they would probably support the building of the transcontinental branch by way of Atchison provided by the 1862 law. [32]

Kansas City promoters also played a part in Hallett's decision. Representatives of the Chamber of Commerce conferred with him during the summer of 1863. As part of his plans for the future, Hallett had agreed tentatively to support the building of a line from Leavenworth to Cameron in order to connect the Union Pacific, Eastern Division, with the Hannibal and St. Jo. To forestall this, the Kansas City leaders, acting through the Chamber, offered him control of their Cameron project. In support of this move, on September 14, 1863, a short while before Hallett moved to Wyandotte, the City Council, "in order to facilitate the speedy resumption of the work," voted unanimously to appoint Hallett a proxy to vote the shares of stock owned by the city in the Kansas City, Galveston, and Lake Superior Railroad Company. Since private shares were almost nonexistent, this of course gave him control of the Kansas City company.[33]

Hallett may have contemplated the development of a regional system of railroads. He obtained direction of the Parkville and Grand River Railroad, a paper company authorized to build north of the Missouri River, and attempted to gain control of the Pacific Railroad of Missouri during the winter of 1863–1864. These companies could have provided the basis of a logical system with Kansas City at its center.[34]

Late in September of 1863, Hallett started work on the Union Pacific, Eastern Division, below the mouth of the Kansas River across the state line from Kansas City. For the promise to construct a short spur to Wyandotte's river landing, he obtained a $100,000 subscription from the county. Optimistically, Hallett set a goal of fifty miles of railroad completed by the first of January. The *Journal*, indicating that Hallett had given proper assurances to local promoters, began offering fulsome praise of the way Hallett was conducting the enterprise. Everything was being done in the most economical fashion; all bills were being paid in cash; laborers were hired without regard to color. Hallett was a man fired with "lofty enthusiasm;" he would build the road in accord with its importance as a great national undertaking. He had successfully resisted all the "clamors and seductions" of local interests in its location: this, translated from the rhetoric of the day, meant that Leavenworth, like Kansas City, had wanted to be the terminus of the road. "His experience is large—his energy is indomitable, and his resources ample. Success must crown his efforts." [35]

Hallett's actual conduct of the enterprise was much less magnificent. His financial manipulations led to further fights within the company. Without adequate capital to complete the first forty-mile section necessary to begin to collect the federal subsidy, Hallett launched a money-raising plan. He first got the directors of the company to grant a contract giving him exclusive right to construct the railroad. By promising a share of the construction profits and by giving up some of his shares in the company, he next negotiated a series of loans with John D. Perry, president of the Exchange Bank of St. Louis, other St. Louis investors, and with Thomas C. Durant, of the Union Pacific. Perry extended the largest loan, $750,000. During his negotiations with the St. Louis capitalists, Hallett apparently worked out agreements so that his line could be conveniently joined with the Pacific Railroad of Missouri.[36]

Hallett made these transactions during the winter of 1863–1864 without the consent of Frémont, and the two men broke. Frémont and his associates began to support the claims of the old construction company, Ross, Steele, charging that Hallett had obtained his construction contract illegally. They also began to line up support among the holders of certificates issued earlier by Stone. At two separate meetings in Leavenworth on April 5, 1864, conflicting stockholder groups elected different boards of directors. The Hallett–St. Louis faction re-elected the old directors, who had approved Hallett's transactions, and named Perry to replace Frémont as president. The rival group selected a completely new set of directors with Frémont as president.[37]

In the controversy that ensued, the Hallett faction had a friend in power: John Palmer Usher, who had been Secretary of the Interior since January, 1863. Usher, in dealing with the roads benefited by the Pacific Railway Act, had vigorously supported the Union Pacific, Eastern Division, from the beginning; his first annual report as Secretary lavished praise on the railroad. When Hallett's manipulations aroused criticism during 1863, Usher and Postmaster General Montgomery Blair issued a public letter that commended Hallett, expressed the "good will and cordial support" of the government, and promised full assistance to further the rapid completion of the railroad.[38]

In the fight the next year between the Hallett and Frémont factions, Usher lined up with Hallett. When Fielding Johnson of

Leavenworth became one of the directors on the Frémont board, Usher removed him from his office as Indian Agent of the Delawares. Johnson vigorously denounced the Secretary, charging that he was using his official position to line his own pockets. Johnson took his case to Kansas and Missouri newspapers, and the episode became a minor scandal of the Lincoln administration. The *Journal* of Kansas City, firmly behind Hallett, interpreted the removal of Johnson to mean that the government officially backed the Hallett faction and would not permit any interference with the great national project. The newspaper demanded that Leavenworth and other parties stop harassing the railroad. The unhappy Trowbridge, who failed in his efforts to wrest control from Hallett, supplied another analysis of the episode: he asserted that the rascality of the railroad and the "infamous conduct" of Usher made up "an amount of villainy unparalleled in any business transaction I ever heard of." Trowbridge exaggerated. Public promotion of private enterprise led logically to ties between government officials, capitalists, and promoters. Although in the long run mixed enterprise may have been an efficient method to promote economic growth, corruption was an integral part of the system. During the nineteenth century, when government support of railroad building was common, numerous railroad entrepreneurs—large and small—engaged in practices similar to those of Hallett and the other promoters in the Union Pacific, Eastern Division.[39]

Through the federal government's support and through negotiations with Frémont, the Hallett group gained full control of the company. But new problems developed immediately. When Hallett moved to Wyandotte, he fixed a route that crossed the Kansas River just west of Wyandotte and then ran straight to Fort Riley on the north side of the river. Because of the southward jogs in the river, this route would mean that the railroad would bypass both Lawrence and Topeka, located on the south side of the Kansas. All evidence indicated that Hallett intended to build forty miles of line as quickly as possible in order to realize payment of the federal subsidy without regard to the future operating profits of the railroad.

Hallett's plans, however, conflicted with those of Senator James Lane, who had been instrumental in getting the Kansas railroad included in the Pacific Railway Act. Lane had a master plan to make Lawrence rather than Kansas City the regional railroad center. He circulated a petition requesting that the road pass through Lawrence and obtained the signatures of thirty-four senators as well as the endorsement of Lincoln. Lane's move had popular appeal; Lawrence had become a national symbol of the Union cause as a result of the brutal Quantrill guerrilla raid on the town in 1863. Hallett, hardly the type to be moved by sentimental appeals to patriotism, argued that the change would be too costly and demanded large subsidies from both Topeka and Lawrence. After several meetings between Lane, Perry, and Hallett, during which Lane threatened to block the federal subsidy, Hallett backed down. He wrote Lane on June 13, 1864, that he would accept the latter's demand and run the road to touch the Kansas River opposite both Lawrence and Topeka.[40]

The Pacific Railway Act of July 2, 1864, which increased the subsidies for the building of the authorized transcontinental roads, specifically required that the road touch opposite the two Kansas towns. Through the efforts of the Kansas delegation, the law also required that the railroad reach Leavenworth: if it was not feasible to build the main line by way of Leavenworth then the company had to build a branch from there to unite with the main line at or near Lawrence.[41]

After the passage of the law, construction moved along rapidly. Hallett laid plans for celebrating the completion of the road to Lawrence on August 18 and sent out invitations to high governmental officials and men of wealth. The *Journal* in commenting on the forthcoming celebration enthusiastically proclaimed that the vision of the early transcontinental railroad prophets had at last begun to be realized. The cause to which Gilpin had devoted "the energies of his manhood," a transcontinental by the central route beginning at the juncture of the Missouri and Kansas rivers, was at last achieved. The iron horse had started on its iron track to the "final West." [42]

The celebration never came off. On July 27, 1864, as Hallett was returning to his offices in Wyandotte after lunch, he was shot in the back and killed by Orlando A. Talcott, who had earlier been chief engineer of the road. Apparently, Talcott's motive was revenge. Frémont had originally employed him. When Hallett took over the company, he fired Talcott, who then wrote a letter to Lincoln asserting that the road was so poorly constructed that it would not meet the standards required for the federal subsidy. He charged that Hallett was perpetrating "the Bigest [sic] swindle yet." Lincoln referred the letter to Usher, and a copy reached Hallett, then in Washington. Angered, Hallett telegraphed his brother to "slap" Talcott. This he did, and Talcott bided his time waiting for Hallett's return.[43]

After the death of Hallett, John D. Perry and his group gained control of Hallett's construction contract and through a cash settlement with Fremont stabilized the organization of the company. Perhaps, in view of some of Hallett's maneuverings, there was a measure of poetic justice in the fact that Perry through years of complicated litigation, finally settled in the Supreme Court in 1879, was able to eliminate any claims of Hallett's widow to a share in the profits of the railroad. On December 19, 1864, the railroad opened service between Kansas City and Lawrence. With Usher out of the cabinet and James Harlan, a supporter of the Union Pacific and an opponent of Hallett's policies, in office, the company had difficulty collecting its first federal subsidies. Initially, government inspectors refused to approve Hallett's construction, but in the latter part of 1865 after certain changes and improvements had been made the company began to receive government payments.[44]

From then on construction proceeded rapidly across Kansas. On July 3, 1866, the government authorized the company to change its route west of Fort Riley to build up the Smoky River to Denver. The road eventually joined with the Union Pacific at Cheyenne. In 1869 Congress authorized the company to change its name to the Kansas Pacific, and eleven years later it consolidated with the Union Pacific and the Denver Pacific under its present name of the Union Pacific.[45]

The Kansas Pacific gave Kansas City an outlet to the west and provided a crucial link in the system of railroads that eventually made
the city a leading transportation center. Achievement of this long-
dreamed of hope of Kansas City promoters—a railroad up the Kansas Valley—came about through a complex series of events. The
decision as to where to begin the line had resulted from the congressional action of 1862. That this requirement was written into
the bill was largely the result of the work of Missouri leaders in
Congress, who supported St. Louis' demand for continued control
of the western trade. They were able to muster greater support for
their demand among those who favored a central route than could
the Kansas leaders who wanted a Leavenworth or an Atchison terminus. In this regard, the years spent by Kansas City leaders in
echoing the Benton-Gilpin argument about the significance of the
juncture of the Missouri and Kansas had importance, for by 1862
the merits of the location had been woven into the rationale for the
central route. But geographic logic had nothing fundamental to do
with the decisions in the Pacific Railway Act of 1862. These resulted
from months of logrolling among a variety of local and sectional interests. Although the act did require a branch of the transcontinental
to begin near Kansas City, this was not decisive. Because of the act's
ambiguities, Leavenworth could still have been a point on the line,
and given the right turn of circumstances, a road between Leavenworth and Kansas City could have become a relatively insignificant
branch. Later railroad developments demonstrated the reality of
this possibility. That Hallett chose to build the main line straight
along the Kansas River, in violation of his commitments, related to
the fight within the Union Pacific, Eastern Division, and to the fact
that his opponents successfully stirred up sentiment against him in
Leavenworth. Kansas City promoters played a part in offering inducements to Hallett that he found attractive. Moreover, his relationship with St. Louis investors made a tie-up with the Pacific
Railroad of Missouri at Kansas City logical. In short, political negotiation, corporate intrigue, and local maneuvering—not the logic
of geography or location—shaped this key development in Kansas
City's growth as a railroad center.

The Kansas Pacific tapped a rich agricultural market. It contributed to the rapid rise of Kansas City as a livestock and meat-packing center. As John T. K. Hayward had predicted before the war, owners of the huge Texas herds, which had multiplied rapidly because of the collapse of markets during the war, shipped their cattle eastward during the late sixties and seventies from railheads on the Kansas Pacific. At first, however, these herds passed by way of Leavenworth over the Leavenworth-Lawrence branch required by the Pacific Railway Act of 1864. In the end, the rich promise foreseen by early Kansas City railroad prophets of a railroad up the Kansas Valley was to be realized to a greater extent than even they with all their exuberant dreams had predicted. But before the potentialities of the Kansas Pacific could be realized, new links in a regional system had to be built and Kansas City promoters had to counter many railroad schemes of rival communities.

5

Railroad Revival
The Stage is Set

THE Pacific Railway Act of 1862, with its provision for a transcontinental branch beginning at the juncture of the Missouri and Kansas rivers, focussed attention on the uncompleted Pacific Railroad of Missouri. If St. Louis and Missouri were to continue to profit from the Western trade, which had long been a mainstay of the state's economy, quick completion of the line was necessary. During the early years of the war, as the Pacific attempted to obtain relief from its enormous debts to the state, promotional argument in Kansas City emphasized an old theme: If St. Louis did not support the Pacific with more money, she faced the danger of losing to Chicago the rich plains trade that rightfully belonged to her, and Kansas City would further this outcome by throwing all her support to the Cameron connection unless assistance was rapidly forthcoming. The threat was even emptier than it had been in the past. The amount of aid that war-impoverished Kansas City could extend to any railroad was negligible. The principal program of the community leaders during the war was to obtain a moratorium on taxes, so that property holders could save their city additions and other real estate. Nevertheless, the discussion of the problem of the Pacific threw considerable light on the trade patterns that had begun to develop during the war.

A *Journal* editorial of May 2, 1863, provided a detailed and typical analysis of the Chicago–St. Louis rivalry for the commerce of the West. The writer found several reasons to explain why St. Louis businessmen were in the process of losing the lucrative trade of Kansas to Chicago. Pro-Southern guerrillas, encamped in thickets along the Missouri River, had made steamboat navigation unsafe. The Hannibal and St. Jo.—Chicago, Burlington, and Quincy system provided a direct, quick, and efficient connection to Chicago. Most important, however, was the superior energy and enterprise of Chicago; the businessmen of that city were alive, wide-awake, alert, and always on the lookout for new trade. Chicago interests would never allow a large business to be lost through failure to complete some sixty miles of railroad. If Chicago had the problem of the Pacific to deal with, the road would be finished in a year. St. Louis could do the same thing; she had wealth enough but not the enterprise. Natural forces had given St. Louis the trade of the West. But in "days of grand competition for the trade of future empires," natural advantages were no longer enough. They had to be supplemented by enterprise, sagacity, and wise, liberal expenditures.[1]

Now that the Pacific had definitely fixed Kansas City as the railroad's western terminus, the three local representatives in the General Assembly—Van Horn, Payne, and E. M. McGee, platter of McGee's Addition and one of the more imaginative of the town's real-estate developers—became railroad legislators and led the effort in the 1862–1863 session to push through proposals that would ease the burden of indebtedness to the Pacific. Van Horn, for example, introduced a bill that would have cancelled the debt of the various state-aided roads and substituted stock of the companies in payment. Although his measure as well as several others that would have provided drastic relief did not pass, railroad supporters obtained a law that prohibited the governor from selling any of the railroads of the state for nonpayment on bonds for a period of three years. A letter from one of the three Kansas City representatives, signed "Spectator," warned that something would have to be done to complete the road, and quickly. Otherwise, all the trade of Santa Fe, southern Kansas, and Colorado would soon pass to Chicago. Railroads out of that city had been rapidly reducing freight charges on goods shipped from Kansas towns in order to undermine the river trade and to fix patterns of commerce that could not easily be altered in the future.[2]

During the next summer, the directors of the Pacific made plans to resume construction. George R. Taylor, president of the company, wrote to Payne, who during the war assumed leadership of the local railroad movement, that a substantial portion of the line would be ready for business before the next winter was over. The completion of the remaining segment would then depend on favorable action by the legislature at its next session. Taylor commended Payne for his zeal on behalf of the state railroads. Robert Campbell, a director of the Pacific, in writing to a local resident, also praised highly the actions of the Kansas City legislators in seeking to extend assistance to the Pacific during the preceeding legislative session.[3]

For the rest of the year, the *Journal* continued to emphasize the need for greater state support of the Pacific. Before the legislature met, the local promoters called another of their public meetings to drum up enthusiasm for a new measure to suspend the state lien. The resolutions adopted embodied the by now all-too-familiar theme: the trade of the plains, by natural geographic right, belonged to Missouri, and it would be suicidal for the state to allow this commerce to be diverted elsewhere.[4]

During the session, local leaders frequently expressed the fear that the legislature again might not approve this measure. But as before they found hope in the alternative of the Cameron road. Loyalty to Missouri, a convenient argument to use since Missouri-Kansas antagonism had been intensified by the war, had little force in the city. In December, for example, the *Journal* told the businessmen of the city that if they would just take hold of the Cameron project in the proper spirit, they would be able to finish the line. The necessary amount of money was entirely within the capacity of the city to raise. Then let the trade pass to Chicago, the *Journal* said. "We have been calling on Jupiter long enough, now let us help ourselves." [5]

The forecasts that the bill to aid the Pacific would fail proved unduly pessimistic. After a long fight with opponents who favored foreclosure and sale to private parties, the assembly passed a measure suspending the state's first lien on the railroad and substituting a second mortgage. This permitted the Pacific to sell a first-mortgage bond issue as a means of raising more funds. The directors' report issued the next month predicted that the road would be finished by the end of the year. Through the efforts of Payne, who made a trip to St. Louis to consult with Pacific officials, the company agreed to begin building immediately on the Kansas City end of the line. Again, there was celebration, marked by the usual oratory and "jollification," as construction began just outside of Kansas City. But this time the festivities were quieter; war and the frequent disappointments of the past had tempered the community's exuberance.[6]

Late in the summer of 1864, a minor breach in the community's unity developed over the railroad's requested right-of-way along the levee. Opposition came from two sources. Landholders in the south end of the town favored a route through McGee's Addition; some merchants and traders feared that a railroad along the levee would ruin their stakes in the river trade. Although this disagreement presaged a division among city sectional interests that was to become intense in the future, on this occasion the dispute was settled with relative ease. On September 17, the City Council submitted to the voters an ordinance granting the right-of-way along the levee for a cash payment of $25,000. Proponents of the proposition gained considerable support through the argument that the city badly needed the $25,000 offered by the Pacific for the improvement of streets, which had fallen into bad disrepair during the war years. In the ordinance submitted to the people, the money was specifically allotted for this purpose. A few months later, however,

Cameron officers obtained control of this money and used it to pay off the interest on the city bonds held by their prewar contractor. In the cause of obtaining railroads, local promoters frequently resorted to this kind of extra-legal practice.[7]

Once more the community was disappointed. The release of the state's first mortgage did not ensure the completion of the Pacific. Although the company finished the Kansas City–Independence link, the road again encountered financial difficulties, intensified by damage caused by General Sterling Price's raid into Missouri in 1864. Most of the money obtained from the sale of first-mortgage bonds was used to repair the already constructed portion of the road in western Missouri. The company began a campaign for more funds. Legislative action on January 7, 1865, permitted the County Court of St. Louis to issue new bonds to the railroad in the amount of $700,000. With this new benefaction, finally on September 21, 1865, the line opened from St. Louis to Kansas City. After nearly fifteen years of agitation and effort, Kansas City had its eastern connection. "The 'long roll' of . . . rumbling wheels heard for the first time in the history of our city," the *Journal* commented, "announced the arrival of the 'advance guard' of the grand army of enterprise, commerce, industry and progress, hereafter to assemble at this the railroad centre of the Missouri Valley." [8]

But Kansas City's longtime urban rivals were far from willing to accept this assertion as fact. The start of construction of the Union Pacific, Eastern Division, had revived the prewar programs of Kansas towns to obtain railroads. In the years 1865–1873, the new state experienced the second phase of an intense railroad boom. Notable among the many plans developed in the closing years of the war was that of Senator James Lane, whose professed hatred of Kansas City as a center of proslavery sentiments seems to have been real, to make Lawrence rather than Kansas City the regional metropolis.

Violent, ruthless, vulgar, utterly cynical, perhaps even paranoic, Lane was perhaps the most colorful politician in the history of a state noted for colorful politicians. He had begun his career in Indiana, winning the lieutenant governorship as a result of a distinguished military record during the Mexican War. As a member of the House of Representatives, his vote for the Kansas-Nebraska Act wrecked his chances of re-election, and in 1855 he came to Kansas to repair his fortunes. Initially a Democrat, he shortly went over to the Free State Party, and won great popularity during the Border Troubles for his flamboyant, intemperate attacks on Border Ruffians. In his lifetime, he became, through powerful oratory and tremendous personal magnetism, a Kansas folk-hero of the Free-State cause.[9]

Although Lane perhaps gained less wealth than other Kansas politicians of the period from using his political power to promote his own financial interests, he was deeply involved in many of the corrupt railroad-land transactions that were so much a part of Kansas political life in the 1860's. Thomas Ewing, Jr., had enlisted his assistance in getting the treaties through the Senate authorizing the Leavenworth, Pawnee, and Western to purchase Indian reserves under most favorable terms. Ewing wrote at the time that these were being considered that Lane would not want anything for himself, "but his Kansas friends must be provided for." And they were. For his services, Lane did receive land near Lawrence from the Delaware reserve.[10]

When construction of the Union Pacific, E. D., was underway, Lane by threatening to block the railroad's congressional subsidy had forced Samuel Hallett to build by way of Lawrence. This railroad was to provide the east-west link in the system he planned. North-south, the key line was the Leavenworth, Lawrence, and Fort Gibson, a prewar Lawrence paper railroad company which in 1858 had received a charter authorizing construction to the southern border of the territory. Since the project would provide Leavenworth an outlet to the south, it was also supported by interests there. The original promoters planned eventually, like those in Kansas City, to extend the line to the Gulf of Mexico, and they shortly renamed their company the Leavenworth, Lawrence, and Galveston. Lane took over the presidency in 1865. Through his support, in September the company obtained a $250,000 subscription from Douglas County, of which Lawrence was the seat. Franklin County, directly below Douglas, voted a $125,000 subscription to the project during the year. Lane made a speaking tour in the South, traveling to Memphis, Vicksburg, and New Orleans, in an unsuccessful attempt to raise additional capital from private investors. Finally, with promised support from Chicago and New York capitalists and an increase in the Douglas County subscription to $300,000, the company began building south of the Kansas River in 1866. The Leavenworth-Lawrence branch of the Union Pacific, E. D., which Lane had been able to make a requirement of the 1864 transcontinental railway law, was to provide the part of the road north of the river.[11]

The Leavenworth, Lawrence, and Galveston competed directly in southeast Kansas with an important new Kansas City project: the Kansas City and Neosho Valley Railroad (shortly renamed the Missouri River, Fort Scott and Gulf). This represented the postwar revival of the Kansas City promoters' plans for a road to Galveston Bay. As a result of the railroad enthusiasm that developed in southeastern Kansas during the summer of 1865, a company with Coates as president, was organized in Kansas City early in September to build through the tier of Kansas counties along the Missouri border to the Oklahoma line. Kansas City immediately voted a $200,000 subscription. In November, two Kansas counties each approved subscriptions of the same amount.[12]

In addition to facing the rivalry of Lane's Gulf road, the Missouri River, Fort Scott, and Gulf also encountered opposition from another of his proposed lines, the Pleasant Hill and Lawrence Railroad. This represented a new effort to realize the possibilities of the cut-off to the south of Kansas City, which had plagued local promoters from the first days of Missouri's railroad program. Projected to intersect the Pacific of Missouri at Pleasant Hill, Lane's line would be able to move east-west freight twenty-five miles south of Kansas City on the more direct route to St. Louis. Lane attempted to gain the support of the Pacific for the project and to undermine the Missouri River, Fort Scott and Gulf in southeastern Kansas by promising an alternative outlet to the east.[13]

There were signs during 1865 that Lane's plan might be successful, but the next year he suffered some sharp political reverses. Hoping to establish the same type of close relationship he had enjoyed with Lincoln, he supported Johnson's Reconstruction program in return for continued control of federal patronage in Kansas. Kansans in general supported the Congressional Radicals, and public sentiment turned against him. In the same period, newspaper articles exposed his ties to a corrupt contractors' ring in the Indian Territory. Lane fought to protect his power, but late in June he collapsed in St. Louis. While recuperating on a farm near Leavenworth, he put a pistol in his mouth and shot himself. He died ten days later. Although Lane's business associates lacked his vigor and influence, they attempted to carry through his railroad plans. As matters stood at this point, railroads had been provided that would open to Lawrence the markets of southern Kansas and establish a direct outlet to St. Louis. One further step was necessary: if Leavenworth could be connected to the Hannibal and St. Jo. and thus to Chicago, the Lane scheme to circumvent Kansas City and to make Lawrence the regional metropolis might be realized.[14]

Developments beyond the control of the Lawrence promoters gave Kansas City rather than Leavenworth this connection. Nevertheless, the completion of the Lawrence and Pleasant Hill road several years later, in 1872, demonstrated the possibilities that had been posed by the Lane plan. The Missouri Pacific immediately supported the project by providing equal through rates to St. Louis from Lawrence and Kansas City. By this time, however, railroad rivalry in the region had been settled in Kansas City's favor. Another major line between St. Louis and Kansas City, the St. Louis, Kansas City, and Northern, had been constructed, and this railroad exerted its influence to force the maintenance of a rate differential between the two towns. This destroyed the last hope of Lawrence to overtake Kansas City.[15]

Kansas City successfully attracted railroads. Lawrence made a good try and failed. The result was local disillusionment with promoters and all their works. Editorials in the mid-seventies even expressed the view that railroads were "of doubtful utility to a town."

A sadly amusing letter to the *Lawrence Daily Journal* of December 18, 1880, reflected this disenchantment. The writer said he could recall when Lawrence had no railroads. At that time, the citizens of the town had assumed that if they could get the Kansas Pacific to come that their fortunes would be made. It came. The town leaders next decided that a railroad to southern Kansas would make that rich section Lawrence's tributary, so $300,000 was voted to the Leavenworth, Lawrence, and Galveston. But this railroad did not help the town's fortunes either. Then it was decided that what the city really needed was a competing eastern outlet; the citizens voted $450,000 to the Pleasant Hill line to kill Kansas City and make Lawrence the commercial center of the Kansas Valley. "Unfortunately for our hopes," he went on, "the grass soon grew over the track of that road." The next panacea was a road to the coal fields of Osage County; this would make Lawrence a great manufacturing center; the town voted $200,000 to build a road to Carbondale. Finally, local promoters decided that it was not really railroads at all that the town needed, but rather a dam across the Kansas River. If it were built, they argued, Lawrence would become a second Fall River. "And here we are," the writer concluded, "still poor and dissatisfied." [16]

Other postwar railroad developments were also significant in establishing the basis of the final battle for regional supremacy. As soon as the Pacific of Missouri was completed to Kansas City, it employed the Kansas charter of the Missouri River Railroad to extend the road to Leavenworth. It reached the city in July, 1866, and immediately began construction toward Atchison. Adopting a policy that boded ill for the future of Kansas City, the Missouri Pacific—as it was now known—began to move freight from the east destined for Lawrence and beyond by way of Leavenworth, and also posted a schedule of freight and passenger rates favorable to Leavenworth. [17]

In Atchison, Senator Samuel C. Pomeroy had revived a number of prewar railroad projects with which he was associated, designed to improve his own as well as Atchison's fortunes. Pomeroy was willing to use all his great political influence and whatever corrupt means were necessary to realize his involved land and railroad schemes, but unlike many of the more sanctimonious representatives of the period, he conducted these operations with an engaging frankness and good nature. Mark Twain made an apt choice when he selected him as the model for the Gilded Age promoter-politician, Senator Dilworthy from the "Happy Land of Canaan." Pomeroy had come to Kansas in 1854 as an agent of the New England Emigrant Aid Company, and like most of the prominent free-state leaders became interested in town development, turning his attention toward the close of the Border Troubles to the proslavery stronghold of Atchison. In an 1857 letter to his business associate, Thaddeus Hyatt, he reflected clearly the fact that ideology was usually an afterthought to profit in the development of Kansas. He wrote that the two of them now owned every alternate lot upon 330 acres adjoining the town and a number of lots and buildings within the town itself. They had also acquired a half-interest in the town's leading newspaper, operated by a dedicated slave-stater B. F. Stringfellow. Only after enumerating these material accomplishments at some length did Pomeroy see fit to add, "We have hoisted a *Free-State Flag*." [18]

Pomeroy also instructed Hyatt on how to deal with promoters who might want to invest in this kind of speculative venture. During the summer of 1857 a group of Kentucky investors came to Atchison with a plan to develop a town across the river; Pomeroy rather gleefully recounted that they had found that he had already bought the best 200 acres at the potential site. If there is to be a new town, he wrote, "I am to control it." He had insisted on retaining timber rights on the land and also on developing it through the device of a land company, in which he would keep a controlling number of shares. He asked Hyatt to suggest a name for the new town but warned him to publish nothing. Show the map of Atchison around, he said, for that would demonstrate that the promotion was doing well. But, he cautioned, "talk of the new town only to those who will interest themselves and advance money." [19]

Like any effective town promoter, Pomeroy recognized the vital relationship between real-estate profits and railroad planning. In

1857 he had concentrated his attention on obtaining a connection for Atchison with the Platte County Railroad in Missouri. "If the Rail Road can be put through next season—," he wrote to Hyatt with characteristic frankness, "we can sell lots enough to make such sinners as we are rich as *sinners ought to be.*" [20]

As part of the prewar Kansas railroad planning, Pomeroy and his associates obtained charters for companies to build from Atchison to Pikes Peak, to Topeka, and to Fort Riley. These were later consolidated into two companies, the Atchison and Pike's Peak and the Atchison, Topeka, and Santa Fe. As president of the Atchison and Pike's Peak, Pomeroy negotiated with the interests controlling the Hannibal and St. Jo. and obtained control of the subsidies granted to the latter under the Pacific Railway Act of 1862 in return for the promise to operate the new line as an extension of the Hannibal and St. Jo. In 1863 he maneuvered through the Senate a highly favorable treaty which gave his company control of the valuable Kickapoo Indian reserve. A political enemy later offered evidence that Pomeroy had received 50,000 acres of the reserve for his part in the negotiations, and, as was often the case, relatives of government officials were rewarded with tracts. For one dollar, the company conveyed 640 acres of the holding to the wife of the Commissioner of Indian Affairs. With these benefactions in hand, the company began building westward from Atchison at the end of the war. For the second of the lines, the Atchison, Topeka, and Santa Fe, later to become one of the major railroads of the West, Pomeroy gained bond subscriptions totalling $950,000 from Kansas counties. Actual construction of the line, however, was delayed until 1868 when he was able—again through much devious maneuvering—to gain control of the Pottawatomie reserve for the railroad, even though its route ran nowhere near this Indian holding.[21]

In Missouri in the immediate postwar period, a number of projects important to Kansas City's interests were being revived or initiated. Before the war short lines had been built between Weston and Atchison and between Atchison and St. Joseph; these had been consolidated into the Platte County Railroad, authorized to build between St. Joseph and the western terminus of the Pacific of Missouri. Early in 1864 the legislature ordered the sale of the state-aided Platte County because of its failure to make payments on its state bond loans. The two small roads that had been absorbed into the company successfully resisted this action and reorganized as the Missouri Valley Railroad in 1867. The litigation that resulted from these developments delayed construction of this railroad and of the reorganized and renamed Platte Country Railroad. In 1864 the North Missouri, another prewar state aided line, laid plans to run a branch to Leavenworth from Moberly, on the north bank of the Missouri in the central part of the state. Leavenworth voted $250,-000 to the railroad in August, 1864, with the stipulation that its line would pass no closer to Kansas City than three miles. When the road the next year decided to build by way of Kansas City, Leavenworth withdrew its subscription.[22]

Early in 1866 Van Horn's *Journal*, with customary comprehensiveness, summarized the prospects of the river communities. The writer recognized that four towns had a chance to gain regional supremacy: Atchison, St. Joseph, Leavenworth, and Kansas City. He paid the customary tribute to Kansas City's superior natural advantages, and then quickly dropped the subject. The *Journal*—reflecting Van Horn's comprehension of the significance of technological change—had early recognized that railroads could decisively alter natural patterns of city location and growth. Railroad connections, the writer asserted, would ultimately determine the location of the great regional metropolis, and all the towns had made considerable progress in obtaining them. St. Joseph had the Platte Country to be built north in the direction of Council Bluffs and southward toward Kansas City. She was also of course the western terminus of the Hannibal and St. Jo. Atchison had a connection to the Platte Country through the Weston-Atchison line. She would be a point on the Missouri River Railroad (the extension built by the Missouri Pacific from Kansas City to Leavenworth and extended northward.) The Atchison, Topeka, and Santa Fe would provide a connection to the Union Pacific, E. D. Leavenworth also had a number of proposed connections. The city was a point on the Missouri River Railroad, and its branch of the Union Pacific, E. D., required by the Pacific Railway Act of 1864, would be finished within a few weeks. Leavenworth had also made plans for a road to Cameron, to connect with the Hannibal and St. Jo.

The Kansas City system, however, was far more comprehensive than any of these, the writer argued. It had both the Pacific roads. It was the terminus of the Missouri River Railroad and the proposed terminus of the Platte Country. A road to the Gulf of Mexico—the Kansas City and Neosho Valley—was under way. Because the city was located farther south than her rivals and could build on an unobstructed course south of the Kansas River, Kansas City would have a monopoly of trade in that direction. The other three towns, in spite of their connections, would only be able to divide trade north of the Kaw. This proved to be a prophetic analysis of eventual regional trade patterns.[23]

From the complex array of railroad projects that developed in the region at the end of the war emerged a design, which contemporary writers only occasionally and only partially comprehended. The equation defining this design contained five significant factors: three railroads—the Union Pacific, E. D., the Missouri Pacific, and the Hannibal and St. Jo.—and two metropolitan markets—St. Louis and Chicago. In attracting railroads, Kansas City had a major locational advantage in relation to the rich areas of south and south-central Kansas. Atchison and St. Joseph were located in better position to the Chicago market, but were too far north to be readily accessible to St. Louis. Enterprise could pull railroads from their natural pathways; even the Lane plan to make Lawrence the victor in the struggle for regional urban supremacy could succeed. But measured in terms of the logic of location, only Leavenworth seemed to have a real opportunity to compete with the strategic position of Kansas City. In order to move freight efficiently to and from the Chicago market, somewhere the Missouri River would have to be bridged. If the bridge was built at Leavenworth, the two branch roads—the extension of the Missouri Pacific up the west bank of the Missouri River and the division of the Union Pacific, E. D., between Leavenworth and Lawrence—could reasonably become the main lines of traffic. In fact, during 1866 this already seemed to be taking place. The stage had been set for the two towns to do battle over rival connections to the Hannibal and St. Jo. The attempt to build the Kansas City–Cameron and to obtain support for the building of a bridge at Kansas City supplied local promoters with their greatest challenge.

6

We Had Like To Have Been
Too Late
The Road to Cameron

D URING the early years of the Civil War, Kansas Citians, who
had to concentrate on surviving, forgot the disastrous attempt to build a local railroad northward to the Hannibal and St.
Jo. But during 1863, with the stabilization of the military situation
along the border and the resumption of railroad activity in the region, interest in the project began to revive. Owing to the wartime
diversion of western trade from St. Louis to Chicago, the road to
Cameron quickly assumed even greater importance than before the
war. In the summer of 1863, St. Joseph experienced a business revival; sizable amounts of livestock and packed hogs were shipped
from there to Eastern markets over the Hannibal and St. Jo. Kansas City leaders expressed the fear that the city's prewar position
as a western trading center would be seriously threatened unless it
quickly obtained a northern connection.[1]

As usual, the Kansas City Chamber of Commerce, which consisently represented the policies of the inner group of town builders, initiated action on the problem. On November 28, 1863, the Chamber appointed Johnston Lykins, Kersey Coates, and Theodore S. Case to try to reorganize the Kansas City, Galveston, and Lake Superior Railroad, under whose charter the Cameron project had been started before the war. Lykins and Coates, of course, had been active in local promotion for several years. Case was to play a particularly significant part in the postwar negotiations of Kansas City leaders with Eastern business interests.[2]

Born in Ohio in 1832, Case had come West after graduating from a Columbus medical college in 1856. After losing a few dollars in an unsuccessful Kansas town promotion, he arrived in Kansas City in 1857 and although still a young man quickly found a place among the leaders of the community. Like Lykins, Gilpin, or Van Horn, Case had far-ranging intellectual interests and capacities that equipped him to express the aspirations of local promoters. Throughout his career, he found time for literary and scientific pursuits. In 1860, with another local physician, he established the *Kansas City Medical and Surgical Review,* which they published for twelve months before war forced its abandonment. In the postwar era, he founded the *Kansas City Review of Science and Industry,* a publication of considerable merit, and edited the journal for nearly a decade. He also compiled a massive history of the city published in 1888 and during the latter years of his life held the chair of chemistry in the Kansas City Medical College.[3]

As part of its prewar promotional program, the Chamber of Commerce in 1859 requested Case to record his impressions of the town upon his arrival two years earlier. Although never published, this document, which provided a vivid description of early-day Kansas City, demonstrated that the business leadership had quickly selected Case to help propagandize the interests of the young community. As a Northerner and a Republican, Case, like the Pennsylvania Quaker Kersey Coates, sought to refute the charge that Kansas City represented pro-Southern sentiments. Shortly before the war,

Horace Greeley, the editor of the *New York Tribune*, launched an attack against Kansas City as a stronghold of slavery. He emphasized particularly an incident in which Henry C. Titus, the hotel keeper who often entertained the assembled business leaders of the town, had brutally assaulted Samuel C. Pomeroy, the Kansas free-state leader who happened to be passing through Kansas City. Recognizing that this kind of charge "might do incalculable harm among Eastern people whom we were then trying to attract," Case wrote a series of letters to Greeley that tried to show that Kansas Citians decried violence and were earnestly trying to build up a free-state city. Greeley was unconvinced: he replied that he knew that Kansas City "was a malignant stronghold of persecution and violence;" throughout the Kansas struggles, the town had assumed the position of "bitter and lawless hostility to the free-state cause." Later, however, when Case pointed out to Greeley that Kansas City had organized a Republican club to support Lincoln in 1860 and particularly early in the war when he wrote that Kansas City had organized a company of Union volunteers, Greeley underwent a change of attitude.[4]

Because his loyalties could not be questioned, Case, like Coates, played an active wartime role in the town. He enlisted as a private in Van Horn's battalion, but soon rose to the position of Chief Quartermaster of the Military District of the Border, which included Kansas City. In this capacity in the war-torn community, he tried to protect the property of pro-Southern business leaders, denounced outlawry on both sides of the struggle, and vigorously defended the loyalty of the town. At war's end, he took advantage of the rapid growth of Kansas City to build a fortune in real-estate.

Aside from reviving interest in the Cameron project, the Chamber of Commerce committee accomplished little of a concrete nature through its early efforts. In December, 1863, the three men called a stockholders' meeting of the Kansas City, Galveston, and Lake Superior, at which Coates was elected president of the company. Coates set about finding out the condition of the roadbed and the financial status of the company. He also went to Chicago to see if support could be obtained from railroad investors to complete the roadbed or to equip it once it was finished. The promoters' prewar contract with the Hannibal and St. Jo. had required that the road-bed to Cameron be completed in two years. This, of course, they had not been able to do, and the contract had expired in 1862. At one of their infrequent meetings, the directors instructed Coates to write to officers of the Hannibal and St. Jo. to see if there was any possibility of making a new agreement with the Boston owners of the railroad.[5]

These actions indicate the historical inaccuracy of an important aspect of the Kansas City bridge legend. Various local accounts—particularly the later ones that celebrate the triumph of local enter-prise—have assigned great significance to the lost prewar contract. Suddenly at a key moment during the deliberations in Boston, the story goes, the members of the Kansas City delegation brought out a copy of the contract to the great surprise of the owners of the Hannibal and St. Jo. These versions of the legend overlook the fact that the contract had expired and that there was never any claim on the part of the Cameron leaders that the Boston company was in any way bound by its terms. When the Kansas Citians reorganized their company in 1863, they immediately began to negotiate anew with various railroad interests to try to gain support. Moreover the leg-end strongly implies, in virtually all its presentations, that the fa-mous Boston meeting represented the first attempt since before the war to approach the Hannibal and St. Jo. A vital element in the legend is sudden surprise on the part of the Boston capitalists that the Kansas City company even existed.

Through 1864 and 1865 desultory negotiations continued. In April, 1865, for example, the directors offered to turn the railroad over to the North Missouri to serve as part of its projected west branch, but the company rejected the proposal. In May, 1865, the company elected a new president, W. C. Ransom, a local commis-sion merchant. He made a trip to Chicago and reported that rail-road interests there might be persuaded to build the road, provided that the Missouri River could be bridged at Kansas City. From this point on, plans for a bridge played a vital part in the local effort.[6]

Before the war, Kansas City promoters had not been concerned with the problem of bridging the Missouri River. Railroads at that time ordinarily employed ferries across major rivers. In 1860, while construction of the roadbed was under way, the Cameron officers had negotiated a contract with a local ferry company to transport freight and passengers for the railroad once it was completed. During the war, however, the inefficiency of ferries for this purpose had been widely demonstrated. With the revival of interest in the project, the Kansas City promoters obtained a charter during the 1863–1864 legislative session, which granted the Kansas City Bridge Company, made up of four incorporators including Milton J. Payne and Robert T. Van Horn, a twenty-year franchise to construct and to operate a bridge across the Missouri at Kansas City. Although the company was authorized to capitalize at $1,000,000, the promoters did not of course seriously propose to build a bridge at the time. They were merely obtaining another elaborate charter to use in their negotiations with Eastern investors. When Ransom reported the possible interest of Chicago railroad men in the Kansas City project, the Cameron company hired an engineer to examine the river bed and to determine the feasibility of bridge construction.[7]

The local engineer, as might be expected, submitted an encouraging report that stressed the ease with which a bridge could be built on the solid rock bottom of the river channel. Van Horn's *Journal* commented that the results had exceeded the most optimistic expectations. The report had exploded the universal belief that the river bed of the Missouri was a mass of shifting sand bars and quicksands without bottom. "To build a bridge here," the editor concluded, "is a very easy matter."[8]

The report on the bridge, issued in September of 1865, came during a period of intense railroad activity in the region. The Pacific completed its line the same month and immediately made plans to extend the railroad to Leavenworth. The Union Pacific, Eastern Division, was rapidly being built across Kansas. With the war ended, all the river communities had revived their earlier railroad plans. Newspapers in the region continually reported local railroad planning and emphasized the dangers posed by the schemes of rival communities. In November, for example, the *Journal* commented that "tremendous efforts" were being made in Leavenworth to induce the Hannibal and St. Jo. to connect with the Union Pacific, E. D., by way of Leavenworth and Lawrence. The editor observed that were it not for Kansas City's acknowledged position as a great railroad center, these efforts might have some chance of success.[9]

During this period, over a year before the eventual bridge decision, representatives of both Leavenworth and Kansas City met with officials of the Hannibal and St. Jo. It was natural that they should. The Hannibal and St. Jo. was the most significant railroad in the region and from the time of the passage of the Pacific Railway Act of 1862 had been concerned with the problem of obtaining westward connections across the Missouri River. The Kansas City promoters offered to turn over the assets of their Cameron company to the Hannibal and St. Jo. provided the latter would agree to build the local line. The company did not accept this proposal, but the Leavenworth leaders obtained a vague agreement, whereby the Hannibal and St. Jo. promised to guarantee the first-mortgage bonds of the Leavenworth-Cameron company, once it had managed to complete its roadbed.[10]

While these negotiations were pending, the Cameron directors made plans to resume construction on the road in the event that the Hannibal and St. Jo. did not accept their offer. Accordingly, in December they worked out a settlement with William Qualey, the prewar contractor, and arranged for him to resume work. His contract had provided that he be paid in cash and in Kansas City bonds in a seven-to-ten ratio. The company still owed him cash payments of $13,644.42; with accumulated interest over the years, this now amounted to $18,556.40. On the total amount of city bonds authorized for the prewar work ($89,050.00), the city owed Qualey interest of $36,213.87. Of the principle in bonds, $45,000 had not been issued to him.

For the interest due on the bonds, Qualey agreed to accept a payment of $25,000 in cash with the remainder of the amount to be paid in six months. The city was to issue a new set of bonds to provide for the principle in bonds still due him, since the originals had been burned as a precautionary measure when an invasion of Kansas City seemed imminent, and the records in relation to the issue had been lost. Sale of the Clay County bonds were to provide the cash payments.[11]

Coates presented this settlement, worked out by the company officers, to the City Council of Kansas City, which approved it immediately. The cash payment of $25,000 to pay the interest was significant, for the council provided that Qualey should be given the securities paid to the city by the Missouri Pacific for its right of way through the town. In the ordinance authorizing the right of way, this money had been set aside for street improvements, and the voters had approved it in part because of this provision. In this as in other instances, however, the City Council merely ratified the policies deemed essential by the railroad promoters. The local leaders could and did manipulate public funds as if they were their own. The reappropriation was accomplished without controversy.[12]

As a result of the costly prewar effort, the company was in a poor financial position to resume the work. The total assets actually in the hands of the treasurer at this date amounted to $68,508. Kansas City still owed approximately $110,000 of its pledged subscription of $200,000; Clay County $50,600 of its $150,000 subscription. A share of these assets, however, had to be used to provide the cash payments due Qualey for his prewar work.

Private subscribers had supposedly purchased $21,500 in stock in the company, but of this amount only $1,530 had actually been paid. From time to time, the company tried to collect these individual obligations and on one occasion initiated legal proceedings to compel payment. In the end, however, the directors apparently wrote them off as uncollectable. Like all other railroad companies organized in Kansas City during the period of local promotion, the Cameron company was financed almost exclusively through public rather than private funds.[13]

Again as before the war, the marketing of Kansas City bonds proved the principal problem for the company. Sands W. Bouton, a director, went East in March, 1866, to try to sell a portion of them, but wrote back to Ransom that he had been unsuccessful. Eastern capitalists, he said, were unwilling to recognize the solvency of the city. He suggested that the only way that they might be marketed would be to obtain private endorsement of them in Kansas City.[14]

Shortly thereafter, Ransom submitted a discouraging report to the officers of the company. Since there seemed to be no way to raise the cash portions of the payments that would have to be made to Qualey for additional construction, the contractor had actually done no further work on the roadbed. Ransom said that he was unwilling to incur any new liabilities unless he could be sure that the means would be available to meet them. If the work was to continue, the company would have to obtain private endorsement of the Kansas City bonds. Moreover, the company would need a new city subscription. Ransom estimated that $225,000 would be required to complete the roadbed and to lay the track ready for operation. If this could be done, a "powerful corporation" stood ready, he said, to provide rolling stock and to operate the road on advantageous terms.[15]

There were repeated vague assurances of this sort that the Hannibal and St. Jo. would make an agreement with the Cameron company once it had finished its roadbed. The *Journal* reported in December, 1865, for example, that the Eastern company would help to build the Kansas City road and had no interest in a Leavenworth-Cameron project.[16]

At about this time, three executives in the Hannibal and St. Jo.— John T. K. Hayward, James F. Joy, and John W. Brooks—began to play an important part in shaping the course of events that led to Kansas City's emergence as a railroad center. Their actions and their misfortunes demonstrated how little the logic of entrepreneurship, technology, or geography really influenced the critical developments that assured Kansas City's future.

Through the war years, John T. K. Hayward, who had been influential in the early negotiations of the Kansas Citians with the Boston investors, had continued as the general superintendent of the Hannibal and St. Jo. and had also retained his position as an agent of the Cameron company. It was apparently he who assured the local promoters that the Hannibal and St. Jo. would eventually support their project. In August of 1865, Hannibal and St. Jo. officials initiated steps to remove him from the superintendency on the grounds that the company needed "new blood" and that he lacked "system & *method* enough properly to run the road." He was to be retained in some position where he could "look after the general interest & policy of the co." Hayward did not accept the change with good grace and aroused the ire of the managers by refusing to co-operate with the new superintendent. However, the company continued to employ him as a kind of general negotiator.[17]

In this capacity Hayward went to Leavenworth in the fall of 1865 to examine local charters and to work out a compromise between two groups who held rival charters authorizing a railroad to Cameron. There was nothing secretive about this effort. Leavenworth newspapers reported his activities, and Van Horn reprinted the stories. Moreover, Hayward retained his position with the Kansas City company. As late as May of 1866, the directors instructed him to assist the president of the Cameron in negotiations for a new contract with the Hannibal and St. Jo. to furnish iron and rolling stock. Hayward later admitted, however, that during the previous year he had decided that the Kansas City project was "practically dead" and had agreed to help with Leavenworth's road. In most versions of the bridge legend, Hayward has filled the position of the traitor who tries to sell out Kansas City to the enemy Leavenworth. Granting the degree of dramatic license necessary to legend, this interpretation is reasonably accurate.[18]

While Hayward was surreptitiously acquiring an interest in a Leavenworth connection, James F. Joy, a man of much greater power, found himself with a reason to support the claims of Kansas City. By the fall of 1865, Joy had established a reputation as a national railroad leader and was engaged in developing the first major system of Western railroads. A graduate of Dartmouth and of the Harvard law school, Joy had begun practice in Detroit in 1836. He became counsel for several railroads; eventually president of the Chicago, Burlington, and Quincy, running from Chicago to the Mississippi River; and an influential figure in the Burlington-controlled Hannibal and St. Jo. His personal holdings in these and a number of related railroads were small, but because the actual owners—a Boston investment group directed by John Murray Forbes—had great faith in his ability, he made many of the significant decisions for the growing Burlington system.[19]

In the Kansas City bridge legend, Joy is introduced on the scene in the summer of 1866, unaware of the circumstances surrounding the rivalry between Leavenworth and Kansas City. He faces the problem of deciding on the claims of the two towns for a connection. In the fashion of the able man of affairs, he familiarizes himself with the facts by making a rapid inspection trip to the two towns. After this, he makes the decision necessitated by the logic of geography or, as some versions have it, of reasoned entrepreneurship. The actual events, unsurprisingly, were much more complicated.

In reality, Joy was familiar at an early date with the various railroad companies organized in the river towns, since they offered a possible means for the extension of the Burlington system westward. He had, for example, taken some part in the negotiations of the Kansas City and Leavenworth companies with the Hannibal and St. Jo., and Coates had supplied him with detailed reports on the circumstances of the local road.[20]

Early in 1866, several months before the eventual decision to support Kansas City, Joy became interested in Kansas City real estate, and through an intermediary, Theodore S. Case, began to purchase shares in the West Kansas City Land Company. This was a company that had been organized in the late 1850's in an effort to develop the river-bottom land located west of the hills upon which the town was being built. Investors from Independence had originally owned it. Before the war, their efforts to obtain the Pacific depot in their holdings had caused a fight with Kansas City landholders, who had developed their city additions on the hills. During the war, a group of Kansas Citians, including Charles E. Kearney, a leading Western trader and grocery dealer, John R. Balis, Thomas Swope, and others, had acquired control of the company. How much of an interest in this venture Joy obtained at this early date is not known; in two years he was the largest individual stockholder. The acquisition proved highly profitable; late in 1870, for example, on an apparently rather small initial investment, he obtained a dividend on his holding of $20,000, and other dividends had already been voted during the year. Obtaining stock in the West Kansas City Land Company was clearly in accord with Joy's consistent policy as a railroad entrepreneur of using his knowledge of where railroads would be built to buy cheap land and later to resell the property at a substantial profit.[21]

In a letter of March 26, 1866, in which he wrote about the affairs of the land company, Case also discussed—in apparent answer to a query of Joy's—the arrangements being made to elect new officers in the Cameron railroad. He told Joy that he would be happy to serve as a director of the company during the next year and would do all that he could to see the road through. Joy's exact relationship to the road at this time cannot be determined. Nonetheless, the bridge legend is certainly inaccurate in emphasizing the sudden nature of Joy's decision to support Kansas City. It is reasonable to assume, moreover, that at this early date, he had some concern with completion of the road, for it seems unlikely that he would have invested in a town that was to be denied railroad connections.[22]

The third railroad leader important to the bridge decision was John W. Brooks, president of the Michigan Central, a key railroad in the Burlington system. Working closely with Joy, Brooks, from his Boston office where he kept in close touch with the investors forming the Forbes group, served as a kind of general co-ordinator of the system. In their attempt to get the Hannibal and St. Jo. to furnish iron and rolling stock for their road, the Kansas City promoters with the assistance of Hayward had apparently dealt chiefly with him. In May of 1866 Brooks was struck down by a serious illness. The Boston group informed Joy that for several months he would be unable to receive any correspondence—that he must either "rest or die." They told Joy that he would now have to make all decisions on his own and asked him to assume temporary official representation of the Hannibal and St. Jo. Brooks was not in Europe, as the bridge legend has had it, but he was totally incapacitated, barely alive, and being fed forcibly by his doctors at the time of the famous Boston meeting. As a result, co-ordination broke down between Joy and Boston, and the company temporarily lacked unified direction.[23]

Meanwhile after Ransom's report in April on the troubles of the Cameron road, the local promoters moved rapidly to get construction started. At his suggestion, they launched an effort to obtain private endorsement at par of $60,000 in Kansas City bonds held by the company. The endorsers were to be repaid through a new city subscription to the company. At a railroad rally in mid-May, pledges were obtained for $52,300 of the old bonds, and on May 26, Van Horn reported that all but $3,000 of $56,000 in pledges had been collected. On June 19, Kansas City voters approved a city subscription of $180,000 to the Cameron. Of this amount, $60,000 was to be paid immediately in cash and used to repay the endorsers of the bonds. The rest of the subscription was to be in bonds issued to the company as they were needed for construction.[24]

From this point on, the city's issuing of bonds became extremely complicated. A few years later, an investigating committee found it impossible to disentangle the details, for city records did not distinguish between reissue of old bonds, which had been burned early in the war as a safety precaution, and the new issues. With the city subscription approved, the Cameron company solicited a grant of $25,000 from Jackson County.[25]

During the course of these efforts, Reid wrote to Coates and others who were conducting the Cameron's negotiations in the East that the private endorsement of the city bond issue was moving along well. He suggested that Coates write to Brooks immediately that the "Cameron Road is a certainty *at last* & in a few months." Showing his capacity for devious and complicated scheming, Reid also suggested that his correspondents propose to Brooks and Hayward a plan he had thought up to force the Missouri Pacific to break freight at Kansas City instead of running through trains to Leavenworth. Reid proposed that the Hannibal and St. Jo. buy up overdue coupons on the Missouri Pacific's bond issues. Since the railroad held no Kansas charter of its own, Reid thought it possible in this way to attach the property of the railroad in Kansas. Speed was necessary, however, so that Brooks could be prepared "to seize the first train that crossed the line." This letter clearly indicated Brooks' familiarity with the Kansas City project before the Boston meeting. It is also reasonable to assume that the quick effort to raise the $60,000 in cash resulted from some pending arrangement with Brooks.[26]

A few days earlier, the directors had reorganized the Cameron company. Dissatisfaction had been expressed with the conservative way Ransom was running the project, and Charles E. Kearney was picked as his successor. Kearney had taken little part in the prewar railroad movement, but he now had an incentive to do so, since during the war he had acquired a large holding in the West Kansas City Land Company and had become its president. The hoped-for industrial development of the bottom lands held by the company could be obtained only through railroads. In any case, his salary of $5,000 per year, exorbitant by prevailing standards for the presidency of a small local railroad, was reason enough for him to head the company.[27]

With action begun on the new city subscription—and popular approval only a formality—Kearney and the directors made immediate plans to resume construction. On May 23, Qualey accepted a new contract, which provided that he would receive $225,000 for completing the roadbed, one-half the amount to be paid in cash and the remainder in Kansas City bonds. A week later the directors instructed Case and Reid to go to Boston to close an arrangement with the Hannibal and St. Jo. for the purchase of iron and rolling stock, and authorized them to execute the first-mortgage bonds of the company to be issued on the completed roadbed in payment.[28]

From this followed the Boston meeting, the climax of the bridge legend. During the illness of Brooks, Hayward took advantage of the Boston group's lack of knowledge of the policies of Brooks and Joy to try to negotiate a contract for the Leavenworth group, with which he was now tied. R. S. Watson, treasurer of the Hannibal and St. Jo., supplied Joy with detailed reports of these developments that indicated how close Hayward came to succeeding. On June 4, 1866, Watson sent Joy two contracts for his examination and approval. Two days later, at the instigation of Sidney Bartlett and Nathaniel Thayer, members of the Boston group, he wrote again explaining that the contracts were those that the Hannibal and St. Jo. had considered making with a delegation from Leavenworth. But, he continued, the very next day after they had been sent to Joy, "three very respectable gentlemen from Kansas City made their appearance" and asked the Hannibal and St. Jo. to renew a contract made with them in 1860. (Coates, who had been in Washington, joined Case and Reid, but his hurried trip to Boston ahead of the rest of the delegation is apparently imaginative.) They had said, Watson continued, that Hayward had known about their project from the beginning and had assured them that the contract would be readily renewed or that an even more favorable one could be obtained. The delegation had been optimistic about finishing their line and had contended that they had sufficient money to complete the roadbed by October. Watson admitted that this development put the Hannibal and St. Jo. in a bad position. If the Leavenworth group honored all the particulars of their proposed arrangement, the company might be obligated to support their line. But the directors felt that the Kansas City connection could well prove more beneficial, and Watson requested Joy's judgment on this point. Joy wrote back immediately asking the directors not to make a final decision until he had an opportunity to visit Kansas City. Watson agreed that they would delay taking any immediate action.[29]

During the following days, Thayer and Bartlett consulted further with both the Kansas City and Leavenworth groups. They found that in order to complete the Leavenworth road, a large part of the company's county bonds would have to be underwritten by the Hannibal and St. Jo. This would be hard to manage, Watson wrote, but if Joy thought the Leavenworth plan better perhaps the Hannibal and St. Jo. stockholders "might be screwed up to do something." The Kansas City leaders, in spite of the great financial difficulties they were having, had apparently been able to convince the Boston officials that their Cameron project was a going concern and that they were perfectly capable of finishing their roadbed in a matter of months.[30]

On his way home, Case stopped at Detroit to consult with Joy, who then immediately went to Kansas City. During his brief visit there, Joy apparently told local promoters that their project would probably be supported. On June 17, Reid wrote to Van Horn, who had been elected to Congress in 1864 and was then attending the session in Washington, that Joy had just left the city and that success seemed sure. He had gained a most favorable impression, and this made it certain, Reid felt, that the Boston people would approve the Kansas City proposals. "We had like to have been too late," he continued, "as Hayward for Leavenworth had almost concluded an agreement, but we are satisfied we have beaten them." Joy had emphasized the importance of passing a federal law to authorize a bridge over the Missouri River at Kansas City. Reid also told Van Horn that it was essential that he work for the pending authorization for a Burlington bridge at Quincy, Illinois. In return, Joy had promised to muster support for Van Horn's bill to provide a Congressional land grant to the local promoters' Missouri River, Fort Scott, and Gulf Railroad, which had been organized the year before to be built from Kansas City into southeast Kansas. Joy had said that the line "would be a very important connexion for them at this place." To make matters easier for Van Horn, Reid enclosed a draft for a bill authorizing a Kansas City bridge.[31]

Kearney wrote at the same time to emphasize the importance of getting the bridge bills through Congress. He assured Van Horn that he would have all the friends of the Hannibal and St. Jo. be-

hind him. If the two bridge authorizations could be passed, the promoters "would be out of the woods." [32]

After his trip, Joy wrote to Boston recommending a Kansas City
rather than a Leavenworth connection but suggesting that the company delay a decision until after Congress acted. Watson, speaking
for the Hannibal and St. Jo. directors, instructed Joy to find out
the best contract the Kansas Citians were willing and able to make
that would embrace bridge construction. Since the Leavenworth
group had been unable to demonstrate that they could raise adequate means to finish a roadbed, the directors did not now feel
"morally bound" to support their project in spite of the earlier
agreements. Watson added that he had written James Craig, chief
of the formidable crew of Burlington lobbyists, to suggest that the
right to bridge at Kansas City be added to the Quincy bridge bill. [33]

The bridge legend gives great weight to Van Horn's "fast political footwork" in pushing through the authorization. In reality,
his efforts were rather routine. Of critical importance was the decision by the Burlington interests to throw their support to the proposition.

For some time, Burlington roads had experienced trouble in operating across rivers with ferries. C. W. Mead, Hayward's successor
as superintendent of the Hannibal and St. Jo., wrote in December,
1865, of the difficulties the road had experienced in getting cargoes
across the Mississippi. He pointed out that during the winter
weather freight had sometimes been delayed for several weeks and
that passengers had been forced to lay over for as long as four days.
The company had received innumerable complaints from Western
businessmen who had not received their holiday merchandise. Of
most concern to the officers in the system was the building of a
bridge across the Mississippi at Quincy, Illinois. A short railroad
had been constructed between Quincy and Palmyra, Missouri, a
point on the Hannibal and St. Jo. Once the bridge was constructed,
through connections could be maintained from Chicago to the Missouri River. A bridge at Kansas City would, of course, open the
whole southern plains area to the system. [34]

Railroad bridges could and had been built under state charters. Unless federal authorization was obtained, however, there was danger that Congress might exercise its prerogative over interstate commerce to pass legislation that would establish standards forcing them to be torn down. The chief opposition to the Quincy bridge bill came from representatives of Mississippi steamboat interests and spokesmen of St. Louis, who feared properly that the bridge would strengthen Chicago's position. But Craig did his work well. He gained the support of John D. Perry, of the Union Pacific, E. D., distributed railroad passes, and tried to bring pressure to bear of one kind and another. In one of his letters, he pointed out that in spite of the efforts of St. Louis interests, he had lined up the entire Missouri delegation in the House with the exception of the two St. Louis representatives. Therefore, in working for the Kansas City bridge authorization, Van Horn had the full support of the powerful railroad and financial interests backing the Quincy bridge bill.[35]

Upon receiving his instructions from Kansas City, Van Horn promptly introduced his bill on June 26. An omnibus bridge bill, which included provision for the Quincy bridge, had already passed the Senate on April 30. This was presented on the floor of the House on July 14. Van Horn offered his measure as an amendment; the House approved it as it had others. Then he made two motions: first, to reconsider the vote by which his and a previous amendment had been passed and then to table that motion. The House approved this second motion, meaning that the motion for reconsideration of the vote was tabled. This was standard parliamentary tactics. The effect was to provide that when the House voted on the whole bill, the amendment for the Kansas City bridge would have to be included. But this in no way precluded the possibility of further amendments, as the legend has had it. Nor was there any mention in the record of debates of any attempt by Kansas representatives to add further amendments. The Washington correspondent of the *Daily Times* of Leavenworth did not deem the bridge debate even important enough to mention in his reports from the Capital.[36]

In its final stage, the bill contained authorization for seven bridges. While it was again being considered in the Senate, the Kansas Senators did not try to provide for a bridge at Leavenworth. With only minor opposition, led by John Henderson of Missouri, the bill passed late in July. In short, Van Horn's brilliant congressional coup, so well entrenched in local history, was little more than a good story.[37]

A second action of Van Horn's at this session, somewhat underemphasized in interpretations of Kansas City history, was equally important in shaping the outcome of urban rivalry in the Elbow region. In writing to Van Horn, Reid had emphasized Joy's interest in the Congressional land grant to the Missouri River, Fort Scott, and Gulf. Over considerable opposition from Kansas interests, especially from Kansas City's longtime enemy, James Lane, the bill providing ten sections of land on each side of the track for each mile of the road constructed passed on July 23, 1866.[38]

The public evaluation of these measures was extensive and significant. A few weeks later, the *Journal* commented that the passage of the two laws had been responsible for great interest in Kansas City on the part of Eastern capitalists and railroad builders. The legislation had acted "like a force of natural gravitation to draw to the great bend of the Missouri" nearly all contemplated lines in the region. Negotiations concerning both the Cameron and Fort Scott had awaited this outcome; now these projects could be quickly carried through. Still pointing to relative advantages—but largely advantages created through enterprise, not those of nature—the writer emphasized the fact that Kansas City was the only point on the Missouri to have both state and national authority for bridging the river. This advantage, he said, along with a number of others, would "tell all in the future." [39]

Van Horn considered the laws of comparable significance. Writing from Washington, he asserted that bridges at Kansas City and Quincy would for practical purposes put Kansas City as near to Chicago as to St. Louis. The southern road, with its generous land grant, would help Kansas City capture the trade to the south and west. No longer would it be possible for the Union Pacific, E. D., to run away to Leavenworth to find a connection with Chicago, nor would the Missouri Pacific go anywhere else to find a road to Galveston. "The point for the meeting of all these roads," he wrote, "and the concentration of business . . . is thus settled and for all time, and settled at *Kansas City*." [40]

"Kaw," the Washington correspondent of the *Journal*, thought the land grant singularly important. In getting it, Kansas City had "secured the richest prize yet sought for you in your ambitious railroad schemes." Without it, the city would have been just a way station on the line of the Missouri Pacific. "Kaw" commended Van Horn for overcoming the skill and cunning of Lane, who had rarely, if ever before, been beaten in a square and open fight. Van Horn's victory meant that Lane's plan for a road to Galveston could be "classed among those idle speculations which men soon forget." [41]

These contemporary comments made clear the inter-relation between the bridge bill, the land grant, and a whole series of railroad developments that had begun to take place in the region. The congressional land grant was considered just as significant and perhaps more significant than the bridge authorization. The contention that winning the Hannibal Bridge made Kansas City a railroad center is only partially true. The analyses also demonstrated the changing character of the central argument of town promotional polemics. The writers still paid tribute to natural advantages, but in a perfunctory, almost offhand way. Emphasis had begun to shift to the role of initiative and enterprise in shaping favorable turns of events through the creation of artificial advantages.

In spite of these helpful laws, prolonged negotiations still proved necessary. Right after the Boston meeting, the Cameron officers had taken steps to effect a contract with the Hannibal and St. Jo. They gave Kearney full power to negotiate on his own for the purchase of iron, the provision of rolling stock, and the construction of the bridge. In spite of Joy's assurances, the promoters still had doubts. They urged him to force an immediate decision, for they suspected that certain members of the Boston group still sympathized with the Leavenworth plan. During July they sent Case to see Joy. He made two offers to the Kansas City leaders as a basis for a possible contract: either to turn over the stock of the local company outright to the Hannibal and St. Jo. or for the Hannibal and St. Jo. to accept and sell the first-mortgage bonds of the company issued on its completed roadbed, then to iron and equip the road for a percentage of earnings. Reid wrote to Joy that the directors could not accept the proposal to transfer the stock. Although the approval of the City Council of Kansas City could readily be obtained, Clay County would object, and the latter's bonds were essential for completion of the roadbed. After the road was finished, it would be an easy matter to obtain the necessary approval, Reid asserted, for the argument could then be used that taking this action would ensure that the Cameron connection would become the main line of the Hannibal and St. Jo.[42]

During July and early August, the Hannibal and St. Jo. directors debated the decision. Hayward continued his determined efforts on behalf of Leavenworth, and argued with Bartlett and Thayer that a bridge at Kansas City would cost just as much as one at Leavenworth. Even though the river was wider at the latter place, the bridge at Kansas City would have to be built at an angle, thereby increasing its length. He also sent Joy statistics showing that considerably more western freight passed through Leavenworth than through Kansas City. Apparently, there was controversy in the company over the decision. C. W. Mead, Hayward's successor as superintendent of the Hannibal and St. Jo., favored the Leavenworth connection. "In the multitude of concillors there will be safety," wrote Treasurer Watson, "if too many cooks do not spoil the broth."[43]

In mid–August, Joy made another trip to Kansas City, Leavenworth, and other Kansas towns with the ostensible purpose of finally deciding the issue. An associate who accompanied him, Charles Perkins, later to become president of the consolidated Burlington system, wrote to his wife during the trip that in all likelihood Joy would decide on Kansas City, and the decision was really his to make. It seems quite clear that Joy supported the Kansas City connection from the beginning of the discussions in the company. Well before this trip, he took Hayward to task for his machinations with the Leavenworth group, telling him apparently that he had made it impossible for the Hannibal and St. Jo. ever to build that road. Moreover, sometime during the period of negotiations, Kearney went to work for Joy buying miscellaneous pieces of land in the area and trying to obtain more shares in the West Kansas Land Company. Much of the delay in completing a contract may well have resulted from an effort on the part of Joy to obtain favorable terms for his own, as well as railroad company, land purchases.[44]

Finally, on November 19, the Boston directors of the Hannibal and St. Jo. authorized the president of the company, James Craig, to draw up a contract—with the approval of Joy—to provide rails for the Cameron road and funds for bridge construction. The directors of the company approved the agreement a month later, and on February 4, 1867, the Kansas City and Cameron officers executed a mortgage to a committee of trustees—Joy, Thayer, and Bartlett—representing the Chicago, Burlington, and Quincy—Hannibal and St. Jo. companies.[45]

A circular issued by the trustees discussing the settlement pointed out that the two railroad companies had taken a number of steps to arrange an unbroken connection with the Union Pacific, Eastern Division, and southern Kansas. These included a bridge at Quincy, the acquisition of the Palmyra Railroad (running from opposite Quincy to Palmyra on the Hannibal and St. Jo.), and an agreement with the Kansas City and Cameron. The circular made it clear that the support of the Kansas City and Cameron was one part of an over-all plan of the Burlington system to establish a unified line to the West.[46]

In rather moving rhetoric, Van Horn in his *Journal* triumphantly proclaimed a victory. "The work is done," he wrote. "The anxiety and toil of ten years is ended!" The bright anticipations of the people had finally been realized. In spite of the "various and malignant influences" that had to be overcome, Kansas City had emerged as "the city of the Missouri Valley." "Let the heathen rage." Leavenworth and other towns in the region had done their worst; cities to the east had tried to build up local rivals to Kansas City. But in spite of war and carnage and all else that had stood in the way, Kansas City had at last come through triumphant. No longer was the future of the city in doubt. Her rivals had been bested. "Sunk in the turbid waters of the river, are many of the cities of this valley. Oblivion has sealed the fate of many a place deemed immortal." [47]

In a sense, the Kansas City leaders had proved their mettle as promoters, for there was no overriding reason why the Hannibal and St. Jo. connection with the West could not just as well have been made at Leavenworth. Eclectic interpretations of events are seldom satisfying, but in this instance, a number of considerations—involving geography, Joy's actions, and the nature of local effort—were critical. The Burlington system was attempting to reach the rich trade of south-central and southern Kansas; here Kansas City's position below the Missouri River provided an advantage. Moreover, the Missouri was slightly narrower at Kansas City than at Leavenworth. But this technological consideration had little influence on the outcome. In truth, construction of a bridge at Kansas City proved exceedingly difficult, and required significant engineering innovations to complete. The land grant to the Missouri River, Fort Scott, and Gulf apparently provided an inducement to Joy to support Kansas City's Cameron connection. Furthermore, Joy had acquired a personal stake, albeit a limited one, in Kansas City's future. His decision to invest in the city may in turn have been influenced by geographical and locational considerations.

The delegates to Boston played a part in the outcome, for they were able to convince the Hannibal and St. Jo. officials that their roadbed was nearly finished, which was far from the truth, whereas the Leavenworth interests admitted that they would be unable to finance the completion of their roadbed without a loan from the

Hannibal and St. Jo. Here a difference in the two communities was important. The Kansas City promoters could always count on their City Council to supply as many bond issues as they needed, because they virtually controlled the community. In Leavenworth, on the other hand, obtaining a bond issue involved a complex factional fight, and the voters often defeated local subscriptions. The Kansas City leaders could thus afford to be more expansive in their promises than the Leavenworth group. The two elements that receive so much emphasis in local historical evaluation—natural advantages and the ability of Kansas City leaders—do offer insight into why Kansas City became a railroad center. But the two are interrelated in such a complex manner that any simple interpretation of the events that led to the winning of the bridge is impossible.

OPENING THE HANNIBAL AND ST. JOSEPH BRIDGE, JULY 3, 1869
Courtesy the Kansas City Museum, Kansas City, Missouri P1629, PCI.229, OD8

MAIN STREET, KANSAS CITY, 1868
Courtesy Native Sons Archives, N10-412, Western Historical Manuscript Collection, Kansas City

MAJOR ROBERT T. VAN HORN

KERSEY L. COATES

COL. WILLIAM GILPIN

THEODORE S. CASE

*Courtesy: Gilpin, State Historical Society of Colorado; Van Horn, Coates, and Case,
Native Sons Archives, Western Historical Manuscript Collection, Kansas City*

Map 1. Principal Western Railroads circa 1880.

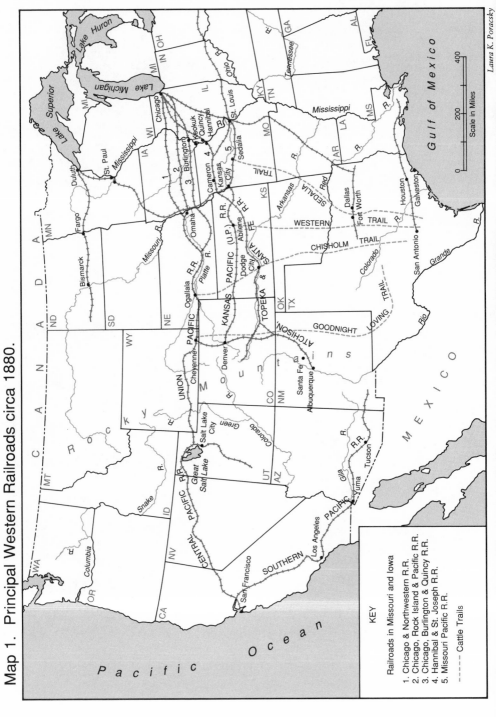

Laura K. Poracsky

KEY

Railroads in Missouri and Iowa

1. Chicago & Northwestern R.R.
2. Chicago, Rock Island & Pacific R.R.
3. Chicago, Burlington & Quincy R.R.
4. Hannibal & St. Joseph R.R.
5. Missouri Pacific R.R.

- - - - - Cattle Trails

Scale in Miles
0   200   400

Map 2. Missouri Railroads circa 1860.

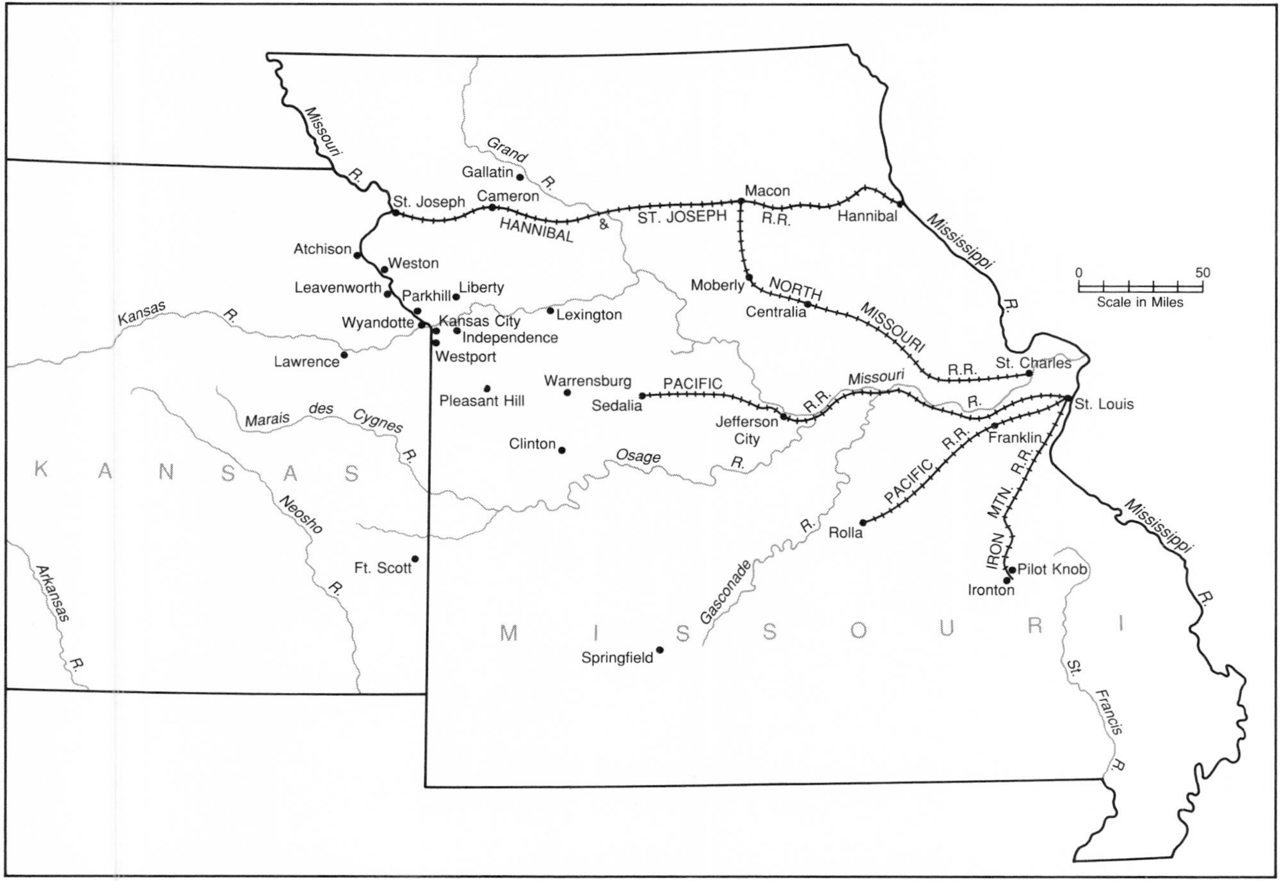

Laura K. Poracsky

Map 3. Kansas Railroads circa 1880.

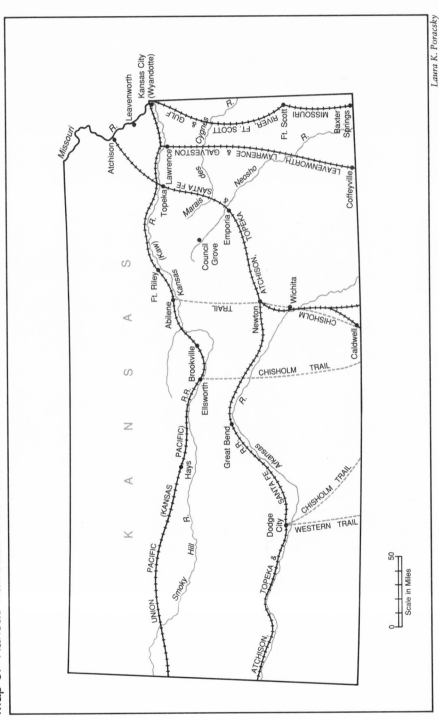

Laura K. Poracsky

: 7 :

Kansas City Becomes
A Railroad Center
The Joy System

AS a result of their successful negotiations during 1866, Kansas
City promoters obtained the support of the powerful railroad and financial interests that controlled the Burlington system.
This did not entirely solve their problem, however, for their contract with the Hannibal and St. Jo. provided that the local company must complete its roadbed. The Kansas City railroad leaders
were always much better promoters than they were builders. Even
with the support of the Joy interests, the Cameron company found
it impossible to complete the line with local funds.

During the summer of 1866, as the Hannibal and St. Jo. debated the claims of Kansas City and Leavenworth, the Kansas Citians had instructed their contractor, William Qualey, to begin work
again on the roadbed. But they immediately encountered a series of
difficulties. Because of well organized rural opposition, county vot-

ers at an election of August 7 turned down the company's request
for a $25,000 subscription from Jackson County, which the direc-
tors hoped would supply some readily marketable bonds. Qualey
submitted construction bills that proved much higher than his original estimates. During the course of negotiations with the Hannibal
and St. Jo., the company required a change in the grade of the
roadbed of the Cameron; this necessitated additional expense.
After a quarrel with Qualey in the fall of 1866, the company paid
him for the work that he had completed, but he was unhappy with
the settlement and threatened legal action. The directors then became embroiled with Qualey's subcontractor, Hunt, Miller, and
Company, which tried to collect from them debts owed by Qualey.
Hearing of these difficulties, Joy early in 1867 questioned whether
the roadbed would be completed as provided in the agreement.
Both Reid and Kearney assured him that it would be, that everything was going well. The company had let new grading contracts
and had 450 men now at work on the roadbed. The unfavorable reports, Kearney said, were just another example of the company
again having been "willfully maligned with no other purpose than
to defeat our enterprise." [1]

During January, Kearney and Reid went to Chicago and attempted to sell $100,000 in Kansas City bonds to investors. Their
success, although greater than in the past, was limited, for they were
able to market only about $10,000 of the total. The promoters un-
successfully attempted to raise a subscription in Clinton County, at
the northern end of the line. Again they appealed to Jackson
County, this time for $30,000. In spite of an intense campaign de-
signed to overcome the opposition of farmers with the appeal that
the railroad would greatly increase the value of their lands, county
voters again turned down the subscription late in March. Although
throughout Missouri, as throughout much of the nation, there was a
great expansion of county aid to railroads during the period 1865
to 1872, Kansas City promoters, who so clearly represented a group
narrowly concerned with urban real-estate speculation, were generally unsuccessful in the postwar period in overcoming the resist-

ance of farmers to their program. The realization that railroad aid often benefitted only an inside group of manipulators in part accounted for a general revulsion against local aid that developed in the 1870's, when many states enacted constitutional restrictions prohibiting any kind of municipal or county assistance to private companies.[2]

In spite of the difficulties experienced by the Cameron company, Joy's plan for a system of regional connections with the West depended on completion of the road. At his suggestion, the local directors early in 1867 had hired Octave Chanute to take charge of the bridge construction. Chanute, a largely self-educated engineer who before coming to Kansas City had been chief engineer of the Chicago and Alton Railroad, played a significant part in the regional developments that led to Kansas City's growth as a metropolis. After several unsuccessful experiments with conventional methods of construction, he introduced new techniques from Germany that made possible the completion of the Kansas City bridge in 1869. In addition, he built the main Joy lines in Kansas. As Joy's chief lieutenant in the region, he supervised his holdings in the West Kansas Land Company, bought other property in Kansas City on his behalf, conducted negotiations for Kansas land, and dealt with local town and railroad promoters in the region. Joy relied on his judgments; his abilities helped to ensure the successful organization of the Joy system. Late in his career, Chanute won national prominence for his experiments in aviation and his writings on principles of aerodynamics, both of which contributed to the Wright Brothers' achievement.[3]

Upon his arrival in Kansas City in 1867, Chanute found that little work had been done on the bridge. But after paying off some confused accounts and after taking a new survey of the river bed, he got construction under way early in the year. Because of the seemingly chaotic condition of the company's affairs and the likelihood that the roadbed would not be completed, Joy wrote to the Cameron directors in March proposing that all assets of the local company be turned over to the committee of trustees of the Hannibal and St.

Jo.—C. B. Q., who held the Cameron's first-mortgage bonds in accordance with the earlier agreement. If this were done, Joy promised that the trustees would finance the completion of the roadbed,
and, in addition, would probably assist in the construction of the
Missouri River, Fort Scott, and Gulf as well. The directors of the
Cameron had anticipated this development; in fact, at the time of
the original agreement, Reid had indicated that a transfer of stock
could probably be arranged once construction was well underway.
To make this easier, they had obtained a modification of their charter from the legislature to permit the Cameron to consolidate with
other railroad companies.[4]

Early in April, the City Council of Kansas City, acting after customary easily-gained popular approval, voted to turn over the
Cameron stock held by the city. Transferring the Clay County stock
proved more difficult. Both Kearney and Reid had to go to work to
influence the judges of the County Court, who were responsible for
this stock. "We had a much more difficult time than I imagined,"
Kearney wrote to Joy, "two of the judges were quite obstinate but
after the pressure was brought to bear made the . . . order." On
August 9, the Cameron directors turned over all local bonds and
other company assets to the Joy-Bartlett-Thayer committee. Not
until February 21, 1870, after the completion of the bridge, was
the Cameron company officially made a part of the Hannibal and
St. Jo., for this step involved the settlement of certain legal tech-
nicalities that had developed. From the time of the 1867 agreement,
however, construction and control of the road rested entirely in the
hands of the group of trustees headed by Joy, and it was quickly
completed during the year.[5]

Kansas land, inextricably related to most significant railroad developments in the region, delayed until 1868 the acquisition of the
second of the local lines, the Missouri River, Fort Scott, and Gulf.
Joy's interest in the Fort Scott was closely related to his effort to acquire the Neutral Tract of Kansas—an 800,000 acre, fifty by twenty-
five mile strip of land in southeastern Kansas originally held by the
Cherokee Indians. The railroad would provide a way to develop

the Neutral Tract quickly and thereby, of course, cause a sharp rise in the price of the land. Profit from Indian land was the *raison d'être* for a substantial share of the Kansas railroad companies of the sixties and seventies. The Cherokees had ceded the Neutral Tract to the government on August 19, 1866, during the period of negotiations concerning the Cameron. Shortly before leaving office, Secretary of the Interior James Harlan had arranged the sale of the land to the American Emigrant Company, a Connecticut corporation. Chiefly through the influence of Thomas Ewing, Jr., who represented the Cherokees, the government declared the sale invalid on the grounds that it violated the terms of the treaty.[6]

At this point, four railroad groups attempted to buy the Neutral Tract. Joy, because of his close relationship with the new Secretary of the Interior, Orville H. Browning, and because he was able to exert greater pressure on Congress than his rivals, won final control after many months of maneuvering with the passage of a supplemental treaty by the Senate in June of 1868. During the course of this effort, Van Horn played an important part in Washington in prosecuting Joy's interests.[7]

In the meantime, Kersey Coates, who had invested in the Joy land syndicate, and the other Kansas City railroad leaders had gone ahead with an attempt to build the Fort Scott. The Boston group showed little interest in supporting the project for the time being because of the difficulty they had been having in marketing the Cameron first-mortgage bonds; Joy was inclined to wait until the purchase of the Neutral Tract was confirmed before taking action. As usual, the local leaders encountered extreme difficulty in trying to construct a railroad. Coates, who had assumed the presidency of the Fort Scott, had little success in selling the bonds subscribed to the road, and through 1867 entreated Joy on several occasions to extend some measure of assistance. In December he threatened to form an alliance with other railroad groups unless Joy indicated firm interest. Early the next year, with the effort to obtain the Neutral Tract proceeding well, Joy initiated arrangements eventually to take over the road. When he began to investigate the status of the company, he found that Coates, who was a member of the land syndicate, had used a substantial share of the money raised in bond issues for the railroad to pay expenses connected with the acquisition of the Neutral Tract. Coates admitted that he had spent $14,000 of Fort Scott funds on legislative expense for this purpose, much of it to keep James Blunt, a Kansas land speculator, in Washington for a year as a full-time lobbyist.[8]

The officers of the Fort Scott also voted themselves salaries that seemed exorbitant to Hannibal and St. Jo. officials. R. S. Watson, the treasurer, checked the financial statements of the Kansas City railroad and wrote to Joy asking that someone work through Coates' vouchers, for he had found some "very Flemish looking" accounts. Whether Watson meant this archaic phrase in its technical sense of accounts actually short is uncertain, but he did indicate that there were many irregularities. He pointed out also that $6,300 had been paid to directors who had no real duties. Coates had received $5,000 in salary and the treasurer of the company over $2,000. Both of these amounts seemed excessive to Watson for this kind of limited local enterprise.[9]

During a dispute with Coates over the salary he was to receive once the Hannibal and St. Jo. took over the company, Joy provided a frank opinion of the railroad activities of the Kansas City promoters. He wrote to Coates that he had *"never known* a new company organized to build 150 miles of road to pay such salaries as your company has been paying." Had he known the true state of affairs earlier, the Hannibal and St. Jo. would never have embarked upon the project. "It really seems," he wrote, "as if the organization was made rather to pay salaries to numerous parties primarily & secondarily to build the road." But this dispute was settled, and Coates continued to work closely with Joy. In the warfare that broke out on the Neutral Tract between the Joy forces and squatters who had settled there during the period the disposition of the tract was being considered, Coates played a leading part in arranging the support of newspaper editors, distributing free railroad passes, importing detectives, and conducting espionage against the Cherokee Neutral Land League organized to fight for the squatters' interests.[10]

Once Joy made his decision to absorb the Fort Scott, the transfer of ownership proved only a formality. On August 7, 1868, the City Council of Kansas City appointed Reid its agent to turn over the stock it held with the requirement that by September 1, 1869, the company should complete eighty miles of line. Later in the month, the Fort Scott was reorganized with the Hannibal and St. Jo.— C. B. Q. trustees in control.[11]

During the next few years, as Joy developed an integrated regional system of railroads, Kansas City quickly became the center of the lines he controlled. The Leavenworth, Lawrence, and Galveston, which had been organized to compete with Kansas City's Fort Scott, was acquired on June 30, 1869. Reid, the behind-the-scenes negotiator, successfully discouraged competing Chicago railroad interests from investing in the road. Through a series of short connections in Kansas acquired by Joy, the trains of the L. L. G. were routed into Kansas City over the Fort Scott line. Thus Kansas City rather than either Lawrence or Leavenworth—in contradiction to the intentions of the original Kansas organizers of the project— became the real terminus of the road. North of the Missouri River, the Joy group gained control of the North Missouri and the various small lines that made up the Platte Country Railroad. In the course of negotiations with the Platte Country, James Craig, of the Hannibal and St. Jo., indicated some of the problems involved in gaining favorable terms for the transfer of local railroad companies. He wrote to Joy that a campaign for a bond issue for the railroad would be getting under way in earnest on the next Saturday, but he anticipated some trouble. Two St. Joseph newspapers were still silent, for the "D——d mercenary editors wish to be bribed." "I will try to see," he continued, "that they don't come out against us." Another editor had been paid $100 but had not as yet said anything in favor of the subscription. One other newspaper owner had left for the East but, said Craig, "his partner is with us—I have promised him $100 & some more if the vote is carried." [12]

After the Platte Country was acquired, the Joy trustees renamed it the Kansas City, St. Joseph, and Council Bluffs, and extended the line into Iowa. Joy negotiated arrangements so that all the lines in his system north of the river could use the new bridge and reach Kansas City. As a result of these acquisitions, Joy had assured the Burlington system an unbroken connection between Chicago and the West and was able to maintain a unified policy on through business from the region.

Kansas City was on its way to supremacy in the lower Missouri Valley. By 1870, the city had become the major reshipment point for cattle shipped from the West. With the establishment of the Armour plant in 1871, it began its rapid growth as a meat-packing center. Joy played a significant part in both these developments. Through promising favorable rates on cattle shipped from Kansas City to Chicago, the Hannibal and St. Jo. encouraged the plan of Joseph G. McCoy to set up a marketing center in Kansas to which Texas cattlemen could drive their herds. McCoy had been sharply rebuffed when he submitted his proposition initially to the Missouri Pacific. Because of his large interest in the West Kansas City Land Company, which held much of the bottom land suitable for stockyards and meat-packing plants, Joy was able to acquire blocks of land that could be sold in large tracts to investors. Chanute reported in 1868 that he had been successful in getting forty-one and a half acres of land for depot grounds for the Kansas City and Cameron at a reasonable price. He assured Joy that the terms "could not have been made as favorable for the R. R. co. had you not purchased the stock of the land co.; as people are rapidly getting crazy about that property." The program of purchase and resale of land was conducted as surreptitiously as possible. Chanute held in his name much of the property that belonged to Joy. On this occasion, Chanute indicated that he had been having difficulty keeping secret Joy's holding in the land company, for Kearney had failed to keep quiet the fact that he had sold out his interest.[13]

It was through the efforts of Joy and other Hannibal and St. Jo. officials that stockyards were built at Kansas City in 1870. Up to that time, as the business expanded enormously because of the increase in the number of Texas cattle shipped to railheads in Kansas, feeding and reshipment was handled through the small yards operated by the railroad companies themselves. The provision of adequate centralized facilities caused an immediate large-scale expansion of the local livestock industry. The Joy holding provided the land for such outside meat-packing firms as that of Thomas J. Bigger, who set up a small specialty plant in Kansas City in 1868, and then two years later built a large plant at a bottom site. More importantly, Joy furnished the necessary acreage to conduct a major operation to Armour, Plankinton, and Company, whose decision in 1870 to build a plant at Kansas City was the single most important step in the growth of the local meat-packing industry. In tying themselves to Joy, an entrepreneur of ability, Kansas City promoters had assured the realization of their dream of building a city.[14]

Local boosters in the rival towns along the Missouri River had always found population growth the most satisfying index of progress. By this standard, the city's success was exceptional. From 4,418 inhabitants in 1860, it had grown to 32,260 by 1870. Since it had declined sharply in population during the Civil War, the increase was all the more striking. By 1880, the population stood at 55,785. As early as 1870, Leavenworth and the other urban rivals in the region had been left far behind.

There were less tangible, but just as meaningful, indications of the significance of the post-Civil War railroad developments. In May, 1867, R. C. Watson, the Hannibal and St. Jo. treasurer, visited Leavenworth and Kansas City. Like so many of the travelers of the period, he found Leavenworth an attractive place. "I was very much impressed with Leavenworth," he wrote to Joy, "which *pro rata* is as much a wonder as Chicago & it seems to me that it will not do to turn a cold shoulder on that place." He admitted that it was impossible for the Hannibal and St. Jo. to make an agreement to build Leavenworth's connection because of the company's contract with the Kansas City and Cameron. He hoped, however, that some liberal arrangement with Leavenworth could be made in the future. Two years later, Octave Chanute reported on Leavenworth. He had been approached by a prominent group of businessmen from there who had proposed to him that they move their warehouses to the state line opposite Kansas City and "build a new town in Kansas at that point." They had sounded out Chanute to determine if side tracks could be built to their proposed new location. For over ten years Kansas City boosters had talked of merchants deserting the decaying village up river, and yet Leavenworth had continued to grow and prosper, often at the expense of Kansas City. But the Cameron road decision, and the developments that followed naturally from it, had made the wildest exaggerations and the most exuberant dreams of the early prophets of railroad progress come true.[15]

The cost to Kansas City of obtaining its railroad system and assuring metropolitan dominance in the region was not excessive. About $740,000 was issued in subscriptions, none of which produced any direct return to the city, but in a period when local governments provided a substantial part of the total capital investment in American railroads, this was not a large amount compared to the expenditures of other cities. In the postwar years alone, Louisville extended over $2,500,000 in railroad aid. Baltimore during the nineteenth century provided about $18,000,000 to railroads. Although an occasional city such as Philadelphia or Cincinnati profited from certain of their investments in railroads, in general they did not. In turning over to railroad companies all the stock purchased by its subscriptions as an additional inducement to get railroads built, Kansas City followed a practice often observed by municipalities during the era of local promotion.[16]

The two significant Kansas City local roads were the Cameron and the Fort Scott. To the latter, the city issued a subscription of $200,000. The financial arrangements with the Cameron were much more complicated. City ordinances authorized a total of $380,000 in subscriptions. An investigating committee checking the actual payments a few years later found, however, that the total bonds issued seemed to have gone beyond that amount by nearly $14,000. But the committee could not be sure, for the complicated terms of the subscriptions, the highly informal accounting procedures, and the reissue of old bonds burned during the Civil War had left the financial records of the city hopelessly confused. Because of the close co-operation maintained between the officers of the Cameron and the city council, the council doled out bonds much as they were asked for. The 1872 investigating committee concluded that the "secret history of those times (and there seems to be one) will in all probability never be known." Present municipal records, although in good order, permit no fuller evaluation of the financial relations of the city to the Cameron than that made by the committee. But provided the principle is accepted that city growth represents a desirable goal, no Kansas Citian could have argued that a bad bargain was made in turning over public assets to the local promoters, for in the long run, they had succeeded admirably.[17]

Although the promoters demonstrated little brilliance or efficiency in the way they conducted their projects, it is doubtful that there was any flagrant corruption or dishonesty in the attempts to build either the Fort Scott or the Cameron. Most of the money received by the Cameron seems to have been spent on legitimate construction costs. But Kearney received an inflated salary for serving as its president, and Coates and other local leaders voted themselves excessive salaries from the funds of the Fort Scott. Moreover, Coates used money specifically appropriated to build a railroad to promote a personal interest in the land syndicate headed by Joy that was attempting to buy the Neutral Tract. This, however, ultimately worked out well for Kansas City's interests.

Although the fiction of private investment was zealously maintained, local Kansas City railroads were essentially public enterprises. The amount of private subscription to all the Kansas City projects combined could not have totalled over a few thousand dollars. A handful of men who controlled these projects were able to use the resources of a city to promote essentially personal ends, the building of the value of their real-estate holdings through the acquisition of railroads.

To what extent this should constitute an indictment is debatable. It is the essence of democratic government that rival economic groups should be allowed to contend for their own interests within a

framework of representative institutions. And superficially there is
something of the classic purity of the town meeting in the way
early-day Kansas City government functioned. On the surface, programs were initiated at public meetings and approved at popular
elections, and the city council accepted the verdicts of the people. Of
course this was not really the case, as it never is. The "iron law of
oligarchy" dictates that an inner group always makes the decisions,
no matter how democratic the procedure may seem to be. But to
the extent that popular mandates are possible, the Kansas City railroad leaders had one. The community agreed wholeheartedly with
their argument that in promoting railroads they were advancing the
general interest. Through a careful channeling or manipulation—
and whether it was one or the other depends largely on one's point
of view—they were able to unite the city behind their actions and
policies. At a later time, Kansas City underwent an experience with
real dishonesty in the building of the Memphis road, a local project
conducted by essentially the same group of men. Nevertheless, the
Kansas City railroad leaders—Van Horn, Coates, Reid, Kearney,
and the rest—were still considered local heroes and have remained
so to the present day. Perhaps in the delicate balancing of the complexities of principle and result, of time and changing business
ethics, a community's own verdict should bear as much weight as
any other.

The Era of Pools
A Community's Search
for Alternatives

BEFORE the Civil War, the arguments of Kansas City promoters had rested on the assumption that railroads would bring a
golden age to the community. Local writers and orators had consistently expressed an almost mystical faith in the benefits to be
brought by the iron horse. With the construction of the Hannibal
Bridge, their exuberant predictions began to be realized. The city
grew rapidly; new lines were added to its already imposing railway
system; old urban rivals recognized that Kansas City had won the
struggle to become the metropolis of the lower Missouri River valley. But the community leaders who had struggled so long to
bring railroads to the city were by no means satisfied with what they
had accomplished. During the 1870's a complex series of pooling
arrangements among western lines affected the city's welfare.

These combinations often operated to the detriment of the community's economic interests. Even when they did not, they still fostered the conviction among local leaders that they were no longer masters of the destiny of their city.

During the 1870's Kansas City served as the center of the Joy system of railroads, which during the period had few equals in strength or magnitude. Although Joy lost his personal authority over the Burlington lines in 1875 when John Murray Forbes withdrew the support of the Boston group, his power was fully intact at the time Kansas City began to develop as a railroad center. In eastern financial circles, he was frequently referred to as the "Vanderbilt of the Southwest." Joy shared the common view of the business giants of the post-Civil War era that competition was inherently destructive and should therefore be restricted as much as possible. In accord with this view, he and the organizer of a potentially competitive railroad system, John Tracy, president of the Rock Island, set about organizing the famous Iowa Pool, which successfully regulated western business passing from Omaha and Kansas City to Chicago. Although there were a number of complicated realignments among the various railroads represented in the pool, it functioned effectively until 1884 and served as the prototype for similar organizations in other parts of the country.[1]

During the early seventies, the roads running between St. Louis and Kansas City also maintained pooling arrangements, which were somewhat more flexible than those of the Iowa Pool. Co-operation between the St. Louis, Kansas City, and Northern and the Missouri Pacific was responsible during the decade for the fact that Lawrence failed to realize any benefits from the completion of the Lawrence and Pleasant Hill Railroad. This effort to control competition resulted in the formal organization of the Southwestern Railway Rate Association in August, 1876.[2]

Pools had a significant effect on the character of the Western freight-rate structure, on the building of new lines into the region, and on governmental policies toward railroads. They also influenced drastically the community programs of western cities, such as

Kansas City, which became major railroad centers. Before 1870 Kansas City leaders had been almost exclusively concerned with attracting railroads to the city. Now they had to deal with them. During the decade, they reshaped old concepts relating to railroads and formulated plans for alternative methods of transportation. For the most part, their proposed solutions proved ineffectual, but this in itself was significant, for it demonstrated the declining scope of local promotion in a period when business consolidation and monopoly were on the rise.

As early as 1869, the year the bridge was completed, local railroad polemics began to reflect a growing insecurity about the community's achievements. The Kansas City Board of Trade in a report issued in August warned that in spite of the bridge and seven railroads on their way, the city could not afford to rest on past triumphs. Old rivals were still at work. Tireless community exertion would be necessary to continue the successes of the past. Re-emphasizing the prewar attitude of local leaders toward partisan politics and factionalism, the report admonished the community above all else, to "beware of the rock of internal discord on which so many prosperous cities have been wrecked. Our very danger lies in our prosperity, and that in our vain glory we may go mad and destroy ourselves by disunion and apathy." [3]

In addition to reflecting this kind of insecurity bred of success, community leaders during the 1870's began to express ambivalent sentiments about the value of railroads. Their pronouncements differed markedly from the exuberant paeans to the iron horse of the early promoters. The postwar leaders still recognized that the future of Kansas City was dependent on railroads and still more railroads. Therefore, the community would have to support new lines with new bond issues and other assistance. Each time a new railroad proposal came before the community, local advocates of further aid expressed the ardent hope that the building of the line would foster the competition necessary to the city's continued growth. But this did not happen. New railroads built into the region were assimilated into old pooling arrangements, and the rates set by pools often proved detrimental to important economic groups in the city. Consequently, community business leaders—at the same time they continued to urge the attraction of new lines—began to express a resentment of railroads as dangerous monopolies.

An 1873 *Kansas City Times* editorial reflected these new community attitudes. The writer asserted that every citizen should be grateful for the city's rapidly maturing railway system, for it had been responsible for great local growth and prosperity. Still, he said, conditions could not be considered entirely favorable, for there were visible indications of the rise of dangerous railroad monopolies that could seriously injure the trade of Kansas City. In particular, the writer singled out for attack James Joy, whom Kansas Citians had considered a national business hero because of his support of the city's aspirations. It was true, the writer admitted, that the city owed more to Joy than to any other railroad man, but the tendency toward monopoly was particularly evident in the lines that he controlled. He had failed to show a proper regard for the community that had given him so much. He had allowed detrimental clashes to develop within his system. His "stubborness . . . his insatiate greed . . . would now kill the goose that laid the golden egg." In short, the writer concluded, the people of Kansas City were being "fleeced" by an "unrighteous monopoly" kept up for the benefit of Joy and his friends.[4]

During times of stress—in late 1877, for example, when the Southwestern Pool imposed a temporary embargo on Kansas City grain—this always smoldering opposition to railroads flared up in blistering attacks. The wheat embargo, the *Times* declared, "was a vital stab at the business interests of the city." The energetic community lay "prostrate and paralysed at the feet of the hydra headed railroad pool." The paper pointed out that during the great railroad strike earlier in the year, a group of Kansas Citians had stood guard over railroad property to prevent any outbreak of violence. But the next time, the editorial warned, the railroads would be completely at the mercy of anyone who might choose to take advantage of trouble. In fact, the writer hinted that if the embargo was not repealed, community leaders would not discourage laborers who had been thrown out of work from resorting to violence.[5]

Even Robert T. Van Horn's *Journal of Commerce*, always a friend of capital, frequently attacked railroad monopolies. During 1874, for example, his paper urged on several occasions that Congress pass a law to forbid pooling. In general, Van Horn, as a good mid-continentalist in the Gilpin vein, took the position that the monopolistic practices affecting Kansas City resulted from the policies of Eastern railroad companies. In order to avoid extortionate freight charges, the region should protect its own Western roads. As much business as possible should be sent to the Gulf of Mexico, thereby keeping Western trade out of the clutches of the Eastern lines. An attempt to reach the Gulf ports eventually became a main aspect of local transportation policy.[6]

An 1873 report of the Internal Improvements Committee of the Kansas City Board of Trade supplied the most detailed presentation of Kansas City's changing position toward railroads. The committee, after an extensive examination of freight charges prevailing between Kansas City and a number of Kansas towns, asserted that railroads had instituted a series of unjust discriminations to the detriment of local trade interests. Because of the connivance of railroad companies, the schemes of Chicago and St. Louis merchants to encroach on Kansas City's regional business were succeeding. The whole regional system of rates was a "whirlpool of confusion and turbulency," characterized by a complete indifference to the interests of Kansas City. The report particularly attacked the always unpopular Missouri Pacific. The company had been responsible for the pool among lines running between St. Louis and Kansas City. Its policies, so harmful to Kansas City merchants and justified by no principle save force, stemmed only from the railroad's cupidity.

What could be done about these unfavorable conditions? Not a great deal the writers admitted. To attempt to fight soulless corporations directly would always be unsuccessful. The only weapon that could be used against railroad combinations was competition.[7]

During the 1870's, Kansas City leaders directed their efforts toward finding ways to compete with railroads in the hope that trunk lines would thus be forced to institute a rate structure beneficial to the city. The Board of Trade, in making specific the reason for these attempts, supplied a theory of city growth that demonstrated how far the community leaders had departed from their earlier use of doctrines of natural advantage: "the question of transportation determines the supremacy and future of all cities and must decide our own destiny. . . . The success and superiority of one man, or of one city over another, must for all time depend largely upon the margin obtained on freights." [8]

The principal agency responsible for the translation of these new programs into community policy during the 1870's was the Kansas City Board of Trade. Toward the end of the Civil War, the Chamber of Commerce, the prewar agency of the Kansas City business leadership, had been revived. Active in promoting the immediate postwar railroad program, it had ceased to function after 1866. William H. Miller argued that having once secured the objects that it had set out to obtain, the need for the organization had passed. In his estimate, the city had entered the era of prosperity that the Chamber had so long sought to initiate.

The Board of Trade, founded in 1869, was originally organized to represent the "general welfare"—as the leaders interpreted it —in the same fashion as had the Chamber. Initially, it considered such matters as the improvement of streets, the establishment of a fire department, and the obtaining of a new city charter. But the organization, like the Chamber before it and perhaps for much the same reason that there was less need for such an agency in times of prosperity, became moribund during the year. By the time it was reorganized in January, 1872, new and more specialized interests— meat packers, cattlemen, wheat dealers, and bankers—were represented in the Kansas City business community, a reflection of the city's rapid economic development. These groups demanded new services such as financial reports and information on cattle and wheat-market prices. Owing to the variety of interests represented in the Board, harmonious, decisive action was seldom possible. By the end of the decade, it had become an unwieldy body and was eventually to develop into a specialized agency representing grain dealers and cattlemen. At no time, did it express the consensus of a united business community on general public issues as had the Chamber. Nevertheless, the Board of Trade did keep a vigilant eye on the city's railroad rate structure during the seventies and sponsored the transportation programs of the local business leadership.[10]

The first plan developed to try to foster competition involved building narrow-gauge railroads. The narrow-gauge (usually considered a three-foot road in contrast to the four-foot eight-and-a-half-inch standard gauge) was unknown in the United States before 1870. A paper that year called, "The Gauge of the 'Railways of the Future' " read by Robert J. Fairlie at a meeting of the British Railway Association, aroused widespread attention and enthusiasm in this country. Proponents argued that narrow-gauges would be cheaper to build and would require less upkeep than standard-gauge railroads. With more cars on the line, they could haul the same amount of freight as standard-gauge roads and do it more cheaply. The *Boston Commercial Bulletin*, for example, stated that narrow-gauge roads would prove especially suitable for the opening of the resources of new regions, where the traffic was not great enough to justify the building of a standard-gauge road. In addition they would serve as cheap feeders to trunk lines.[11]

These arguments struck a responsive chord in the minds of Kansas City leaders. During the early years of the decade, almost every issue of the city's newspapers contained at least one article strongly urging their construction. Generally an attack on railroad monopoly accompanied this advocacy: the most important function foreseen for the new lines was to restore competition.

A *Times* editorial late in 1872 provided a typical statement of local arguments. The writer first observed that the fundamental tendency among national railroads was consolidation. And consolidation, he pointed out, damaged interior cities by fostering rate discriminations. The obvious answer to this problem was locally owned railroads controlled by local citizens. These would force the trunk lines to offer concessions. Moreover, they would help to develop manufacturing and could be used to expand local markets. One locally owned railroad, the editorial asserted, would be more valuable to a community than a dozen trunk lines.

Broad-gauge roads were beyond the means of interior cities to build, the writer declared. (Something, at least, had been learned from the years spent in futile effort to construct local railroads.) No matter how liberally communities might subscribe to them, through lines would always be controlled by outside capital and would discriminate against the cities that helped to build them. Kansas City afforded a striking example of this self-sacrifice for the benefit of others. In the future, if interior cities were to survive, there would have to be cheaper transportation. The narrow-gauge, inexpensive enough to be built with local capital, would provide this.[12]

Robert T. Van Horn, showing his talent for keeping abreast of all economic, commercial, and technological developments, became an early advocate of the narrow-gauge. In the summer of 1871, he announced that after more than a year of study of the subject he was ready to present his findings. He published these in a series of long statistic-filled articles, which in general argued the inexpensiveness and satisfactory operation of the new-type railroads. He asserted that the lines could be built for less than half the cost of a standard-gauge. Maintenance and operating costs, moreover, would not exceed 40 per cent of gross earnings, in contrast to upwards of 60 per cent for standard-gauges. The lines would expand local merchandising in areas not reached by the major railroads and would promote manufacturing in the city by bringing in cheap raw materials, especially coal, from outlying areas.[13]

The original community plan developed through the Board of Trade conceived of a number of narrow-gauge railroads radiating from the city in all directions. After several years of effort, one such line was built from Kansas City to Independence, and extended on to Lexington, Missouri. The construction of this one railroad involved a multitude of difficulties and complications.

During the height of the agitation, which developed late in 1871, Kansas City business leaders organized two local companies: the Kansas City, Independence, and Lexington Railroad to build between the three named cities; and the Kansas City, Wyandotte, and Northwestern Railroad to be built toward the northern border of Kansas and eventually to be extended into Nebraska. As might be expected, Leavenworth strenuously opposed the latter project, which would open to Kansas City a local trade area still tributary to the northern river towns. Although the *Times* dismissed this opposition as another "childish whine" on the part of the "decaying neighbor," just one more foolish cry made "while her walls are crumbling, her merchants deserting her, and her streets becoming silent . . . ," the Kansas City leaders decided initially to concentrate their efforts on the eastward project. The directory of the Lexington road petitioned the City Council of Kansas City for a subscription of $75,000. The Council submitted this proposition to popular vote, but owing to the vigorous opposition of the south section of the city, the bond issue was soundly defeated in April, 1872. The influential real-estate developers from that part of town by now insisted that any new lines coming into Kansas City from the east would have to be built near their holdings. Growth had intensified the problem of sectional rivalry, which had only been slightly felt in the prewar days of railroad promotion.[14]

This setback shifted city attention to the projected road into Kansas. F. C. Eames, the president of the company, "instead of bumming among the Old Fogies of New York," as the *Times* reported it, had traveled to London to attempt to win support there in financing the railroad. He assured local leaders that he could market all governmental bonds in England at no more than a 10 per cent discount from face value. The directors of the project launched a vigorous effort to raise subscriptions in the counties and towns along the route.[15]

The frenzied narrow-gauge movement produced occasional dissent, reflecting a growing opposition to local railroad promotion and promoters. A correspondent calling himself "Progress," sent a letter to the *Times* that stood in marked contrast to the ordinarily ponderous railroad polemics of the day. His purpose in writing, he professed, was to call the attention of readers to the startling importance of building a line to Lone Jack, Missouri, a totally insignificant hamlet a few miles south of Kansas City. Kansas Citians, "flushed with victory," he wryly warned, must not rest too secure in "their already acquired lands" and allow Emporia, Paola, and Shawnee Mission (small Kansas villages near the state line) to rob their city of the Lone Jack trade, which was legitimately hers. "Can we afford to lose this opportunity to connect ourselves with the thriving city of Lone Jack? Can we afford to turn our back upon this trade which is waiting to pour the rich treasures into our lap? Shall we stint ourselves in the matter of taxes merely to accommodate a few old fogies, when glory beckons us onward! No sir, we protest!" The writer called for an immediate subscription of $200,000 for this magnificent road, and then turned to an indirect attack on the Kansas City real-estate interests, who had consistently promoted the local railroad boom. The Lone Jack road, he said, could not be considered a "carpet-bag enterprise." Although its promoters had not yet gained membership in the Old Citizens' Society, they had been in the area long enough "to learn the value of railroads and the unapproachable sublimity of push." Their hopes were as bright and their spirits as gay as those of earlier promoters.[16]

In spite of occasional protest of this sort, the narrow-gauge movement went ahead. After they had obtained sufficient signatures on a petition circulated in the city, the promoters persuaded the Jackson County Court to adopt a proposal to allow Kaw Township, which encompassed Kansas City, to vote on a subscription of $150,000 to the Kansas City, Wyandotte, and Northwestern. The court made the subscription conditional on the road's obtaining $300,000 more in bonds from Kansas counties and stipulated that bonds would be released in installments as construction progressed. Kaw Township voted overwhelmingly in favor of the proposition: 1,299 to 45.[17]

Because of conflict with rival narrow-gauge projects in Kansas, the requisite subscriptions could not be raised in the neighboring state. Consequently, an effort developed early in 1873 to transfer the local subscription to the eastward narrow-gauge road. By specifically promising that the line would be run through the south end of the city, the promoters overcame the earlier opposition to this project, and the transfer was approved by a vote of 1,601 to 113.[18]

In January of 1874, the directors of the Kansas City, Independence, and Lexington negotiated a construction contract with a group of New York and English capitalists. After having completed a part of the road, the company backed away from its commitment to build into Kansas City by way of McGee's Addition in the south part of town and announced that it would seek right of way along the levee. South–end business leaders obtained an injunction delaying the issue of the rest of the county subscription. Finally, however, after considerable heated controversy, the Jackson County Court paid the whole sum. The company completed the railroad between the outskirts of Kansas City and Lexington in the summer of 1876. After several months of debate in the Board of Trade and in the City Council, the latter settled the question of the railroad's route through the city by providing the company its desired right of way along the levee. The intense struggle within the city over the narrow-gauge project had not shown a significant diminishment of popular support of the community's railroad program. The leaders could still muster the overwhelming majorities of the past when they were themselves united. But with the rapid growth of Kansas City, conflict among interest groups had developed which made it impossible to obtain the same kind of business community consensus as had existed before the Civil War.[19]

Through the decade, local leaders initiated a number of other narrow-gauge projects. Extensions of the Lexington line were also contemplated. None of these efforts ever got beyond the discussion stage. By the time the one local narrow-gauge railroad was built, the national vogue for narrow-gauges had about ended, for they had realized few of the benefits predicted for them. The Kansas City line was no exception. It was shortly acquired by the Missouri Pacific of Jay Gould. He changed its gauge to the standard width, and the railroad became a relatively insignificant branch. In no way did the narrow-gauge movement provide any kind of competitive threat to the monopolistic trunk lines.

No more successful was the second alternative of the decade: the attempt to establish barge lines on the Missouri River for the hauling of grain. William H. Miller, who had become commercial editor of Van Horn's *Journal* in 1871, formally launched this movement in a long editorial of April 23, 1872. Miller pointed out that the coming of railroads had caused such a drastic decline in steamboating on the Missouri River that the trunk lines no longer faced a competitive threat from water transportation. Barges would help to overcome this problem by providing cheap rates for some classes of products, especially grain. Their use would bring to Kansas City the agricultural produce of a vast territory in Nebraska, Iowa, and Kansas and would enable St. Louis and Kansas City merchants to supply the area with merchandise. Because of railroad practices, Miller pointed out, Chicago had gained control of this rich region to the west of Kansas City. Octave Chanute prepared a report for the Board that after extensive analysis came to the conclusion that the operation of barges on the Missouri was feasible.[20]

Although throughout 1872 the Board of Trade considered the proposal, it was not until the next year that the Kansas City business leaders made serious attempts to obtain barges. The *Times* early in the year began to argue that the project had become crucial. Although Kansas City was located in the heart of the finest agricultural region in the world and had ten railroads, this was of little consequence, an editorial declared, when the "producing classes—the bone and sinew of the land, and the basis of all prosperity—are from year to year growing poorer and poorer." If something was not done to make farming remunerative, grass would soon grow in the deserted streets of once flourishing cities in the West.[21]

In March the Committee on Internal Improvements of the Board of Trade issued a report recommending that $5,000 be raised to test the practicality of barge-line operations. Although the Board of Trade approved this proposal, its fund-raising committee had little success in obtaining the money. By April only $1,525 had been secured, and the Board reduced the minimum sum necessary to $3,600. The president of the Mississippi Valley Transportation Company, which operated on the Mississippi River, visited Kansas City and offered to provide barges for a test run. The Board rejected his proposal as too expensive. Late in the summer, however, the company accepted a guaranty of $2,700 for a test trip. Because of crop failure that year, by the time a large enough cargo could be obtained, adequate insurance could not be purchased, and the trial was abandoned. However, one of the barges hauled a load of stones back to St. Louis. For years, supporters of barges cited this trip as evidence that the plan was feasible.[22]

In 1878, at a time when the rates established by the Southwestern Pool were particularly detrimental to the city's grain dealers, Kansas City business leaders attempted to organize a local barge-line company. The promoters set a goal of $5,000 in subscriptions and got enough support to sponsor several barge trips down the river. Although they argued that the practicality of barges had been fully shown, the experiments had actually demonstrated that barges could only be operated satisfactorily when the Missouri was abnormally high. Nevertheless, the plan was tried again in 1880. Local businessmen organized a company with a capital of $100,000 and purchased two barges and a large boat. In the end, these operated only on the Mississippi. The company soon recognized that the successful use of barges on the Missouri rested on extensive river improvement, and the firm went out of business in 1882.[23]

Although the effort to establish a system of river transport failed to provide a competitive regulator to trunk-line railroads, the dream of such a plan intrigued local leaders throughout the 1870's. Kansas City businessmen consistently argued the necessity of establishing barges. Howard M. Holden, for example, one of the most important figures in Kansas City's postwar business history, called attention frequently to the need for continued exertion to institute a system of river transport if the city was not to become a mere "whistling station." The leading wheat dealer of the city, Henry J. Latshaw, vigorously denounced the ruinous rates on grain imposed by railroads and became a forceful advocate of barges.[24]

A *Times* editorial in 1878 provided a typical summation of the public consensus of the community. Railroad pools and combinations, the writer asserted, had operated to destroy the legitimate trade of Kansas City. Nevertheless, these monopolies had one good effect: they had created the impulse among the persevering people of Kansas City to seek permanent relief. For years, the writer said, local leaders had talked about barge lines to Memphis, St. Louis, or New Orleans. But just when a project showed signs of being successful, railroads reduced rates and temporarily suspended pooling. This in every case had resulted in the collapse of the barge-line effort; little or nothing could be done until the next pool agreement took effect. For years, therefore, Kansas City had found itself "tied up hand and foot," unable to move freight except at unfavorable rates. This state of affairs would continue until the community established some alternative to railroad transportation. With the river as a "regulator," however, railroads would no longer be indispensable to trade.[25]

Another *Times* editorial, published a month later, discussed the relationship of water transportation to city growth in a manner that reflected the changing character, and the ambiguity, of local theories concerning railroads and urban development. The newspaper asserted that the city could not afford to abandon the barge-line movement; whether it proved practical or not, it was worth its cost alone as an advertisement. Not to carry through the plan would make it appear that Kansas City had repudiated its faith in the greatest of its natural advantages, a navigable river to world markets, and that she had accepted the rank and function of an inland railroad town. If a system of river transport was not developed, the general faith of the country in the city's mid-continental destiny would be destroyed: "Take the Missouri river away from Kansas City, or destroy the general belief that it is to become the principal freight highway for the products of the New West, and what is left to account for the general faith that this is the site of a future great city? It doesn't make any difference how many railroads we have. All the great cities of the continent are, and always will be on navigable waterways. Capital can build railroads anywhere. It has built railroads and cut-offs all around us and can make more railroad centers anywhere to compete with us. Man makes railroads at will, but God made our river and made it ours forever. No human can take it away from us, and . . . so long as we neglect to use that river, Kansas City will be nothing but a remote interior cross roads town, dickering with a sparsely settled country that is kept uncultivated and impoverished by railroad tariffs." [26]

This editorial expressed an inconsistency that reflected the ambivalence in community attitudes. The doctrine that natural advantages created great cities had held sway too long for it to be abandoned easily. But it could not be harmonized with the reality that the writer recognized: that railroads could make cities anywhere. His argument that Kansas City's natural advantages would have to be developed at whatever cost if the city was successfully to compete with cities built only through railroads did not really provide a reconciliation. As did the entire unrealistic movement to reassert the importance of the river, the editorial reflected the nostalgia for a bygone era of a community whose outlook had been fundamentally shaped by a continual reiteration of the doctrine of natural advantages.

A third aspect of Kansas City's search for alternatives embodied an effort to reach ocean outlets on the Gulf of Mexico as a means of avoiding Eastern markets and Eastern railroad connections. In this way, it was argued, Western products could be shipped directly to Europe, and the community could avoid paying tribute to the monopolistic Eastern railroad lines. This program reflected one of the oldest dreams of the Kansas City business community. The project to build a railroad to Galveston had been advanced in these terms. Before the Civil War, the Chamber of Commerce had expended considerable effort in investigating the feasibility of importing goods directly from Europe through Gulf ports. The plan for a Middle Confederacy, which during the days before Secession had considerable support in the city, had been based on the idea of a block of mid-continent states with outlets to the south.[27]

The construction of the Missouri, Kansas, and Texas Railroad supplied the impetus for the revival of this idea in the 1870's. This line won the right over Joy's Missouri River, Fort Scott, and Gulf to build through Indian Territory, and on March 18, 1873, connected with the Houston and Texas Central running to Galveston. From 1872 on, the Katy, as it was generally called, sought a connection with Kansas City, and the trains of the railroad ran into the city after August, 1874.[28]

Late in 1872, as the Katy was being constructed southward, the Board of Trade sent a delegation to northern Texas to see what business arrangements could be made in the region. At first, this effort was directed toward opening new markets for Kansas City merchants. The delegation reported optimistically to the Board of Trade, emphasizing that owing to the extensive agricultural emigration into the region, the country offered rich possibilities for the sale of farm implements and other goods.[29]

During the course of the panic of 1873, local interest shifted from the opening of new trade areas to the development of Galveston as a major ocean port. The *Journal of Commerce* suggested in May that a commercial convention that would include representatives from western Missouri, Iowa, Kansas, Nebraska, Arkansas, Texas, and the western territories be held in Kansas City to formulate policies for building up port and trade facilities in the Texas city. The *Times* enthusiastically seconded the proposal. Nothing immediate came from this effort, but late in the year the program received formal statement when a United States Senate Committee, headed by William Windom of Minnesota, came to St. Louis to take testimony in its investigation of national transportation needs and facilities. The Board of Trade appointed Van Horn and William H. Powell, the president of the organization and a prominent grain dealer, to represent Kansas City at the hearings. The two men drew up a memorial, dated October 25, 1873, under the title "The New West—Its Resources, Agricultural Interests, Commerce and Transportation Needs." For the rest of the decade, the phrase the "New West" was in common use. Sectional spokesmen contended that the region defined by the term was one of distinct economic interests and that the products of the area would have to find their outlet through the Gulf.[30]

The Van Horn–Powell memorial defined the New West as a region that included western Missouri, western Iowa, Nebraska, Kansas, Colorado, the Indian Territory, and New Mexico. The region was unified through a system of trunk railroads having its locus at the mouth of the Kansas River. It was an area of exceptional fertility, embracing the largest, most productive corn and winter-wheat raising section in the world. Adopting the Gilpin theory of the plains, they declared that the New West also contained the "only natural pastoral region in North America"; the area to the west of Kansas City was rapidly filling with the "cattle of civilization." Marshaling a great many statistics to show its wealth, they argued that a region so important was entitled to a voice in shaping national transportation policies.

Despite the concentration of trunk railroads at Kansas City, the memorialists argued that the New West was practically cut off from both foreign and domestic markets. Only when prices were unusually high, in times of crop failure east of the Mississippi or in Europe, could grain profitably be shipped to the Atlantic coast. It was not strange, they said, that corn was burned for fuel when the margin left to the shipper and the farmer amounted to only six to eight cents per bushel.

What remedies were available? The memorialists stated that barge lines on the Missouri and Mississippi rivers offered a possible but as yet unproven alternative. The best solution would be railroad connections reaching the Mississippi far enough south to avoid winter freeze-ups. Accordingly, they demanded some type of federal support for a railroad from Kansas City to Memphis. Such a line would shorten the distance to New Orleans by about 200 miles over existing routes. The memorial also recommended federal removal of obstructions interfering with navigation at the mouth of the Mississippi and the improvement of the harbor at Galveston so as to open the port to ocean-going vessels. The writers estimated that these measures would enable the farmers of the New West to ship grain to Europe by way of New Orleans for about thirty-two and-a-half cents less per bushel than by way of rail to New York. The approximate savings on corn or wheat shipped by way of Galveston would be about a quarter of a dollar per bushel. These Gulf rates could be reduced even more in the future.

In their testimony, Van Horn and Powell both pointed out that only on meat products could satisfactory rates be obtained from Kansas City to Eastern markets, and this was solely because cattle dealers and packers had been powerful enough to obtain special concessions from Eastern railroads. Van Horn observed that the New West could not compete with Illinois, Indiana, and the Northwest in grain crops. Up until recent times, the western, mountain, and Indian trade had absorbed the surplus of the region, but now the rapid settlement of the West had forced the farmers to seek new markets. A short cheap outlet for the products of the New West had become mandatory.[31]

Although Congress took no action on the proposals of the Kansas Citians, during the next two years the effort to open southern ports became intense. This was particularly true after the Katy began to run trains into Kansas City. "There is a tide in the affairs of cities, as well as those of men," Van Horn wrote, "which taken at its flood leads on to prosperity, power and greatness." Kansas City's chance for urban greatness lay in the Gulf movement. In May of 1874 the Board of Trade sent a delegation of city business leaders to Galveston and Houston. This set off a round of visits back and forth, meetings with other boards of trade in the New West, and petitions for federal river and harbor improvement.[32]

During August 1875 the Kansas City Board of Trade met with officials of the Mississippi Valley Trading Company, a London firm organized to promote direct trade between the central United States and England. Thomas D. Worrall, the managing director, told an enthusiastic Kansas City public meeting: "The drones in the markets of New York and the East are getting to be too numerous. They all want to live on the West. The worst of it is, they are now masters of the situation. They are making the people of the West and South hewers of wood and drawers of water." Worrall was only restating a position frequently expressed in the city.[33]

Van Horn called the attempt to open trade to the Gulf a commercial revolution. A long editorial on the subject took its argument from the theories of Gilpin and demonstrated the continuing pervasiveness of the ideas that the early prophet of Kansas City represented. Western development, Van Horn argued, had reached a distance so far from the Atlantic seaboard states that the West's surplus products could no longer be profitably transported there. In the past, immigration had absorbed this surplus, but, owing to the increased productivity of the West, this was no longer possible. A national railroad system had been substantially completed; but this was of no real help, for only world markets could absorb the West's agricultural products. Freight rates were simply too high for them to be shipped abroad by way of Eastern markets. For this reason, the Gulf movement had developed. For all the United States west of the Mississippi River and south of Minnesota, the Gulf would provide the outlet to world markets. "The old thraldom of the East over the West must speedily give way" in the face of this new trade pattern. Moreover, the route would soon be responsible for opening new markets in Central and South America. In the end, this would "liberate" both Latin America and the Midwest from the "commercial thraldom of Europe." Here was Gilpin's mid-continentalism, opposition to the East and to Europe, and emphasis on the West in a world setting emphatically stated.[34]

The "Galveston Movement," as it came to be called, proved unsuccessful. The railroad to the Texas city was owned by several companies, operating different gauge roads. Through connections proved impossible to establish. The *Times* observed in 1875 that these companies were "managed by very short-sighted old grannies . . . and the Galveston trade movement will have to wait until it can be renewed under better auspices." For the rest of the decade, the Board of Trade sponsored frequent trips to Texas in the effort to obtain better facilities. But this movement, like all the other attempts to find alternatives to eastern trunk connections, proved a failure.[35]

Eventually in the mid-1880's, a railroad rate structure favorable to Kansas City was established. The building of new lines into the region, the organization of the Jay Gould system of western roads, and his subsequent war with the Iowa Pool, led to severe competition for Western trade that benefited the city's interests.[36] But Kansas City leaders played little part in bringing this about. As railroads became national businesses, local community programs could no longer seriously affect the location of major railroad lines or the practices of railroad companies. The attitudes and policies of the Kansas City business leaders during the decade of the 1870's demonstrated a point that has increasingly become better recognized: the opposition to railroads that was so much a part of the Western reform crusades of the late nineteenth and early twentieth centuries had its origins not so much in the struggles of oppressed agrarians fighting capital, as older interpretations would have it, but in the attempts of dissatisfied business groups in the cities of the West to protect their interests against monopolistic, consolidated enterprises.

$\cdot 9 \cdot$

So Many Birds of Carrion
The Memphis Road

IF the Cameron road is to be considered the triumph of community policy in Kansas City, then the attempt to build a road to Memphis should be considered its defeat. But the recorded history of Kansas City, which like all American local history tends to commemorate only success, has ignored the chief failure of the town-builders. No city pioneer wrote reminiscences about building the Memphis road; no legend has grown around it. The early Kansas City historians—true to the booster tradition and in some cases themselves involved in the disaster—set about eliminating the story from the city's past by casually dismissing it as unimportant. They admitted that it was unfortunate, of course, that the railroad had not been built, but after all, they argued, depression and other circumstances over which local leaders had no control had stood in the way. Moreover, the failure had little significance when measured against the general success of the whole local railroad movement.

Later historians, bound by motifs incorporated in the accounts

of their predecessors, tended to ignore the Memphis road altogether. Clearly, no part of the city's history harmonized less well
with the "Kansas City spirit." Little significant correspondence
about the project was available for use; probably little of this kind
of material ever existed, for this was not the type of effort in
which participants were likely to set their plans to paper. In short,
it was natural enough that the episode became a forgotten part of
Kansas City's history. Yet, the contemporary public record, although it leaves many questions only partly answered, clearly indi-
cates that the Memphis road was considered one of the most
significant aspects of community policy during the period of local
railroad promotion in Kansas City.

The idea for building a railroad to Memphis originated during
the golden years of railroad promotion following the Civil War,
when throughout the nation local governments greatly increased
the amount of aid extended to private railroad companies. Decisions by national railroad leaders during this period dictated that
Kansas City should become a major American railroad center; in
the years 1865–1870, each significant line organized by the Kansas
City promoters was integrated into a major system. The design for
the Memphis project differed little from that of the highly successful Cameron road: organize a company, mark out a route, obtain a local bond issue, and then unload the railroad on an Eastern
company. But this time no one came forward to help build the
promoters' line.

At long last, the Kansas City railroad leaders, who for years
had talked so grandiloquently of the virtues of local railroads, had
to try to build one with local resources. The Kansas City Board
of Trade, which represented the business elite of the community,
gave its official sanction to the project. The heroes of the Cameron
victory—John W. Reid, Charles E. Kearney, Theodore S. Chase,
Robert T. Van Horn—were intimately associated with it. New
business heroes—the representatives of the rising meat-packing,
grain, livestock, and banking enterprises—lent it their prestige as
well. Only Kersey Coates of the important prewar railroad leaders

still active in city affairs took no part. It was not foresight that caused his abstention. His presidency of the Missouri River, Fort Scott, and Gulf, and his close ties with James F. Joy made it impossible for him to participate in a local project not in accord with Joy's over-all plans.

The result of these efforts of the Kansas City leaders was a total debacle. The community was disrupted; the Cameron heroes fell out among themselves; serious charges of dishonesty and corruption were raised. The end was incredible—at least in terms of the booster tradition. In return for $1,050,000 in county bonds, the citizens of the region obtained a right-of-way, a partially constructed roadbed and a few timbers and pieces of iron, which finally had to be sold at auction for $15,025. And this was on the second try. The first time that the assets of the company were offered for sale the bid was so low that the court administering bankruptcy proceedings rejected it.

The Memphis project spanned two distinct periods in local promotion. It began at a time of prosperity, when railroad enthusiasm ran high, and local governments were willing to extend aid to any enterprise that promised to increase the wealth of the community. But it extended into a period when this enthusiasm had diminished, when local bond issues could no longer be raised, and when depression had created popular animosity against national railroad leaders. This change was reflected in the arguments used to gain support for the road. Initially, the promoters advocated it as another trunk line that would stimulate growth and prosperity in Kansas City and in the neighboring region. Later, they advanced it as an alternative to Eastern railroad monopoly: a people's road to the South that would open markets and provide new outlets for the products of the New West.

The difficulties of the Memphis road also reflected the changing character of Kansas City. As the city grew, rival economic interests developed, and the small inner group of pre-Civil War railroad leaders were no longer able to steam-roller through their proposals without dissent. Much of the controversy associated with the project resulted not from the growing popular opposition to railroads, which was later to flare up in the anti-railroad crusades of the latter part of the century, but from struggles of rival railroad factions within the city.

Moreover, as the early leaders had feared, the city became divided politically. Railroad issues could not be kept separate from politics. Van Horn and the other railroad promoters—as could be expected—became active Republicans, but a strong Democratic faction also developed in the city. Through the seventies a rough equality existed between the two parties. In hotly contested local elections, fought on party lines, politicians exposed the railroad machinations of their political rivals. An influential crusading Democratic newspaper, the *Kansas City Times*, founded in 1868 specifically to give the party a voice, contended with Van Horn's Republican *Journal*, which had always expressed the views of the town-builders. In an effort to increase circulation and to elect Democrats to office, the *Times* was always ready to point to any irregularity on the part of the old-guard leaders and to print criticisms of local railroad policy.

On the surface, the character of the promotional efforts involved in the Memphis road may appear different from that of the earlier projects. Actually, though the promoters perhaps learned more sophisticated methods of profiting from railroad building—the use of the construction company device, for example—their methods did not change radically. They had always handled the public funds that they raised in unrestricted fashion. Nevertheless, there was greater cynicism in the conduct of the Memphis road than in earlier ventures. Up to this time, the leaders had at least made some effort to accomplish what they had pledged themselves to do—build a railroad. However, when it became clear that no Eastern railroad company would support the Memphis road, everyone connected with it tried to use the essentially public project for his own private gain. The promoters' efforts actually to construct a railroad were, at very best, half-hearted. Even Van Horn, who for years had served the causes of the community—as he defined them—with little material recompense, seemed content to sit back quietly and to draw a sizable salary from an exploitative project. In so doing, he reflected the values of the era. This after all was the Gilded Age. Promotions of the type of the Memphis road occurred frequently during the period, and public opinion seldom condemned them. Corporate and governmental corruption were inextricably associated with America's rapid economic growth in the post-Civil War years. And Van Horn had always been adaptable; in fact, one of the chief features of his character was a chameleon-like sensitivity to changing circumstances and standards.

The movement to build a road to Memphis began in much the same fashion as had many of the earlier Kansas City projects—with demands in areas without railroads to establish a connection to the growing regional railroad center. In 1869 agitation developed in Springfield, 150 miles southeast of Kansas City, for the construction of a line between the two cities, which would then be extended southeastward toward Memphis. During the summer, interest grew in Kansas City, and in August the Board of Trade sent delegates to a convention in Springfield, which set up a preliminary organization for the project. After hearing a favorable report from its representatives, the Board recommended city support for the enterprise and appointed a committee, including Reid and Kearney, to solicit private subscriptions in the city.[1]

A convention to back the project met in Kansas City in October. Expanding on themes of William Gilpin, Van Horn, the chief speaker at the meeting, foresaw immense possibilities for a railroad that would permit the exchange of staples of varying degrees of latitude—one of the most profitable and oldest aspects of world commerce. The convention approved a directory for the project that included Kearney and Van Horn and instructed its members to look into the purchase of a paper railroad company possessing a charter that might provide more liberal terms of incorporation than the general statutes permitted.[2]

As a result of the abuses of ante-bellum paper railroad companies, Missouri had begun to make its extremely liberal incorporation policies more stringent. Reflecting the opposition of areas that had not benefited from the massive prewar aid program, the new Missouri constitution of 1865 stated that railroad companies would have to obtain a two-thirds popular vote of approval before a county could subscribe to their stock. Legislation passed after the war required that a new railroad company raise a bona-fide sub- scription of $1,000 a mile with 5 per cent of this amount to be paid at the time of the organization. This requirement could be circum- vented though, for an 1868 law permitted established railroad companies to authorize the formation of branch roads under their old charters.[3]

Initially, the Memphis promoters decided to organize their com- pany as a branch of the Kansas City and Cameron Railroad, which held the Kansas City, Galveston, and Lake Superior charter. Among its many expansive provisions, this charter authorized a line to Memphis. On October 30, the directors of the Cameron, who constituted roughly the same group pushing the Memphis road, approved the formation of the Kansas City and Memphis Railroad Company as a branch road, with the right to build a line to the southeastern border of Missouri. John M. Richardson of Springfield, who had been instrumental in getting the project started, became president of the company, and Van Horn and Kearney were selected as directors. Kearney was also named to a three-man executive committee authorized to handle construction and management. Early in 1870 the City Council of Kansas City appropriated $2,000 for a preliminary survey of the route of the road. In April, the company obtained subscriptions to its capital stock of $250,000 from St. Clair County and $400,000 from Bates County.[4]

In spite of continual urging, the Jackson County Court, which had always opposed the designs of the Kansas City business leaders, did not take immediate action in behalf of the road. This was the first project, however, which would directly benefit the parts of the county below Kansas City, and accordingly considerable pressure developed to support it. After prolonged debate, the court called for an election to be held on October 8 to approve a $300,000 county subscription. In order to protect the interests of the county, the court imposed restrictions on the subscription. The railroad had to follow a specified route south of Kansas City, by way of the towns of Westport and Hickman Mills. The court would withhold payment of the subscription until the Kansas City and Memphis had demonstrated that it had raised sufficient money to finish the road to the southern border of the state, or to connect with another railroad running in the same direction as the projected line. These restrictions allayed the fears of rural voters, and the subscription was approved by the large majority of 4,403 in favor to 940 against.[5]

Again, as they had so often in the past, the Kansas City promoters faced the problem of a competing local line: the Kansas City, Clinton, and Memphis Branch of the Tebo and Neosho Railroad Company (hereafter called the Clinton Company). Business leaders in Clinton in Henry County, Missouri, had also taken advantage of the 1868 incorporation law to organize a branch road under a prewar charter and proposed to build a line southeastward by way of Clinton instead of Springfield. The Clinton Company began soliciting for subscriptions in the same counties as had the Kansas City and Memphis. St. Clair County transferred its $250,000 subscription to the Clinton Company on the grounds that the Kansas City and Memphis had no legal existence since its parent company (the Kansas City and Cameron) had been absorbed by the Hannibal and St. Jo.[6]

This complication forced the Kansas City leaders to obtain authorization from the Hannibal and St. Jo. to build their line. In so doing, they lent support to the charge that they were too closely tied to the investors controlling the Hannibal and St. Jo. Although Kearney and Van Horn vigorously denied associations with the "Boston clique," Clinton Company supporters gained a hearing for their argument that the Kansas City promoters were once again trying to sell out a local railroad company to Eastern interests. "Boston" was still a powerful symbol that could evoke the pro-

Southern sentiments of rural Missourians. Early in 1871 a fight developed over an attempt to transfer the Jackson County subscription from the Kansas City and Memphis to the Clinton Company.[7]

In spite of the public denials, the leaders of the Kansas City and Memphis had clearly hoped to obtain Joy's support for their project. During the previous summer, Richardson had written Joy to inquire whether an arrangement could be made to furnish iron and rolling stock once the local company had completed its roadbed. He also proposed that Joy attempt to get the charter of the Tebo and Neosho Company declared invalid. This company had been absorbed by the Missouri, Kansas, and Texas, which was contending with Joy's Missouri River, Fort Scott, and Gulf for the right to build into Indian Territory. The Tebo and Neosho was of course also the parent company of the Clinton Company. Although Richardson did not make the point, if Joy succeeded in getting the Tebo and Neosho's charter declared invalid, then the Kansas City and Memphis' competitor would be eliminated.[8]

But the Memphis project was not in accordance with Joy's plans for building southeast. At the suggestion of Octave Chanute, early in 1870 he had begun to make plans to construct a line from Baxter Springs, south of Kansas City on the Fort Scott, into southwest Missouri and northern Arkansas.[9]

When it became clear that Joy would not endorse the Kansas City and Memphis project, both Kearney and Reid, who was not an original member of the company but who had been named as director later, enlisted in the effort to divert the Jackson County subscription to the Clinton Company. What inducements the Clinton Company may have offered the two men are unknown, but it was clear by this time in any case that the Kansas City and Memphis had lost popularity because of its connection—however intangible—with the Hannibal and St. Jo.

Reid's actions were particularly disingenuous. In February, 1871, he wrote Richardson that he had just had a letter from Joy. Earlier, Reid said, he had written to the Detroit railroad builder telling him that as he understood Missouri corporation law, the stockholders of the Kansas City and Memphis Company could assert the right to vote for the directors of the Hannibal and St. Jo. Joy had emphatically replied—as he could of course have been expected to do—that the Hannibal and St. Jo. would never under any circumstances consent to this procedure. Reid told Richardson, with feigned innocence, that he had taken this step in order to get the status of the company cleared up before anything more was done on the road. Moreover, he said that he had sent a copy of Joy's letter to the Jackson County Court so that its members would be apprised of the circumstances of the company. Considering the position of the County Court, which reflected rural animosity to Eastern capital, Reid's course could have only one effect—to aid the diversion of the subscription from his own company.[10]

Richardson, who was perhaps more naive than he should have been, seemed mystified by Reid's whole procedure. He sent a copy of Reid's letter to Joy, assuring him that all his company had requested from the Hannibal and St. Jo. was permission to organize. This had been granted. As far as Richardson was concerned the matter was settled. Certainly, there would never be any claim on the part of Kansas City and Memphis stockholders that they had any right to take part in the decisions of the Hannibal and St. Jo.[11]

Richardson soon saw that he was being outmaneuvered and took his case to the Kansas City Merchants' Exchange. During a short period in 1871 when the Board of Trade was inactive, the Exchange functioned as the local businessmen's policy organization. Richardson charged that transfer of the Jackson County subscription would be illegal and sharply attacked Kearney and Reid for supporting the move. As a result of his appeal, the Exchange adopted a resolution opposing the transfer and selected a committee to present this position to the Jackson County Court.[12]

During the next few days, Reid, Kearney, and A. D. La Due, the general superintendent of the Clinton Company, appeared before the Exchange to counter Richardson's appeal. Reid was frank. He admitted that Joy had been approached about the Kansas City and Memphis, but since he had not been interested, the County Court should be left free to decide what to do with the subscription. La Due stated that he had the subscription of Cass County safely tied up; this would be essential to the completion of the road; under no circumstances would Cass County ever subscribe to the Kansas City and Memphis. Kearney praised La Due and the vigorous efforts of the Clinton Company. He agreed that the Kansas City and Memphis would never be able to obtain a subscription from Cass County. Richardson was an honest man but something beyond honesty was needed. "We need," Kearney said, "business energy and tact." [13]

During the course of these reports, Van Horn, who had not been brought into the transfer scheme, denounced the "treachery" of Reid and Kearney in trying to sabotage a company with which they were associated. If these two leading spirits in the Kansas City and Memphis had shown the same "business energy and tact" in behalf of their own road that they had displayed in behalf of La Due's project, the road, he said, could have been built in less time than it would now take to decide on the merits of the two competing companies. He urged the County Court not to yield to the "local Jim Fisks and Vanderbilts," who were "unscrupulous speculators in confidence and public funds." Van Horn also printed a number of letters to the editor criticizing the plan. "Hickman Mills," for example, attacked Kearney as an unsuccessful grocer and gold manipulator who had come into wealth as a creature of Joy. He asserted that it was likely that the county subscription had been sold by the ambitious promoters even before it was issued.[14]

As a result of this controversy among the local leaders, the Merchants' Exchange on March 12, 1871, appointed a committee to look into the transfer and petitioned the County Court to delay action until its investigation was completed. Nevertheless, four days later, the County Court authorized the transfer. Circumstantially, this move was rather suspicious, for the Court imposed little control on the release of the subscription. One-third of the county bonds, for example, could be paid to the construction committee of the Clinton Company as soon as the first ten miles of the roadbed were put under contract.[15]

The Kansas City and Memphis Company obtained a circuit court injunction against the bond transfer and initiated an indecisive legal fight to try to get the charter of the Clinton Company declared invalid. In co-operation with a group of Arkansas promoters who held a charter from that state, a new company was organized in Kansas City in April under the name of the Kansas City, Arkansas, and Gulf Railroad. In the event that the courts held the Clinton Company to be organized illegally, this new company offered to take over the Jackson County bond issue and to build the road to Memphis.[16]

During the summer of 1871, after a series of meetings, the warring promoters got together and worked out a compromise. They organized still another company, the Kansas City, Memphis, and Mobile, which absorbed the Clinton Company. Van Horn went back to work for the road and made a trip to Bates County to try to get county officials to reinstate the subscription that had been held up because of the complications. Late in August, the new company undertook some construction on a roadbed.[17]

Viewing these maneuverings, the Jackson County Court initiated an investigation to determine what disposition had been made of the bonds that it had already issued to the Clinton Company. The Court had released $107,000 of the subscription to the company's construction committee, but found that it was unable to obtain reports of either expenditures or salaries. Until the Kansas City, Memphis and Mobile appointed a new construction committee and supplied full records of past expenditures, the Court asserted that it would issue no more bonds.[18]

The financial agent of the County Court, William Chrisman, a lawyer, banker, and former Whig leader from Independence, who represented the powerful faction in the county seat that had generally opposed the demands of the Kansas City businessmen, began vigorously to attack the railroad promoters. He charged that the Kansas City, Memphis, and Mobile Company had no legal existence. The bonds had been issued to the Clinton Company and could not be transferred without a vote of the residents of the county. The committee appointed to investigate the Clinton Company had found errors amounting to $77,000 in the estimates submitted by Superintendent La Due. The Court had therefore been forced to the conclusion that La Due was either "wholly incompetent or grossly dishonest." Until the "reckless adventurers" who were squandering public funds were gotten out of the way, he was unwilling to see any more aid extended to the much needed Memphis project.[19]

During this period of local uproar in early 1872 when newspapers were filled with charges and countercharges, the Board of Trade also undertook an investigation of the troubled affair. The organization's Committee on Internal Improvements, which had charge of matters relating to railroads, issued a report on April 11 agreeing with the Jackson County Court that the Memphis project had been badly mismanaged. The report recommended the removal of the officers of the new Kansas City, Memphis, and Mobile Company and especially urged that the construction committee —inherited from the Clinton Company—be ousted.[20]

As a result of the Board of Trade recommendations, the new company was reorganized the next month. Van Horn became president, and Howard M. Holden, treasurer. This obviously represented an effort to add some much needed prestige to the organization. Van Horn had long been the leading spokesman for the local business community; as a hero of the Cameron triumph, he enjoyed great personal popularity. Holden had come to Kansas City in 1866 after a successful start in Iowa banking. He invested his accumulated capital of $110,000 in local enterprises—$80,000 of it in the stock of the First National Bank. Under his leadership, this institution, through a highly liberal loan policy, financed the beginnings of the regional cattle and meat-packing industries. Joseph G. McCoy, the pioneer cattle buyer, gave Holden credit for the fact that Kansas City had quickly become the center of the livestock industry. For, unlike most bankers, McCoy observed, he was "willing to let go his ducats without exacting a pound of flesh as surety from next the heart of the borrower." Holden became a local business hero, highly praised for his foresight. He filled the role of the business statesman—predicting that Kansas City was destined to become a great metropolis and offering reassuring statements calculated to bolster the spirit of the community in times of crisis. His name could shore up any tottering local enterprise. The new directory included a number of other principal local business figures: Theodore S. Case, another Cameron hero; James E. Marsh, the most active member of the Internal Improvements Committee of the Board of Trade and a demon watchdog of railroad freight rates; and E. R. Threlkeld, a prominent local merchant of the postwar era. As part of the reorganization, the thoroughly discredited A. D. La Due was removed as superintendent.[21]

The company's organization presented the new officers with their first problem. The Clinton Company had been organized as a branch of the Tebo and Neosho Railroad. The Missouri, Kansas, and Texas had absorbed the Tebo and Neosho. The new Kansas City company—the Kansas City, Memphis, and Mobile—had in turn absorbed the Clinton Company. Consequently, although the legal issue was complicated, the M. K. T. might have control of the local company. Van Horn and Marsh talked to the directors of the M. K. T. in New York and obtained their approval of a quitclaim recognizing the independence of the new company. The officers were also able to arrest bankruptcy proceedings that unpaid creditors had instituted against the Clinton Company. These actions having been taken, the new company requested Chrisman and the Jackson County Court to release the rest of the bonds so that construction could be resumed.[22]

These complex corporate manipulations, even though sanctioned by the inner circle of community business leaders and supported by the Board of Trade were subject to attack. The *Times* printed a good many letters that denounced the whole affair. "Lex," for example, wrote that the new directors had no legal right to the rest of the county bonds; they were "*self-constituted* and self-elected directors of a trumped up railroad company, successors, assignees, etc., etc., of another that never had legal existence." These and similar charges, however, did not represent any kind of important popular protest against the policies of the local leaders. The numerous reorganizations of local companies had left a number of dissatisfied promoters with stakes in one of the earlier ventures. By and large, the battle of newspaper letters was conducted by lawyers representing one claimant or another contending for control of the county bond issues. Even a body as influential as the Kansas City Board of Trade could not impose unity on the struggling power groups within the community.[23]

Treasurer Holden contended that the quitclaim represented a great victory for the city, since undoubtedly the M. K. T. was the legal owner of the franchise of the Kansas City, Memphis, and Mobile. He dismissed as wholly false the charge that the local promoters intended to turn the local company over to the M. K. T. on the condition that the latter iron and equip it. Appealing to an old theme in local promotional polemics, Holden argued that the Memphis road was to be entirely a local project—another people's road. But the assistance of a united community was essential if a railroad was to be built only with local assets. The tenor of both the criticisms and defenses of railroad policy indicated clearly that the past technique of turning over Kansas City companies to Eastern railroad builders had become generally unpopular.[24]

The reorganization of the Memphis project did not impress Chrisman. In spite of numerous appeals during the course of 1872, he refused to release the county bonds to the new officers. The directors reported in November that the company was $85,000 in debt. Since Chrisman refused to issue the bonds, all work had stopped. The section of the roadbed already constructed was falling into disrepair.[25]

Meanwhile, creditors had reinstituted legal proceedings. In December, the United States District Court at Jefferson City declared bankrupt the old Clinton Company. The assignees attempted to compel Chrisman to turn over the bonds that he still held but failed to obtain the necessary court order. While this litigation was pending, the directors of the Kansas City, Memphis, and Mobile made another appeal to the Jackson County Court to save the project.[26]

Finally, the court agreed to a settlement. The company promised to get creditors to delay their claims against the bonds not yet issued. If the directors succeeded, then the Court would hold these in trust until the roadbed was readied to Harrisonville in Cass County and then would pay them in their entirety.[27]

Accordingly, on August 4, 1873, the company resumed work and constructed a magnificent tunnel through the hills outside Westport—made necessary by the route insisted upon by the County Court. Although the company announced in November that the roadbed was ready for iron as far as Harrisonville, actually much work remained to be done.[28]

With construction resumed, the Board of Directors ordered the issuance of a mortgage at $200,000 per mile on the first 100 miles of the road. A committee of Holden, Van Horn, and the irrepressible La Due, who in March had again been named as general superintendent of the road, and members from Henry and St. Clair counties were instructed to purchase rails for the first thirty miles of the road.[29]

Having undertaken some work, the company appealed to the County Court to release the subscription held in trust, even though it was clear that the requirement that the roadbed be completed to Harrisonville had not been met. The court refused. Soden Brothers, the construction firm, had expended nearly $60,000—most of it on the Westport tunnel—and began to pursue their claim in bankruptcy proceedings, as did numerous small creditors.[30]

With the country in the grip of the panic of 1873, which had severe effects on Kansas City, the Memphis project was suspended for several months. In April, 1874, R. C. Ewing, judge of the district court, suggested in his instructions to the convening grand jury that the activities of the Jackson County Court be investigated, for under Missouri law the diversion of railroad subscriptions could

constitute a felony. Since scandalous disclosures had been coming
to light, Ewing thought it well to determine also to what extent
local promoters had used the money appropriated to build a railroad for illegitimate purposes. Although the grand jury took no
action on his recommendations, Ewing's position demonstrated
that the complex corporate maneuverings of the inner circle of
Kansas City leaders did provoke attention and criticism.[31]

Aroused by Ewing's charges, the directors of the Kansas City,
Memphis, and Mobile proposed to the Jackson County Court that
a new offer be made to Soden Brothers to finish the roadbed. They
told the Court that they had negotiated a contract for iron and
rolling stock for the first twenty miles of railroad and for the sale
of the company's first mortgage bonds. They also promised, if the
county bonds were released, to attempt to obtain dismissal of the
bankruptcy suits instituted against the company.[32]

On June 6, the County Court agreed to another settlement.
Once all the proceedings in bankruptcy were dismissed, the Court
would turn over to the company bonds to be accepted at eighty
cents on the dollar for payment of the Soden Brothers' claim of
$57,500 and for the debts of smaller creditors of the road. The
company was then to resume construction. A first installment in
bonds for repairing and finishing the roadbed would be paid when
the work was completed halfway to Harrisonville. A second would
be paid when it was completed half the remaining distance, and the
rest when finished to Harrisonville—provided the bonds held out
that long. The County Court required that the work be completed
by December 1.[33]

The Soden Brothers went back to work. In October they submitted their bill for the construction on the roadbed as far as Belton,
in Cass County, the halfway point to Harrisonville set by the
County Court. The sum amounted to nearly $57,000. This, with
the payment for their past work and the amounts due to other
creditors, more than exhausted the proceeds from the original
$300,000 bond subscription.[34]

Again work on the road was suspended. The Board of Trade,

which since the time of the reorganization had been sponsoring the project, attempted to obtain federal support for the road. La Due, Polk, and Van Horn went to Washington to urge passage of a law to provide a Congressional land grant to the railroad, but they were unsuccessful. At the time of the visit of the delegation from the Mississippi Valley Trading Company, the Board of Trade tried to persuade the English firm to invest in the road with the argument that this would provide an excellent means of opening the trade of the New West to the Gulf of Mexico and to Europe.[35]

During the summer of 1875, the *Kansas City Times* frequently attacked Van Horn and the other managers of the road. The paper charged that La Due and Van Horn had received large salaries for which they had performed little service. Jackson County had issued $300,000 in bonds, and, in addition to the principal, the county would have to pay $24,000 a year in interest until they matured. As chief stockholder in the company, Jackson County might also be liable for payments on the first-mortgage bonds, issued on the first 107 miles of the road at $20,000 a mile for a total of $2,140,000. If the directors had been able to sell any of these, the counties that had issued subscriptions might have to meet payments on them on a pro rata basis. Heavy summer rains were steadily destroying the roadbed, the *Times* observed, and apathy about the project had descended on the region.[36]

As a result of this agitation conducted by the *Times*, the Jackson County Court appointed a committee to investigate the Kansas City, Memphis, and Mobile Company. The report provided a forceful indictment of the methods of the local promoters.[37]

First, the investigators had examined the way the Memphis project had been organized. In order to avoid the large initial stock subscription required by the 1868 general incorporation law, the leaders had first resorted to the expedient of organizing a branch road under the charter of the Cameron company. In forming the new company in 1872, however, they had to meet the law's requirement that an initial subscription of $1,000 per mile be raised. Thirteen of the original incorporators had subscribed $10,000 each and John W. Reid, $5,000. But the books of the company showed that neither the initial 5 per cent nor the balance had ever been paid. The stock had been issued at the time, returned several months afterwards, and then canceled. Later it had been reissued in "payment of pretended services" and was still outstanding. A new director who had joined the company had been issued $10,000 in stock with no payment. In 1875 the company had issued $1,000,-000 in stock to W. G. Ford, and the committee had been unable to obtain any information whatever from the company officers about this transfer. The committee concluded that all these issues of stock had been fraudulent.

The report stated that only the county subscriptions, all transferred from the Clinton Company, had been bona fide. These had been issued in the following amounts: Jackson County, $300,000; Cass County, $300,000; St. Clair County, $250,000; and Henry County, $200,000—a total of $1,050,000. The proceeds from the sales of the bonds issued had totalled $840,000. The company's vouchers showed expenditures of $869,952.69. If the private subscriptions made by the directors had been paid, the company should still have had assets of $115,047.31. Yet the books showed liabilities of $29,620.78, indicating clearly that the company had received only a few dollars from individual investors.

Moreover, the committee asserted, large expenditures were unaccounted for. John W. Polk had handled $10,000 for which there was no separate voucher and no statement of its disposition. Large amounts had been recorded only as contingent expenses. The company's books credited Holden with having been paid in full the sum of $76,000. But when he had been asked for his records he had replied "*positively* that he had nothing whatever to do with any transactions of the company; that he neither received nor paid out as treasurer of said company any sum of money whatever."

Even where the purpose was clear, the committee found many of the expenditures highly questionable. The payment to the contractors, for example, had exceeded the original estimates by $77,000. Officers' salaries had been far too high as well.[38]

In view of these findings, the investigators asserted that it was quite clear that the company's stock had been "fraudulently issued and manipulated to suit the private purposes of the managers" and that the company's funds had been "grossly misapplied to fraudulent purposes and wasted in extravagent payments made to contractors and others." The committee recommended that a receiver be appointed to collect the unpaid private subscriptions and to try to recover the misappropriated money. In this way, the roadbed and right of way might be saved.

President Van Horn had only one comment on the report. He stated that the payment of $1,000,000 in stock to W. G. Ford had been for the purpose of effecting a consolidation with a railroad in Arkansas and represented a gain of real value for the Kansas City road. Van Horn had argued during the course of the Memphis road troubles that his position in the company made it unethical for him to comment on its affairs in his newspaper. More likely perhaps, he hoped, at this time particularly, that the whole episode would be forgotten as quickly as possible.[39]

The *Times* took up the cry of corruption. The report had supplied presumptive evidence of fraud. Every incorporator of the company should be made to pay up immediately for the benefit of the people, whose money had been wasted and stolen. But no action was taken. Early the next year, the *Times* observed that the "grandest road ever proposed from the city" remained as before, "prostrated by the ring of swindlers who plucked the magnificent fund subscribed for construction, with the remorseless greed of so many birds of carrion." [40]

The indignation of the involved counties against the Kansas City promoters reflected in the *Times'* charges was perhaps proper. Nevertheless, the county authorities themselves were partly at fault. The Jackson County Court had turned over the bonds to the company with virtually no control of expenditures. In the last settlement with the Kansas City, Memphis, and Mobile, moreover, the Court assigned the remainder of the subscription even though it was quite clear that it would not be enough to even begin to finish the whole roadbed. The remaining counties followed similar procedures. The terms of the St. Clair County subscription provided that payments could be made only as work actually progressed through the county; but as soon as a construction contract was signed all the bonds were issued. In short, the promoters acquired control of the bond issues without having to demonstrate concrete accomplishment.[41]

In subsequent months, the counties took action to avoid foreclosure of the road, but they were unsuccessful. An auction of the assets of the company was held in Kansas City in December, 1876. The highest bid was $1,100, but the district court administering bankruptcy proceedings refused to approve. The next year the road was sold to J. D. Bancroft, representing a group of Kansas City business leaders, for $15,025.[42]

The counties also failed in their efforts to avoid payment on the county bonds. In spite of the confused charters of the various companies involved in the project, and the dubious transfers of subscriptions, the United States Supreme Court eventually upheld the legality of the subscriptions in a case involving Cass County.[43]

During 1876, Kansas City leaders made half-hearted efforts to revive the project. At one of these meetings Peter Soden of Soden Brothers, who by the turn of the century had found his way onto the lists of Kansas City millionaires, supplied an unintentionally ironic commentary on the episode when he reported that the magnificent tunnel south of Westport, which had absorbed a large share of the construction costs, had caved in.[44]

During the next decade, Kansas City did get a connection with Memphis built by the Fort Scott through Springfield and southeast, in accordance with the plan proposed by Chanute in 1870. This project, of course, bore no relationship to the defunct Kansas City company. As the early advocates of a Memphis road had predicted, the line did provide an important outlet for grain and other products from the region to the west of Kansas City. Again the Kansas City railroad leaders had been proven far better prophets than builders.[45]

An anonymous contributor in a sketch of the county proper supplied for a massive 1881 history of the towns, cities, and citizens of Jackson County provided one of the few assessments of the Memphis road in relation to the era of local railroad promotion in the region. In general, his account, diffuse and verbose like most histories of this type, was several cuts below William Miller's able "History of Kansas City," which formed a part of the same work. But, when the writer turned to the subject of railroads, his anger moved him to something at least approaching eloquence.

Jackson County, he pointed out, had a truly magnificent set of railroads. These lines were responsible for the tremendous development of the region. Because of them, Kansas City had become the gateway to the West. As the farthest outpost of trade and competition, the city would soon be on a footing with St. Louis and Chicago in size. Eventually, St. Louis would become but a way station— as Cincinnati before her—on the route to Kansas City.

The writer found the local effort that had gone into making this system highly commendable. Still, in spite of this great achievement, he could not forget the disaster of the Memphis railroad. It was one of the most important historical facts to be recorded about Jackson County; her citizens and those of neighboring counties had been "fearfully defrauded." For all the money issued to the company "not a dollar of direct benefit had accrued . . . save perhaps a piece of experience with gigantic fraud and wholesale stealing." The writer said he did not know who had committed the frauds or who had stolen the public funds, but he did know that a great wrong had been committed. The scheme had imposed and would continue to impose a burden of taxes for years to come. The county was "deeply humiliated and incensed." [46]

Nevertheless, in subsequent years the inglorious attempt to build a railroad to Memphis was forgotten. No governmental authority tried to take legal action against the officers of the local company. Although the involved community leaders—Van Horn, Kearney, Holden, and the rest—were caught up in local political battles of the 1880's and 1890's, they retained their prestige fully intact. On occasion, political opponents denounced them as enemies of progress but never as dishonest men. In the twentieth century, as these struggles faded, the railroad promoters achieved local apotheosis as heroic town-builders.

The episode of the Memphis road has not been permitted to mar the legend of inspired local enterprise embodied in all subsequent accounts of the city's early history. Regardless of their methods, the Kansas City promoters—through good luck, through ability, or through a combination of both—had achieved their goal of building a city. Their optimistic predictions concerning Kansas City's destiny had been realized. And this, at least in the view of their own community, was sufficient to make them true representatives of the "Kansas City spirit."

The Last Years of
A Town-Builder

ON Saturday mornings in the early 1890's, promptly at ten o'clock, an old newspaperman retired to his office, turned out any lights left on, pulled down the blinds, and with eyes tightly closed wrote a Sunday editorial for his newspaper. In apologetic tone, he would explain to his associates that his son, who had died a few years before at the age of thirty-five, guided his hand. His son had worked for the newspaper and seemed started on a promising career when he was struck by a fatal mental disease. The old man, who had already lost two of his three other boys, never quite recovered from this blow. The pencilled copy that came from these Saturday sessions was legible, but it made little sense. Someone would have to reconstruct the involuted sentences expounding a slightly mad kind of mysticism to make them at least vaguely understandable to the readers of the newspaper.[1]

Robert Thompson Van Horn had fallen on bad days. Though he was still a power in the Republican Party, since 1880 his newspaper had faced the vigorous competition of William Rockhill Nelson's

Kansas City Star. Nelson after his arrival in the city had quickly assumed the position of community spokesman that Van Horn had earlier held, and the circulation and influence of the *Journal* steadily declined. Van Horn had never demonstrated a talent for making money. Unlike his associates in the Kansas City business community, whose interests he had so consistently advanced, he had profited little from the promotional ventures that were a part of city building. He got deeply into debt. Santa Fe railroad interests bought up the *Journal's* mortgage and began to dictate its policies. They retained Van Horn as nominal editor-in-chief, but his authority was gone. Someone on the staff would always kill the occasional conciliatory editorials he wrote about the agrarian crusaders of the 1890's. The *Journal* now spoke for railroads and corporate wealth.

Van Horn's later writings clearly reflected the decline in his powers. In his early years, he had written concretely, simply, and powerfully of railroads and meat-packing plants, of Santa Fe traders, of Indians and mountain men, of the West and settlers pouring onto the frontier, of technology and the growth of an industrial nation. Abstractions, and philosophic concepts, he found useful only to promote specific material ends. Even as a politician, Van Horn had seldom addressed himself to such favorite subjects as democracy, freedom, and justice. A hard-headed businessman-biographer truly observed that his speeches in Congress contained "nothing whatever of 'buncombe' or mere verbiage." Van Horn found his themes in land grants, Indian treaties, and river and harbor improvements. But in his declining years, he lost interest in the down-to-earth. In his editorials and in his contributions to the *Kansas City Review of Science and Industry* and other periodicals, he devoted himself more and more to the popular kind of moral philosophy that was perhaps the most spurious product of a meretricious age. His efforts to weave the scientific discoveries of the period into vague theories about mankind's growing spirtuality were never enlightening and seldom comprehensible.

In the community which he had done so much to build, Van Horn—who for years had railed against opponents of progress, at those unwilling to be up and doing for Kansas City—now ironically found himself cast in the strange role of "old fogey." Nelson, as part of his campaign to develop parks and other recreational and cultural facilities in Kansas City, lashed out at Van Horn and the other town-builders who opposed his programs. They "are in the habit," he wrote, "of looking around, after the manner of the late King Nebuchadnezzer when he remarked, 'This is great Babylon which I have builded,' of speaking of Kansas City as their creation." But these real-estate owners and prominent citizens who claimed to have made Kansas City opposed the very measures necessary to make it a much greater metropolis. Nelson even turned the promoters' old argument of natural advantages against them. They had not made Kansas City, he asserted. Kansas City had started itself. The "finger of Nature" had pointed out the site to man; the meeting place of the rivers had indicated the meeting place of man; Benton had predicted that a great city would grow there; the railroads had found the place immediately. In other words, said he, natural forces had created Kansas City. The town builders had "merely watched a city grow like a man sitting on a river bank waiting for the river to rise and wash his feet for him." [2]

But Van Horn was not long subject to this kind of attack. His retirement from the *Journal* in 1897 removed him from the arena of contention over community policy. Now he could play a symbolic role as first citizen—town builder, military chieftain, and political leader. He wrote occasional reminiscent articles about the early days of Kansas City; the community called on him from time to time to memorialize town leaders who had died, but for the most part he quietly lived out his life. He died in 1916 at the age of ninety-two. Among the souvenirs of an active life—among the military citations, tickets to Republican conventions, and playbills —are two arresting mementos: a crude, pencilled map dating from the 1850's showing Kansas City as the hub of a system of railroads running to all points on the compass and one share of stock in the Kansas City, Galveston, and Lake Superior Railroad.

Notes

INTRODUCTION

[1] Henry C. Haskell, Jr., and Richard B. Fowler, *City of the Future* (Kansas City, 1950), 5.

[2] For a detailed account of the method of construction of the bridge, see Octave Chanute and George Morison, *The Kansas City Bridge* (New York, 1870).

[3] *Weekly Gazette* (St. Joseph), July 8, 1869.

[4] *Kansas City Weekly Times*, July 8, 1869.

[5] *Ibid.*; *Daily Journal of Commerce* (Kansas City), July 3, 1869.

[6] William H. Miller, *History of Kansas City* (Kansas City, 1881), 116–117.

[7] For versions of the bridge victory in city histories, see William Griffith, *History of Kansas City* (Kansas City, 1900), 48–49; Carrie W. Whitney, *Kansas City: Its History and Its People, 1808–1908* (3 vols., Chicago, 1908), I, 252; Roy Ellis, *A Civic History of Kansas City* (Springfield, Mo., 1930), 33; Darrell Garwood, *Crossroads of America* (New York, 1948), 121–122; Haskell and Fowler, *City of the Future*, 46–47.

[8] William J. Dalton, *The Life of Father Bernard Donnelly* (Kansas City, 1921), 89–90. This work collects the oral reminiscences of Donnelly.

CHAPTER 1

[1] *Western Journal of Commerce* (Kansas City), January 9, 1858.

[2] An account of the dinner, including transcriptions of the addresses can be found in *ibid.*, January 2, 1858.

[3] The best sketch of Van Horn in print is contained in Theodore S. Case, ed., *History of Kansas City* (Syracuse, 1888), 432–440. A small but valuable collection of Van Horn papers is contained in the Archives of the Native Sons of Kansas City (Missouri). The collection of Van Horn materials at the State Historical Society of Missouri (Columbia) relates almost entirely to military affairs during the Civil War.

[4] *Meigs County Telegraph*, (Ohio), June 27, 1850; Van Horn to Parents, June 15, 1854, Van Horn Papers, Archives of the Native Sons of Kansas City.

[5] *Meigs County Telegraph*, April 25, 1850; Van Horn to I. Cartwright, February 27, 1858, Van Horn Papers, Archives of the Native Sons of Kansas City.

[6] Albert D. Richardson, *Beyond the Mississippi* (Hartford, Conn., 1867), 28; Case, ed., *History of Kansas City*, 434–435.

[7] *Western Journal of Commerce*, July 25, 1860.

[8] *Ibid.*, January 2, 1858. A major portion of this address is reproduced in William H. Miller, *History of Kansas City* (Kansas City, 1881), 78–80.

[9] John Johnson to William Van Vleit, July 8, 1855. Johnson's wife, in much less formal fashion, also seems to have been affected by the optimism in the community and the certainty of the coming of railroads. A few months after her arrival she wrote to her children in Milwaukee: "I must tell you of the Country I think if you and Jane would come here you would make money fast . . . the next thing is the Rail Road is located to this County and the inhabitants of this place are sure of the terminus will be at this point then of course we shall soon have large Citty." Diana Johnson to William Van Vleit, December 4, 1853. Both letters are among manuscripts belonging to Miss Frances Berenice Ford, Kansas City, Missouri.

[10] The best discussion of the significance of the geography of the Elbow Region is contained in James C. Malin, *Grassland Historical Studies: Natural Resources Utilization in a Background of Science and Technology*, Volume I, *Geology and Geography* (Lawrence, Kansas, 1950), 119–120. Malin's monumental body of work on the plains has influenced many aspects of this study.

[11] B. Drake and E. D. Mansfield, *Cincinnati in 1826* (Cincinnati, 1827), 99.

[12] Alexander Mackay, *The Western World or Travels in the United States in 1846–47* (3 vols., London, 1849), III, 53–54.

[13] Richardson, *Beyond the Mississippi*, 61; see also 58–59; Anthony to Brother, December 15, 1858, in Edward Langsdorf and R. W. Richmond, eds., "Letters of Daniel R. Anthony, 1857–1862, Part Two, 1858–1861," *Kansas Historical Quarterly*, 24:214 (Summer, 1958).

[14] "Cincinnati—Her Position, Duty and Destiny," *De Bow's Review*, 7:363 (October, 1849); "St. Louis—Its Early History," *The Western Journal*

(St. Louis), 2:71–86 (February, 1849); Jesup W. Scott, "Westward the Star of Empire," *De Bow's Review*, 27:132 (August, 1859). For a discussion of Scott's importance, see Henry Nash Smith, *Virgin Land* (New York, Vintage, 1957), 183–186.

[15] *Congressional Globe*, Senate, 1851, 31 Cong., 2 Sess. (December 16, 1850), pp. 56–57. Benton's views toward a transcontinental railroad are discussed in Ethel Osborne, Missouri's Interest in the Trans-Continental Railroad Movement, 1849–1850, M.A. Thesis, University of Missouri, Columbia, 1928, 1–23. Smith, *Virgin Land*, 20–37, contains a perceptive essay on the influence of Benton in shaping American attitudes toward the West. See also, Leroy Hafen and Ann W. Hafen, eds., *Central Route to the Pacific by Gwinn Harris Heap* (Glendale, Calif., 1957), VII: Far West and Rockies Series, 25–71. For an example of the statement of the prophecy, see *Kansas City Star*, August 3, 1913. Some version of the prophecy is contained in almost every history of the city. From extensive examination of the reminiscences of early settlers, it seems clear that Benton made some such statement, but his exact words are debatable.

[16] Bernard De Voto, "Geopolitics with the Dew on It," *Harpers' Magazine*, 188:313–323 (March, 1944), revived interest in Gilpin's work by portraying him as a prophet of manifest destiny and a pioneer of geopolitics. A similar theme is emphasized in Charles Vevier, "American Continentalism: An Idea of Expansion, 1845–1910," *American Historical Review*, 65:325–326 (January, 1960). Smith, *Virgin Land*, 38–46, 49–50, traces the relationship between Gilpin, Benton, and Whitman. Wallace Stegner, *Beyond the Hundredth Meridian* (Boston, 1954), 1–8, 351–367, assesses Gilpin's role in shaping national attitudes toward the Great Plains. James C. Malin, *The Grassland of North America, Prolegomena to Its History* (Lawrence, Kansas, 1947), 177–192, provides a perceptive essay on his influence. Kenneth W. Porter, "William Gilpin: Sinophile and Eccentric," *The Colorado Magazine*, 37:245–267 (October, 1960), discusses the reactions of a German traveler, Julius Froebel, to an 1852 visit with Gilpin in Independence, Missouri.

[17] Gilpin to Elizabeth Gilpin, October 4, 1836, Gilpin Papers, Missouri Historical Society, St. Louis. Several other letters in this small collection, all dating from this period, emphasize the same theme. The only biography of Gilpin available is Hubert H. Bancroft, *History of the Life of William Gilpin* (San Francisco, 1889). One of a series of subscription biographies turned out in assembly-line fashion by Bancroft and his assistants, this work is highly inaccurate. Gilpin paid $1,000 for the sixty-two page study. See John W. Caughey, *Hubert Howe Bancroft, Historian of the West* (Berkeley, 1946), 322. The *Dictionary of American Biography* contains a brief sketch of Gilpin. The Kansas City (Mo.) Public Library contains a valuable file of

clipping material concerning Gilpin. Particularly significant is a long interview with Will C. Ferrill, a Colorado friend of Gilpin, in the *Kansas City Journal*, [n.d., ca. 1892], cited hereafter as Ferrill interview. It is often necessary to piece together parts of Gilpin's life from a variety of scattered sources.

[18] *Missouri Argus* (St. Louis), November 20, 1839; Ferrill interview. See James N. Primm, *Economic Policy in the Development of a Western State, Missouri, 1820–1860* (Cambridge, Mass., 1954), 43, 45–46, for a brief description of Gilpin's role in the Benton organization. *Congressional Globe*, Senate, 1846, 29 Cong., 1 Sess. (May 18, 1846), pp. 831–832. A Gilpin letter on Oregon is contained in "Report of Committee on Post Office and Post Roads on Expediency of Establishing Mail Route to Oregon by Way of Panama." 29 Cong., 1 Sess., *Senate Doc.* 306 (1846) (Serial No. 474), pp. 19–47. "Report of Committee on Post Office and Post Roads on the Expediency of Establishing a Mail Route from Missouri to Oregon," 29 Cong., 1 Sess., *Senate Doc.* 178 (1846) (Serial No. 473), pp. 3–9, reprints an earlier Gilpin letter on the Oregon question.

[19] William E. Connelley, *Doniphan's Expedition* (Topeka, Kansas, 1907), 151; William E. Connelley, "The First Provisional Constitution of Kansas," *Kansas Historical Collections*, 6:105–106 (1897–1900); Vincent G. Tegeder, "Lincoln and the Territorial Patronage: The Ascendancy of the Radicals in the West," *Mississippi Valley Historical Review*, 35:81 (June, 1948); Robert L. Perkins, *The First Hundred Years, an Informal History of Denver and the Rocky Mountain News* (Garden City, New York, 1959), 130; Herbert O. Brayer, *William Blackmore: The Spanish-Mexican Land Grants of New Mexico and Colorado, 1863–1878* (Denver, 1949), I, 65–70, 103–113, *passim*; Earl Pomeroy, *In Search of the Golden West, The Tourist in Western America* (New York, 1957), 20; Bancroft, *Gilpin*, 51.

[20] The articles originally appeared in the *National Intelligencer* (Washington, D. C.), October 13, 15, 22, December 3, 1857. They were reprinted in part in the *New York Times* and *De Bow's Review* (New Orleans). *The Agricultural Capabilities of the Great Plains*, U. S. Patent Office, Agriculture, 1858, pp. 294–296, is a condensation of Gilpin's article on the pastoral character of the Great Plains. Guides to the Colorado gold mines published in various American cities in 1859 relied very heavily on the articles, and they were frequently reprinted in local newspapers. The Gilpin books are as follows: William Gilpin, *The Central Gold Region* (Philadelphia, 1860); *Mission of the North American People* (Philadelphia, published in slightly different editions of 1873 and 1874); *The Cosmopolitan Railway* (San Francisco, 1890).

[21] Gilpin *Central Gold Region*, 36; Gilpin, *Cosmopolitan Railway*, 207.

[22] Gilpin, *Central Gold Region*, 118.

²³ Gilpin, *Cosmopolitan Railway*, 207.

²⁴ Gilpin, *Mission*, 1873 ed., 198.

²⁵ The Ferrill interview contains Gilpin's own account of his years in Independence. See also *Kansas City Star*, February 18, 1900; *Kansas City Journal*, April 23, 1894; *Kansas City Post*, April 13, 1924; "Scrapbook of John Calvin McCoy," pp. 33b-c, Kansas City (Mo.) Public Library; W. L. Webb, "Major William Gilpin, the Prophet of Kansas City," *Missouri Valley Historical Society Annals*, 1:114–118 (October, 1921). Carrie W. Whitney, *Kansas City, Missouri, Its History and People, 1890–1908* (3 vols., Chicago, 1908), I, 666–671, was the first Kansas City historian to attempt to evaluate Gilpin's role in the area. Her material was based largely on interviews with old settlers.

²⁶ The map is reproduced in Whitney, *Kansas City*, I, 667, and in the *Kansas City Star*, May 26, 1901.

²⁷ "The Cities of Missouri," *The Western Journal and Civilian* (St. Louis), 11:31–40 (October, 1853).

²⁸ Gilpin, *Mission*, 1873 ed., 76.

²⁹ For the original article, see *National Intelligencer*, October 13, 1857.

³⁰ Charles C. Spalding, *Annals of the City of Kansas* (Kansas City, 1858, fascimile edition, Columbia, Mo., 1950), 10–14, 60, 70, 111.

³¹ The best sketch of Lykins' life is contained in the *United States Biographical Dictionary, Missouri Volume* (New York, 1878), 48–49.

³² G. W. Ewing to S. Dyer, August 31, 1850; W. G. to G. W. Ewing, December 15, 1850, W. G. and G. W. Ewing Papers, Indiana State Historical Society Library, Indianapolis.

³³ *Railroads Chartered and Projected Centering at Kansas City, Mo., with Many Other Interesting Facts* (n.p., n.d.).

³⁴ *Western Journal of Commerce*, November 20, 1858.

³⁵ *Railroads Chartered and Projected*.

³⁶ *Enterprise*, February 14, 1857.

³⁷ *Ibid.*, November 17, 1855.

³⁸ *Western Journal of Commerce*, February 6, 1858.

³⁹ *Ibid.*, May 24, 1860.

⁴⁰ *Ibid.*, January 24, April 12, 1860.

CHAPTER 2

¹ Edwin L. Lopata, *Local Aid to Railroads in Missouri* (New York, 1937), 9; John W. Million, *State Aid to Railways in Missouri* (Chicago, 1896), 50–53; Wyatt W. Belcher, *The Economic Rivalry Between St. Louis and Chicago, 1850–1880* (New York, 1947), 72.

[2] Robert R. Russel, *Improvement of Communication with the Pacific Coast As an Issue in American Politics, 1783–1863* (Cedar Rapids, Iowa, 1948), 34–53, 95–109; Carter Goodrich, *Government Promotion of American Canals and Railroads 1800–1890* (New York, 1960), 175–182; Belcher, *Economic Rivalry*, 73–75.

[3] *Laws of Mo.* (1848–1849), p. 220; *American Railroad Journal* quoted in Russel, *Improvement of Communication*, 110.

[4] Floyd C. Shoemaker, *Missouri and Missourians* (5 vols., Chicago, 1943), I, 751; *Laws of Mo.* (1850–1851), pp. 265–268; Goodrich, *Government Promotion*, 150.

[5] Missouri, *Compilation of the Laws in Reference to Such Railroads As Have Received Aid from the State* (Jefferson City, 1859), 66; Robert E. Reigel, "The Missouri Pacific Railroad to 1879," *Missouri Historical Review* 18:11 (October, 1923).

[6] Belcher, *Economic Rivalry*, 80.

[7] Missouri, *Compilation of Railroad Laws*, 7–8; Dorothy E. Powell, History of the Hannibal and St. Joseph Railroad, 1847–1883, M. A. Thesis, University of Missouri, Columbia, 1942, 22–23.

[8] Belcher, *Economic Rivalry*, 90; Howard F. Bennett, The Hannibal & St. Joseph Railroad and the Development of Northern Missouri, 1847–1880, Ph.D. Thesis, Harvard University, Cambridge, 1950, 1.

[9] *Enterprise* (Kansas City), December 15, 1855.

[10] Milton J. Payne, "City of Kansas, Early Municipal History of," in Howard L. Conard, ed., *Encylopedia of the History of Missouri* (6 vols., New York, 1901), I, 623–624. At the time, Payne was mayor of Kansas City and a member of the delegation.

[11] Frank S. Popplewell, "St. Joseph, Missouri, As a Center of the Cattle Trade," *Missouri Historical Review*, 32:446 (July, 1938).

[12] For a more detailed discussion of business development in Kansas City, see Charles N. Glaab, "Business Patterns in the Growth of a Midwestern City," *Business History Review*, 33:156–174 (Summer, 1959).

[13] *Western Journal of Commerce* (Kansas City), August 15, 1860.

[14] John Everett to Robert Everett, December 4, 1856, in "Letters of John and Sarah Everett, 1854–1864, Miami County Pioneers," *Kansas Historical Quarterly*, 8:154 (May, 1939), "Report of the Special Committee Appointed To Investigate the Troubles in Kansas," *House Reports*, 34 Cong., 1 Sess., (1855–1856), No. 200 (Serial 869), p. 838. See also the testimony of other Kansas City leaders before this committee and the *Enterprise*, July 5, August 16, September 27, December 15, 22, 1856.

[15] Charles C. Spalding, *Annals of the City of Kansas* (Kansas City, 1858, fascimile edition, Columbia, Mo., 1950), 10.

[16] Daniel R. Anthony to Sister, September 10, 1858, in Edward Langsdorf

and R. W. Richmond, eds., "Letters of Daniel R. Anthony, 1857–1862, Part Two, 1858–1861," *Kansas Historical Quarterly*, 24:208 (Summer, 1958).

[17] Ewing to Thomas Ewing, June 30, 1860; Ewing to E. Peabody, June 9, 1859, June 24, 1860, Thomas Ewing, Jr., Papers, Kansas State Historical Society, Topeka.

[18] "Coates, Kersey," in Conard, *Encyclopedia of Missouri*, II, 36–38; *United States Biographical Dictionary, Missouri Volume* (New York, 1878), 46–48. Considerable material, especially on Coates' role in Kansas, is contained in Laura Coates Reed, *In Memoriam, Sarah Walter Chandler Coates* (Kansas City, n.d.).

[19] William H. Miller, *History of Kansas City* (Kansas City, 1881), 62. For an indication of Coates' prominence during the troubles in Kansas, see Howard Committee *Report*, pp. 36–38, 1152–1153, and Charles Robinson, *The Kansas Conflict* (New York, 1892), 153, 169, 258, 417. For Anthony, see Anthony to Sister, October 20, 1857, in Edward Langsdorf and R. W. Richmond, eds., "Letters of Daniel R. Anthony, 1857–1862, Part One, 1857," *Kansas Historical Quarterly*, 24:24 (Spring, 1958); Anthony to Sister, September 10, 1858, in Langsdorf and Richmond, eds., "Anthony Letters, Part Two, 1858–1861," *Kansas Historical Quarterly*, 24:208 (Summer, 1958).

[20] *Daily Journal of Commerce* (Kansas City), January 27, 28, 1863; Daniel Geary, Reminiscences of Fifty Years in Kansas City, MS., March 8, 1906, p. 13, Archives of the Native Sons of Kansas City (Missouri); "Bullene, Thomas Brockway," Conard, *Encyclopedia of Missouri*, I, 424.

[21] "Reid, John William," in Conard, *Encyclopedia of Missouri*, V, 327–328; *History of Jackson County, Missouri* (Kansas City, 1881), 830–831. A small collection of Reid Manuscripts and a detailed, unpublished biography prepared by his son, William M. Reid, is in the possession of Mrs. Frederick James, Kansas City, Missouri. For Reid's position in the state legislature, see *Jefferson Inquirer* (Jefferson City), July 10, 1858, December 22, 1860.

[22] *Daily Journal of Commerce*, January 1, 1876.

[23] Theodore S. Case, ed., *History of Kansas City, Missouri* (Syracuse, 1888), 390; *People's Tribune* (Jefferson City), November 30, 1881. For a general discussion of the rise of property values in Kansas City, see "Real Estate in Kansas City," in Conard, *Encyclopedia of Missouri*, V, 308–309.

[24] *Enterprise*, August 15, 1857.

[25] *Western Journal of Commerce*, January 12, 1860.

[26] A transcript of the "Minutes of the Chamber of Commerce of Kansas City, Missouri, 1856–1879," is available at the Archives of the Native Sons of Kansas City. Van Horn's memorial is reproduced in Miller, *History of Kansas City*, 81–91.

[27] Miller, *History of Kansas City*, 69.

[28] *Stat. of Terr. of Kans.* (1855), pp. 926–930.

[29] *Enterprise*, February 7, 1857.

[30] *Ibid.*, April 11, 1857. The letter is dated January 23, 1857.

[31] *Western Journal of Commerce*, August 18, 1859.

[32] *Laws of Mo.* (1856–1857), pp. 162–167.

[33] *Enterprise*, July 12, 19, 1856; Fay Hempstead, *A Pictorial History of Arkansas* (St. Louis, 1890), 1044–1045.

[34] *Enterprise*, January 31, 1857.

[35] *Ibid.*, February 21, 1857.

[36] *Ibid.*, April 4, 1857.

[37] *Western Journal of Commerce*, August 4, 1859, April 12, 1860.

[38] *Enterprise*, January 31, 1857.

CHAPTER 3

[1] *Enterprise* (Kansas City), January 17, 1857.

[2] Carter Goodrich, *Government Promotion of American Canals and Railroads 1800–1890* (New York, 1960), 271, 295; Frederick A. Cleveland and Fred W. Powell, *Railroad Promotion and Capitalization in the United States* (New York, 1909), 206; the resolution is cited in Goodrich, *Government Promotion*, 259; John W. Brooks to James F. Joy, January 28, 1871, quoted in Thomas L. Cochran, *American Railroad Leaders, 1845–1890* (Cambridge, Mass., 1953), 279.

[3] Missouri, *Compilation of the Laws in Reference to Such Railroads As Have Received Aid from the State* (Jefferson City, 1859), 18–22; *Jefferson Inquirer* (Jefferson City), June 28, July 5, 12, 1851, for a reprint of the report; *Liberty Weekly Tribune*, February 13, April 2, 1852.

[4] *Jefferson Inquirer*, December 18, 1852; Missouri, *Compilation of Railroad Laws*, 66.

[5] Missouri, *Compilation of Railroad Laws*, 69–70.

[6] "Minutes of the Chamber of Commerce of Kansas City, Missouri, 1856–1879," Transcript, p. 10, Archives of the Native Sons of Kansas City (Missouri), hereafter cited through chapter as Chamber of Commerce Minutes; *Enterprise*, June 6, July 11, 1857.

[7] Letter in *Missouri Democrat* (St. Louis) reprinted in *Enterprise*, September 19, 1857.

[8] *Jefferson Inquirer*, August 1, 1857.

[9] Letter in *Missouri Democrat* reprinted in *Enterprise*, September 19, 1857.

[10] *Enterprise*, September 26, 1857. For the terms of the subscription, see Record of Ordinances of Kansas City, Missouri, Book A, No. 785, Septem-

ber 24, 1859, p. 189, office of the City Clerk of Kansas City, Mo., hereafter cited through chapter as Ordinance Record.

[11] Lela Barnes, ed., "An Editor Looks at Early-Day Kansas: The Letters of
Charles Monroe Chase," *Kansas Historical Quarterly*, 26:125 (Summer,
1960).

[12] Report of March 29, 1858, printed in *Western Journal of Commerce*,
April 17, 1858.

[13] Chamber of Commerce Minutes, 20.

[14] *Laws of Mo.* (1855), pp. 138–139; *Enterprise*, December 27, 1855,
January 5, 1856; clipping from *St. Louis Intelligencer* in *Enterprise*,
January 5, 1856.

[15] *Enterprise*, September 20, 1856. See also July 12, 1856.

[16] *Enterprise*, January 19, June 28, July 26, 1856; letter printed in *Liberty
Weekly Tribune*, August 8, 1856.

[17] *Enterprise*, August 16, November 12, 1856.

[18] *Ibid.*, October 4, 18, 1856; Ordinance Record, Book A, no No., October 6, 1856, p. 156.

[19] Chamber of Commerce Minutes, 3, 5.

[20] *Enterprise*, November 22, 1856.

[21] *Ibid.*, November 15, 29, 1856.

[22] *Jefferson Inquirer*, November 22, 1856.

[23] Chamber of Commerce Minutes, 7; *Laws of Mo.* (1856–1857), pp. 91–
92; *Enterprise*, January 10, 1857.

[24] *Enterprise*, January 10, 31, 1857.

[25] Ordinance Record, Book A, No. 67, May 25, 1857, p. 172; *Enterprise*, July 11, 1857.

[26] *Enterprise*, January 31, February 11, April 11, 1857.

[27] For a contemporary analysis of the effects of depression on the region,
see Van Horn's discussion of "Border Money" in the *Western Journal of
Commerce*, November 11, 1857.

[28] Chamber of Commerce Minutes, 20; *Liberty Weekly Tribune*, March 6,
1855; *Enterprise*, February 7, 1857; *Jefferson Inquirer*, November 20,
1858. For a letter of July 14, 1855, which expressed Reid's view on the
state-lien proposition, see *Jefferson Inquirer*, August 4, 1855.

[29] *Western Journal of Commerce*, May 5, August 7, 1858.

[30] Missouri, *Journal of the House of Representatives of the State of Missouri* (Jefferson City, 1859), Appendix, "Pacific Railroad Engineers Report:
Edward Miller, Chief Engineer, December 24, 1858," 162.

[31] *Western Journal of Commerce*, March 19, May 7, 1859.

[32] *Ibid.*, January 28, February 12, August 11, 18, 1859.

[33] *Ibid.*, August 18, September 1, 1859.

[34] *Ibid.*, September 1, 1859.

[35] *Ibid.*, September 8, 1859.

[36] The disappearance of prewar Jackson County newspapers, especially those published in Independence, makes it difficult to evaluate the character of the opposition to the Kansas City railroad program.

[37] *Western Journal of Commerce*, September 8, 1859.

[38] *Ibid.*

[39] *Ibid.*

[40] Clipping in *ibid.*

[41] *Western Journal of Commerce*, September 8, 15, 1859.

[42] *Border Star* (Westport), September 16, 1859.

[43] Ordinance Record, Book B, No. 1693, November 24, 1859, p. 63; *Liberty Weekly Tribune*, October 16, November 20, 1857, April 27, 1859; Lucinda de Leftwich Templin, The Development of Railroads in Missouri to 1860, M.A. Thesis, University of Missouri, 1915, pp. 127–129 traces the rise of opposition to railroad aid.

[44] *The Internal Improvement System of the State of Missouri Showing the Enormous Frauds Practiced in Obtaining and Expending State Aid* (St. Louis, 1859), 9; *Western Journal of Commerce*, March 27, 1858.

[45] *Western Journal of Commerce*, September 22, 29, 1859.

[46] *Ibid.*, January 12, 1860.

[47] *Ibid.*, March 15, 1860.

[48] *Ibid.*, April 5, 1860.

[49] *Ibid.*

[50] *Ibid.*

[51] *Ibid.*, March 27, April 24, May 22, June 19, August 25, September 22, 29, 1859.

[52] Chamber of Commerce Minutes, 24–25; Annual Report, General Superintendent, Hannibal and St. Joseph Railroad Company, September 1, 1859, Archives of the Chicago, Burlington and Quincy Railroad Company, Chicago, Illinois.

[53] Hayward to Brooks, October 29, 1859, Hannibal and St. Joseph Railroad Company records, Archives of the Chicago, Burlington and Quincy Railroad Company, Chicago, Illinois.

[54] Ordinance Record, Book B, No. 2020, April 10, 1860, p. 119, Book B, No. 2115, May 16, 1860, p. 132; *History of Clay and Platte Counties, Missouri* (St. Louis, 1885), 184–185.

[55] *Liberty Weekly Tribune*, May 18, June 8, 1860.

[56] Minute Books of the Kansas City, Galveston, & Lake Superior Railroad Co., also the Kansas City & Cameron Railroad, pp. 1, 6, Chicago, Burlington and Quincy Archives, Newberry Library, Chicago, Illinois, hereafter cited through chapter as Cameron Minute Books; *Western Journal of Commerce*, August 23, 1860.

[57] Cameron Minute Books, 12, 14; *Western Journal of Commerce*, October 11, 1860.

[58] Copy of the contract can be found in Hannibal and St. Joseph Railroad Company, Book No. 4, pp. 201–213, Archives of the Chicago, Burlington, and Quincy Railroad Company, Chicago, Illinois.

[59] *Western Journal of Commerce*, June 7, 1860.

[60] *Ibid.*, July 22, 1860.

[61] *Ibid.*, July 26, August 16, 1860.

[62] *Western Journal of Commerce*, January 24, 1861; Cameron Minute Books, 54.

CHAPTER 4

[1] For a summary of Kansas' development on the eve of the Civil War, see Albert Castel, *A Frontier State at War: Kansas, 1861–1865* (Ithaca, New York, 1958), 1–16. On Atchison, see also Peter Beckman, "Atchison's First Railroad," *Kansas Historical Quarterly*, 21:153–156 (Autumn, 1954), and Peter Beckman, "The Overland Trade and Atchison's Beginnings," Essay VI in *Territorial Kansas, Studies Commemorating the Centennial* (Lawrence, Kansas, 1954), 148–151.

[2] *Memoirs of Henry Villard* (2 vols., Boston and New York, 1904), I, 101–102; Horace Greeley, *An Overland Journey from New York to San Francisco* (San Francisco, 1860), 25, 48.

[3] For a summary of the history of the city during the war, which emphasizes military affairs, see Joe Klassen, "The Civil War in Kansas City," *Bulletin* of the Missouri Historical Society, 16:134–156 (January, 1960).

[4] Castel, *A Frontier State*, 205; Albert D. Richardson, *Beyond the Mississippi* (Hartford, Conn., 1867), 549–550.

[5] *Daily Champion* (Atchison), March 28, 1865; *Daily Times* (Leavenworth), August 16, 1865.

[6] Castel, *A Frontier State*, 206; *Daily Champion*, May 9, 1865.

[7] Lela Barnes, ed., "An Editor Looks at Early-Day Kansas: The Letters of Charles Monroe Chase," *Kansas Historical Quarterly*, 26:115–118 (Summer, 1960).

[8] William F. Zornow, *Kansas, a History of the Jayhawk State* (Norman, Oklahoma, 1957), 135; George W. Glick, "The Railroad Convention of 1860," Kansas State Historical Society *Transactions*, 9:467–480 (1905–1906).

[9] The same argument of state loyalty is still employed by business interests of Kansas City, Kansas, in their competition with Missouri merchants

in the metropolitan area. Studies of trade of greater Kansas City show a number of determinants of the pattern, but state loyalty is decidedly not one of them.

[10] This discussion of regional geography is based on James C. Malin, *Grassland Historical Studies: Natural Resources Utilization in a Background of Science and Technology*, Volume I, *Geology and Geography* (Lawrence, Kansas, 1950), 337–338.

[11] See Fred Durr, *Population and Labor Force*, Part IV in *Economic Development in South Central Kansas* (Lawrence, 1957), p. 7, table 2, and p. 9., table 3, for population statistics. See James C. Malin, *Winter Wheat in the Golden Belt of Kansas* (Lawrence, 1944), 44, for the expansion of grain acreage in Kansas. For contemporary statements of the above geographical considerations, see *Western Journal of Commerce* (Kansas City), May 28, 1863, February 27, 1864.

[12] Although the Union Pacific, Eastern Division, was an important part of the significant transcontinental system established by Congress during the Civil War, the complex story of the railroad has often been ignored in general railroad histories. Accounts that are available contain contradictions and debatable judgments. John D. Cruise, "Early Days on the Union Pacific," Kansas State Historical Society *Transactions*, 11:529–549 (1909–1910), was written by an early employee of the railroad. It contains valuable documentary material, particularly in the editorial footnotes. Alan W. Farley, "Samuel Hallett and the Union Pacific Railway Company in Kansas," *Kansas Historical Quarterly*, 25:1–16 (Spring, 1959), is based on manuscript sources and on investigation of legal documents that developed from the litigation in which the railroad was involved. Castel, *A Frontier State*, 219–224, contains a brief account of the early years of the project based on manuscript sources. The unavailability of company records makes it difficult to arrive at a full understanding of this important episode in American railroad history. Although I have utilized the above accounts to a considerable extent, my judgment of the available documents has sometimes led me to conclusions that differ sharply from those embodied in them.

[13] *Kans. Terr. Stat.* (1855), pp. 914–920; (1857), pp. 218–219.

[14] Earl J. Maddox, Early Railroads in Kansas, Typescript, 1937, p. 2, Kansas City Public Library, Kansas City, Missouri; Elmo B. Richardson and Alan W. Farley, *John Palmer Usher, Lincoln's Secretary of the Interior* (Lawrence, Kansas, 1960), 123 n.8.

[15] Ewing to Charles Robinson, March 3, 1860, Thomas Ewing, Jr., Papers, Kansas State Historical Society, Topeka; *A Compilation of All the Treaties Between the United States and the Indian Tribes Now in Force*, 1873, 345–350; Richardson and Farley, *Usher*, 15–16. Although the writers consistently try to place all of Usher's actions in the best possible light, this recent biog-

raphy contains a great deal of material on relations of the federal government to the railroad. A definitive work on Kansas land policy during this period is Paul W. Gates, *Fifty Million Acres: Conflicts over Kansas Land Policy, 1854–1890* (Ithaca, New York, 1954). Any writer on Kansas during the nineteenth century is necessarily indebted to this monumental work.

[16] U. S., *Indian Treaties*, 1873, 350–362.

[17] *Ibid.*, 683–689.

[18] Richardson and Farley, *Usher*, 12, 17; "Report of the United States Pacific Railway Commission," *Sen. Exec. Doc.* 50 Cong., 1 Sess., (1887–1888), No. 51, Vol. 3, Pt. 4, (Serial 2506), p. 1673.

[19] Thomas Ewing, Jr., to Thomas Ewing, Sr., September 8, 1860, Thomas Ewing, Jr., Papers: "Report of the Pacific Railway Commission," Vol. 7, Pt. 8 (Serial 2508), 3852.

[20] "Report of the Pacific Railway Commission," Vol. 3, Pt. 4, contains the testimony of Stone, 1595–1622, and of Usher, 1672–1716. Stone's testimony in particular throws a great deal of light on the early operations of the road. The memorandum is contained in pp. 1597–1599. Stone's comment is on p. 1600. Ewing's testimony is contained in Vol. 7, Pt. 8, 3849–3852.

[21] Robert Russel, *Improvement of Communication with the Pacific Coast as an Issue in American Politics 1783–1864* (Cedar Rapids, Iowa, 1948), 294–308, summarizes the debate in Congress over the Pacific Railway Act of 1862. I have used the compilation of the debates prepared in facsimile from the *Congressional Globe* by Uriah Hunt Painter, *The Pacific Railroad Congressional Proceedings* (West Chester, Pennsylvania, 1875). The comment is included in Carter Goodrich, *Government Promotion of American Canals and Railroads 1800–1890* (New York, 1960), 183.

[22] 12 U. S. *Stat. at L.* (1863), pp. 489–498. For general discussion of the act and its effects, see Nelson Trottman, *History of the Union Pacific* (New York, 1923), 10–11; Robert E. Reigel, *The Story of the Western Railroads* (New York, 1926), 70–71; Goodrich, *Government Promotion*, 182–184.

[23] *Daily Journal of Commerce* (Kansas City), May 15, 1862, July 8, 1862.

[24] Copies of the documents relating to the railroad's financial transactions are included in the printed compilation of the records in the case of *Joseph Stewart vs. The Union Pacific Railway Company*, Circuit Court of the United States, District of Kansas. See "Depositions," 5–9.

[25] "Proceedings," *Stewart vs. U. P.*, 49–56; copy of "Order to Ross, Steele, and Co. from Union Pacific, E. D.," September 27, 1863, in James F. Joy MSS., Burton Historical Collections, Detroit Public Library, Detroit, Michigan; hereafter cited through chapter as Joy Papers.

[26] Trowbridge to Joy, September 26, September 27, October 1, 1863, Joy Papers.

[27] Quoted in Cruise, "Union Pacific," K.S.H.S. *Transactions*, 11:35.

[28] Trowbridge to Joy, September 26, October 1, 1863, Joy Papers.

[29] Trowbridge to Joy, September 26, 29, October 1, 2, 1863, Trowbridge [?, signature missing], Leavenworth, Kansas, to Joy, September 29, 1863, Joy Papers; *Western Journal of Commerce*, November 7, 1863.

[30] Barnes, ed., "Chase Letters," *K.H.Q.* 26:150; *Daily Journal of Commerce*, January 6, 1863. See also *Western Journal of Commerce*, August 8, 22, 1863.

[31] Cruise, "Union Pacific," K.S.H.S. *Transactions*, 11:36; Trowbridge [?, signature missing], Leavenworth, Kansas, to Joy, October 2, 1863, Joy Papers.

[32] Brooks to Joy, November 13, 1863, Joy Papers.

[33] "Minutes of the Chamber of Commerce of Kansas City, Missouri, 1865–1879," Transcript, 28, 30, 31, 32, Archives of the Native Sons of Kansas City (Missouri); "Record of Ordinances of Kansas City, Missouri," Book B, No. 3186, September 18, 1863, p. 304; "Proceedings of City Council, April 1859—April 1864," Book B-2, no p. no., action of September 14, 1863; both volumes are in the office of the City Clerk of Kansas City, Missouri; William H. Miller, *History of Kansas City* (Kansas City, 1881), 107–108.

[34] Miller, *History of Kansas City*, 108; *Western Journal of Commerce*, December 5, 1863.

[35] *Western Journal of Commerce*, September 19, 1863.

[36] "Depositions," *Stewart vs. Union Pacific*, 25–28; Farley, "Hallett," *K.H.Q.*, 25:11–12.

[37] "Depositions," *Stewart vs. Union Pacific*, 11; *Leavenworth Conservative*, April 8, 1864, cited in Cruise, "Union Pacific," K.S.H.S. *Transactions*, 11:538–539. Frémont's part in the Union Pacific, Eastern Division, has been neglected by his biographers.

[38] Richardson and Farley, *Usher*, 55.

[39] *Ibid.*, 60–62; *Western Journal of Commerce*, April 16, 1864; Trowbridge to Joy, August 6, 1866, Joy Papers.

[40] Cruise, "Union Pacific," K.S.H.S. *Transactions*, 11:534; *Western Journal of Commerce*, April 16, 1864.

[41] 13 U. S. *Stat. at L.* (1866), pp. 356–366.

[42] *Western Journal of Commerce*, July 30, 1864.

[43] Richardson and Farley, *Usher*, 58–59; Cruise, "Union Pacific," K.S.H.S. *Transactions*, 11:538; Farley, "Hallett," *K.H.Q.*, 25:10–11, quotes testimony describing the shooting. How legends develop about dramatic episodes is illustrated by the interpretations of the shooting. Perl Wilbur Morgan, *History of Wyandotte County* (Chicago, 1911), 450, says that Talcott had a letter in his pocket from some people in Leavenworth offering him money to murder Hallett. On p. 453 the author quotes a letter to the

Topeka Commonwealth, which states that Talcott represented "the capitalists —the principal of whom was John D. Perry of St. Louis; or he may have represented Frémont or both." Maddox, Railroads in Kansas, MS., p. 3, says that Talcott and Hallett quarreled over the dispersal of payments. The most complete effort at reconstruction is in *Wyandotte County and Kansas City, Kansas* (Chicago, 1890), usually called the Goodspeed history, 204–211, which is based on interviews with Wyandotte residents, and agrees with Cruise's and Farley's accounts. A contemporary newspaper account of the shooting can be found in *Daily Journal of Commerce*, July 28, 1864. Later, the *Journal* stated that Leavenworth interests were not surprised by the assassination and sympathized with it. The account hinted that someone there may have been responsible. *Daily Journal of Commerce*, August 3, 1864. Fifteen years later Talcott, who had escaped right after the shooting, was captured in Colorado, returned for trial and acquitted. See *Wyandotte County and Kansas City, Kansas*, 205.

[44] Richardson and Farley, *Usher*, 89–91; Farley, "Samuel Hallett," *K.H.Q.*, 25:14–15.

[45] Farley, "Hallett," *K.H.Q.*, 25:13, 15–16.

CHAPTER 5

[1] *Western Journal of Commerce* (Kansas City), May 2, 1863.

[2] *Daily Journal of Commerce* (Kansas City), January 22, 25, March 19, April 3, 1863.

[3] Letters printed in *Western Journal of Commerce*, July 4, 18, 1863.

[4] *Ibid.*, December 26, 1863.

[5] *Ibid.*, December 19, 1863.

[6] *Ibid.*, April 2, 16, June 25, 1864.

[7] *Ibid.*, July 2, 9, September 17, 1864; Record of Ordinances of Kansas City, Missouri, Book B, No. 3516, September 10, 1864, p. 346½ (pages numbered with ½'s lie between the whole numbers), office of the City Clerk of Kansas City, Missouri, hereafter cited through chapter as Ordinance Record.

[8] Margaret L. Fitzsimmons, "Missouri Railroads During the Civil War and Reconstruction," *Missouri Historical Review*, 35:199 (January, 1941); *Western Journal of Commerce*, January 14, September 23, 1865.

[9] Albert Castel, *A Frontier State at War: Kansas, 1861–1865* (Ithaca, New York, 1958), 20–21; Leverett W. Spring, "The Career of a Kansas Politician," *American Historical Review*, 4:80–104. (October, 1898).

[10] Ewing to John P. Usher, November 19, 1861, Thomas Ewing, Jr., Pa-

pers, Kansas State Historical Society, Topeka; Castel, *A Frontier State at War*, 220; Paul W. Gates, *Fifty Million Acres* (Ithaca, New York, 1954), 133.

[11] *Kans. Priv. Laws* (1858), pp. 128–133; Harold J. Henderson, "The Building of the First Kansas Railroad South of the Kaw River," *Kansas Historical Quarterly*, 15:227–228 (August, 1947); James C. Malin, *Grassland Historical Studies: Natural Resources Utilization in a Background of Science and Technology*, Volume I, *Geology and Geography* (Lawrence, Kansas, 1950), 337–338.

[12] *Western Journal of Commerce*, August 19, September 2, 1865; Ordinance Record, Book B, No. 3860, August 9, 1865, p. 380; Book C, No. 4602, August 14, 1866, p. 63; William H. Miller, *History of Kansas City* (Kansas City, 1881), 112.

[13] *Western Journal of Commerce*, August 19, 26, December 2, 9, 1865. See especially letter from "Roland" in *ibid.*, December 16, 1865, for a contemporary evaluation of the significance of the Lane plan.

[14] Castel, *A Frontier State at War*, 231–232.

[15] Malin, *Grassland*, I, 330; Kenneth A. Middleton, *The Industrial History of a Midwestern Town*, No. 20 in Kansas Studies in Business, Publication of the University of Kansas School of Business (Lawrence, December, 1941), 23.

[16] *Lawrence Daily Journal*, December 18, 1880, quoted in Middleton, *Industrial History of a Midwestern Town*, 47.

[17] *Daily Journal of Commerce*, July 6, August 1, 1866.

[18] Pomeroy to Hyatt, May 18, 1857, Samuel C. Pomeroy Papers, Kansas State Historical Society, Topeka.

[19] Pomeroy to Hyatt, August 6, 1857, Pomeroy Papers.

[20] *Ibid.* See also Pomeroy to Hyatt, July 24, 1857, Pomeroy Papers.

[21] *Charter, Treaty and Contracts of the Atchison & Pike's Peak Railroad* (New York, 1863); *Atchison, Topeka and Santa Fe Railroad Company* (New York, 1864). For a summary of Pomeroy's land transactions, see Gates, *Fifty Million Acres*, 133–140, 142–160.

[22] Paul W. Gates, "The Railroads of Missouri, 1850–1870," *Missouri Historical Review*, 26:138 (January, 1932); Floyd C. Shoemaker, *Missouri and Missourians* (5 vols., Chicago, 1943), I, 768; *Western Journal of Commerce*, August 27, 1864, August 26, September 2, 1865.

[23] *Western Journal of Commerce*, April 21, 1866.

CHAPTER 6

[1] Frank S. Popplewell, "St. Joseph, Missouri, As a Center of the Cattle Trade," *Missouri Historical Review*, 32:447 (July, 1938).

[2] "Minutes of the Chamber of Commerce of Kansas City, Missouri, 1856–1879," Transcript, 31–32, Archives of the Native Sons of Kansas City (Missouri); hereafter cited as Chamber of Commerce Minutes.

[3] The best biographical sketch of Case is contained in Theodore S. Case, ed., *History of Kansas City, Missouri* (Syracuse, 1888), 460–463.

[4] Case's manuscript is located in the Archives of the Native Sons of Kansas City. Excerpts from the correspondence with Greeley, and Case's comments, are printed in Richard L. Douglas, "A History of Manufacturing in the Kansas District," Kansas State Historical Society *Collections*, XI (1909–1910), note 47, pp. 93–94.

[5] "Minute Books of the Kansas City, Galveston & Lake Superior Railroad Co., also the Kansas City & Cameron Railroad," 37–38, 42, Chicago, Burlington and Quincy Archives, Newberry Library, Chicago, Illinois; hereafter cited as Cameron Minute Books.

[6] *Ibid.*, 44, 47, 49.

[7] *Ibid.*, 22, 49–50; *Laws of Mo.* (1864–1865), pp. 238–240.

[8] *Western Journal of Commerce* (Kansas City), September 9, 1865. The engineer's report is printed September 16, 1865.

[9] *Ibid.*, November 12, 1865.

[10] *Daily Times* (Leavenworth), October 31, 1865; *Daily Journal of Commerce* (Kansas City), March 27, 1866.

[11] Cameron Minute Books, 54–55.

[12] Record of Ordinances of Kansas City, Missouri, Book B, No. 4069, December 2, 1865, p. 407, office of the City Clerk of Kansas City, Missouri; hereafter cited as Ordinance Record; Cameron Minute Books, 54–55.

[13] Cameron Minute Books, 59.

[14] Bouton to Ransom, April 8, 1866, printed in *Daily Journal of Commerce*, April 10, 1866.

[15] Report printed in *Daily Journal of Commerce* (Kansas City), April 29, 1866.

[16] *Western Journal of Commerce*, December 30, 1865. See also December 9, 1865.

[17] John W. Brooks to James F. Joy, August 14, October 3, 1865, James F. Joy Manuscripts, Burton Historical Collections, Detroit Public Library, Detroit, Michigan; hereafter cited as Joy Papers.

[18] Hayward to Joy, August 21, 1866, Joy Papers.

[19] Thomas C. Cochran, *Railroad Leaders, 1854–1890: the Business Mind in Action* (Cambridge, Mass., 1953), 38–39.

[20] Cameron Minute Books, 51.

[21] Tax book containing 1857 and 1858 Kansas City tax records, manuscript in the possession of Miss Frances Berenice Ford, Kansas City, Mo.; Case to Joy, March 26, 1866; Memorandum of Affairs of West Kansas Land Company, August 25, 1868; Octave Chanute to Joy, October 21, 1870, Joy Pa-

pers; "The West Kansas City Land Company Minute Book, 1867–1894," 34–35, Archives of the Native Sons of Kansas City.

[22] Case to Joy, March 26, 1866, Joy Papers.

[23] William Boot to Joy, May 26, 1866; R. S. Watson to Joy, June 4, 1866; John M. Forbes to Joy, May 26, 1866; John W. Denison to Joy, May 17, 1866, Joy Papers.

[24] *Western Journal of Commerce*, May 19, 26, 1866; Ordinance Record, Book C, No. 4394, May 11, 1866, p. 28; Book C, no No., July 28, 1866, pp. 57–58.

[25] *Western Journal of Commerce*, May 26, 1866.

[26] Reid to "Gentlemen," May 8, 1866, Archives of the Native Sons of Kansas City.

[27] Cameron Minute Books, 98, 122.

[28] *Ibid.*, 73–77.

[29] Watson to Joy, June 4, 6, 11, 1866, Joy Papers.

[30] Watson to Joy, June 17, 1866, Joy Papers.

[31] Reid to Van Horn, June 17, 1866, Archives of the Native Sons of Kansas City.

[32] Kearney to Van Horn, June 18, 1866, Archives of the Native Sons of Kansas City.

[33] Watson to Joy, June 23, 1866, Joy Papers.

[34] Brooks to Joy, Telegram, January 23, 1865; Mead to Joy, December 27, 1865, Joy Papers.

[35] See debate on the bill in *Cong. Globe*, 39 Cong., 1 Sess., pp. 2268–2274.

[36] *Ibid.*, pp. 3406, 2274, 3811; *Daily Times* (Leavenworth), July 6, 19, 26, 1866. While maintaining the hope that Leavenworth would become the commercial center of the Missouri Valley, the *Times* apparently did not consider the significance of the bridge question at any other time. The major emphasis in the newspaper's railroad discussions was on the importance of the establishment of direct connections with St. Louis by way of the Missouri Pacific. See June 28, 1866, for example.

[37] *Cong. Globe*, 39 Cong., 1 Sess., pp. 3900–3903; U. S. *Stat. at L.* (1866), pp. 244–246.

[38] *Cong. Globe*, 39 Cong., 1 Sess., pp. 1342, 2737–2738, 3334–3336, 4059; 14 U. S. *Stat. at L.* (1866), pp. 236–239.

[39] *Daily Journal of Commerce*, August 19, 1866.

[40] Letter printed in *ibid.*, August 26, 1866.

[41] *Ibid.*, July 31, 1866.

[42] Cameron Minute Books, 82; Reid to Joy, June 23, 1866; Thayer to Joy, June 30, 1866, Joy Papers.

[43] Hayward to Joy, August 18, 1866; Kearney to Joy, July 25, 1866; Watson to Joy, August 6, 1866, Joy Papers.

[44] Charles E. Perkins to Edith Forbes Perkins, August 17, 1866, printed in Richard C. Overton, *Burlington West* (Cambridge, Mass., 1941), Appendix D, 524; Hayward to Joy, August 21, 1866; Kearney to Joy, November 18, 1866, Joy Papers.

[45] Hannibal and St. Joseph Railroad Company, Book No. 4, p. 354, Archives of the Chicago, Burlington, and Quincy Railroad Company, Chicago, Illinois; the contract is printed in *Chicago, Burlington & Quincy Railroad Company, Documentary History* (3 vols., Chicago, 1929), II, 888–894; Cameron Minute Books, 106–107.

[46] The circular is transcribed in Cameron Minute Books, 106–107. A rather complex arrangement for the disposal of the resulting stocks and bonds was provided. The newly chartered Quincy Railroad Bridge Company issued 10,-000 $100-shares, paying 10 per cent interest. These were to be sold to the stockholders of the Hannibal and St. Jo. and of the C. B. Q. The Kansas City and Cameron was to issue its first-mortgage bonds, not to exceed 120 $1,000 shares, payable in twenty years and drawing 10 per cent interest. The two companies agreed to appropriate 40 per cent of the gross receipts from the operation of the Kansas City and Cameron for the purchase of these bonds and the payment of the interest. The right to purchase 10,000 Cameron bonds and 5,000 shares of Quincy bridge stock on a pro rata basis was to be divided equally between the stockholders of the C. B. Q. and the Hannibal and St. Jo. The ratio was set as follows: the purchase of each $1,000 bond of the Kansas City and Cameron would entitle the purchaser to buy five shares of the Quincy bridge stock.

[47] *Daily Journal of Commerce*, December 1, 1866.

CHAPTER 7

[1] *Daily Journal of Commerce* (Kansas City), August 12, 1866; Kearney to Joy, September 17, 1866, January [no day], 1867; Reid to Joy, January 11, 186[7], Joy Papers. The last page of the Reid letter including the signature is missing, but handwriting identification makes it certain it was written by Reid. The letter is dated 1866, but from the contents it is clear that this is an error, the result of the common practice of early-in-the-year misdating.

[2] "Minute Books of the Kansas City, Galveston, & Lake Superior Railroad, also the Kansas City & Cameron Railroad," 103, Cameron Minute Books; Memorandum, January 25, 1867 [list of Chicago investors who agreed to take Kansas City bonds], Joy Papers; *Daily Journal of Commerce*, December 28, 1866, January 29, 31, March 19, 22, 1867.

[3] A sketch of Chanute's life can be found in the *Dictionary of American Biography* (New York, 1930), IV, 10–11. An interesting account of Chanute's experiments in winged flight is contained in Powell A. Moore, *The Calumet Region* (Indianapolis, 1959), 574–585.

[4] Chanute to Joy, January 23, February 8, 1867, Joy Papers; *Daily Journal of Commerce*, March 29, 1867; *Laws of Mo.* (1867), pp. 143–144.

[5] Kearney to Joy, March 27, 1867, August 8, 1867; Reid to Joy, August 7, 1867, Joy Papers; Record of Ordinances of Kansas City, Missouri, Book C, No. 4497, April 6, 1867, p. 134, office of the City Clerk of Kansas City, Missouri, hereafter cited through chapter as Ordinance Record. The actual transfer was made on July 27, 1867; Book C, No. 5321, July 27, 1867, pp. 178–179, 184; Cameron Minute Books, 23. The directors of the Hannibal and St. Jo. approved the consolidation February 14, 1870 (Hannibal and St. Joseph Railroad Company, Book No. 4, p. 354, Archives of the Chicago, Burlington and Quincy Railroad Company, Chicago, Illinois) and the directors of the Kansas City and Cameron on February 21, 1870 (Cameron Minute Books, 127).

[6] *Daily Journal of Commerce*, June 7, 9, 1868. For a definitive discussion of the Neutral Lands Controversy, see Paul W. Gates, *Fifty Million Acres* (Ithaca, New York, 1954), 154–193.

[7] Joy to O. H. Browning, May 11, 1868, Joy Papers; Gates, *Fifty Million Acres*, 158–169.

[8] Thayer to Coates, March 18, 1867; Coates to Joy, March 21, September 9, December 26, 1867, July 8, 1868, Joy Papers.

[9] Watson to Joy, October 16, 1868, Joy Papers.

[10] Joy to Coates, September 2, 1868; Coates to Joy, August 12, 1869, Joy Papers; Gates, *Fifty Million Acres*, 174–177.

[11] Ordinance Record, Book C, No. 6219, August 7, 1868, p. 295; *Daily Journal of Commerce*, September 9, 1868.

[12] Reid to Joy, December 6, 20, 1866; Craig to Joy, July 19, 1867, Joy Papers.

[13] Joseph G. McCoy, *Historic Sketches of the Cattle Trade of the South and Southwest* (Kansas City, 1874), 43; Chanute to Joy, October 27, 1868.

[14] "History of the Kansas City Stockyards," *Hereford Swine Journal* (July 30, 1943), 13; contract, Thomas J. Bigger and Missouri River, Fort Scott, and Gulf, July 11, 1870; Chanute to Joy, February 20, 1871, Joy Papers.

[15] Watson to Joy, May 11, 1867; Chanute to Joy, December 31, 1869, Joy Papers.

[16] Carter Goodrich, *Government Promotion of American Canals and Railroads 1800–1890* (New York, 1960), 237, 254, 273.

[17] Report printed in *Kansas City Times*, January 15, 1873.

CHAPTER 8

[1] Julius Grodinsky, *The Iowa Pool* (Chicago, 1950), 9–10, 13, 17, 150–162. In this thorough, detailed study, Grodinsky examines the rate arrangements affecting Kansas City at great length. See also Thomas C. Cochran, *Railroad Leaders, 1854–1890, The Business Mind in Action* (Cambridge, Mass., 1953), 38.

[2] Robert E. Riegel, "The Southwestern Pool," *Missouri Historical Review* 19:12–34 (October, 1924).

[3] Report printed in *Daily Journal of Commerce* (Kansas City), August 31, 1869.

[4] *Kansas City Times*, September 29, 1873.

[5] *Ibid.*, October 3, 1877.

[6] *Daily Journal of Commerce*, July 4, November 11, 1874.

[7] Report of Internal Improvements Committee of the Kansas City Board of Trade, printed in *Daily Journal of Commerce*, January 25, 1873.

[8] Resolution of Board of Trade, *Kansas City Times*, January 25, 1873.

[9] "Minutes of the Chamber of Commerce of Kansas City, Missouri, 1856–1879," Transcript, 55, Chamber of Commerce Minutes; William H. Miller, *The History of Kansas City* (Kansas City, 1881), 124.

[10] *Kansas City Times*, January 15, 1872. The disunity in the Kansas City business community is made clear by a debate over efforts to reorganize the Chamber of Commerce in 1879 and a subsequent attempt to combine it with the Board of Trade. See Chamber of Commerce Minutes, 36–39.

[11] For a discussion of the general aspects of the narrow-gauge movement, see George R. Taylor and Irene D. Neu, *The American Railroad Network, 1861–1900* (Cambridge, Mass., 1956), 63–66. The *Boston Commercial Bulletin* is cited on 64.

[12] *Kansas City Times*, November 22, 1872.

[13] *Daily Journal of Commerce*, June 6, 7, 8, 9, 13, 1871. See also *Kansas City Times*, June 16, 1872.

[14] *Kansas City Times*, December 17, 1871, February 15, March 5, April 5, 1872.

[15] *Ibid.*, April 6, May 31, 1872.

[16] *Ibid.*, June 30, 1872.

[17] *Ibid.*, July 30, August 21, 1872.

[18] *Ibid.*, February 20, March 18, 1873, January 16, 1874.

[19] *Ibid.*, July 16, 24, 28, 29, 1874, July 30, 1875, August 10, December 19, 1876; *Daily Journal of Commerce*, May 19, 1874.

[20] *Daily Journal of Commerce*, April 23, 1872. Chanute's report is printed in Miller, *History of Kansas City*, 136–142.

[21] *Kansas City Times*, January 21, 1873.

[22] *Ibid.*, March 7, April 12, June 22, August 8, 1873; Miller, *History of Kansas City*, 145.

[23] *Kansas City Times*, February 6, 14, 15, 1878; *Industries of Kansas City, Board of Trade Review* (Kansas City, 1879), 36; Theodore S. Case, ed., *History of Kansas City, Missouri* (Syracuse, 1888), 299–300.

[24] *Kansas City Times*, January 24, 1878.

[25] *Ibid.*, January 19, 1878.

[26] *Ibid.*, February 20, 1878.

[27] Chamber of Commerce Minutes, 18; *Western Journal of Commerce*, December 13, 20, 1878.

[28] V. V. Masterson, *The Katy Railroad and the Last Frontier* (Norman, Okla., 1952), 188–189; *Kansas City Times*, November 18, 1872; Miller, *History of Kansas City*, 156.

[29] *Kansas City Times*, November 12, 27, 1872.

[30] *Daily Journal of Commerce*, May 15, 1873; *Kansas City Times*, May 17, 1873. The memorial is printed in "Report of the Select Committee on Transportation-Routes to the Seaboard with Appendix and Evidence," *Senate Reports*, 43 Cong., 1 Sess., (1874), No. 307, (Serial 1589), Part 2, 639–643. For a typical statement of the "New West" argument see William H. Miller, *Second Annual Report of the Trade and Commerce of Kansas City, Missouri* (Kansas City, 1879), 9.

[31] The testimony of Powell and Van Horn is contained in "Transportation Routes Report," 643–646.

[32] *Daily Journal of Commerce*, April 22, June 6, July 7, 1874; *Kansas City Times*, October 22, 1874, January 5, 1875.

[33] *Kansas City Times*, August 21, 1875.

[34] *Daily Journal of Commerce*, October 23, 1874.

[35] *Kansas City Times*, January 16, April 3, 18, 1875, November 12, 1876; Miller, *History of Kansas City*, 159.

[36] The Economic Base of Greater Kansas City, September 27, 1949, 12, unpublished MS prepared for the Federal Reserve System, used through permission of supervisory author; Julius Grodinsky, *Jay Gould, His Business Career, 1867–1882* (Philadelphia, 1957), 189–200.

CHAPTER 9

[1] *Daily Journal of Commerce* (Kansas City), August 18, 20, 23, 31, September 22, 1869.

[2] *Ibid.*, October 10, 1869.

[3] *Laws of Mo.* (1865–1866), pp. 27–39 (1868), pp. 90–91; Edwin L. Lopata, *Local Aid to Railroads in Missouri* (New York, 1937), 109.

[4] "Minute Books of the Kansas City, Galveston & Lake Superior Railroad Co., also the Kansas City and Cameron Railroad," 125–126, Chicago, Burlington, and Quincy Archives, Newberry Library, Chicago, Illinois; "Office of the Hannibal and St. Joseph Railroad Company—List of Resolutions by Board of Directors, 1870," memorandum, no day, Joy Papers; *Daily Journal of Commerce*, February 8, April 8, 10, 1870.

[5] Jackson County Court Orders of September 15, 1870, October 21, 1870, printed in *History of Jackson County* (Kansas City, 1881), 194. The various County Court proceedings relating to the Memphis road are compiled in this source.

[6] *Daily Journal of Commerce*, June 25, 1870.

[7] John M. Richardson to Board of Directors, Hannibal and St. Joseph Railroad, May 9, 1870; Richardson to James Joy, May 10, 1870; "Office of the Hannibal and St. Joseph Railroad Company—List of Resolutions by Board of Directors, 1870," memorandum, no day, Joy Papers; *Daily Journal of Commerce*, September 21, 1870, December 2, 1870.

[8] Richardson to Joy, separate letters dated August 3, 1870, Joy Papers.

[9] Octave Chanute to Joy, January 31, 1870; William M. Fishback to Joy, March 2, 1870; George Morrison to Chanute, January 29, 1870; John J. Chapman to Chanute, July 1, 1870, Joy Papers.

[10] Reid to Richardson, February 23, 1871, Joy Papers.

[11] Richardson to Joy, February 26, 1871, Joy Papers.

[12] *Daily Journal of Commerce*, March 8, 1871.

[13] *Ibid.*, March 9, 11, 1871.

[14] *Ibid.*, March 11, 12, 15, 1871.

[15] *Ibid.*, March 13, 14, 28, April 2, 1871; Order of March 16, 1871, printed *History of Jackson County*, 197–199.

[16] *Daily Journal of Commerce*, April 4, 14, 26, 29, May 10, 27, 1871.

[17] *Ibid.*, June 24, July 12, 29, August 11, 1871; *Kansas City Times*, September 3, 1871.

[18] Orders of November 15, 16, 20, 1871, January 18, 1872, printed *History of Jackson County*, 201–202.

[19] Letter dated January 29, 1872, *Kansas City Times*, January 31, 1872.

[20] *Weekly Journal of Commerce*, April 12, 1872.

[21] *Kansas City Times*, May 9, 1872; Joseph G. McCoy, *Historic Sketches of the Cattle Trade of the South and Southwest* (Kansas City, 1874), 324.

[22] *Kansas City Times*, August 7, 10, 1872.

[23] *Ibid.*, August 11, 1872.

[24] *Weekly Journal of Commerce*, August 19, 1872.

[25] Reports of John Polk and J. E. Marsh, directors, printed in *Kansas City Times*, November 11, 24, 1872, respectively.

[26] *Kansas City Times*, December 5, 1872, May 5, 1873.

[27] Order of July 23, 1873, printed in *History of Jackson County*, 203–204.

[28] *Kansas City Times*, November 1, 1873.

[29] *Ibid.*, August 10, 1873.

[30] Letter from Van Horn and La Due, printed in *Daily Journal of Commerce*, April 12, 1874; report of La Due to the Jackson County Court, printed *Daily Journal of Commerce*, February 5, 1874.

[31] *Daily Journal of Commerce*, April 26, 1874.

[32] *Ibid.*, April 28, 1874; letter from Van Horn and La Due, May 12, 1874, printed in *Daily Journal of Commerce*, June 7, 1874.

[33] Order of June 6, 1874, printed *History of Jackson County*, 206–208.

[34] Order of October 26, 1874, printed in *ibid.*, 211.

[35] *Kansas City Times*, January 20, 29, August 20, 21, 1875.

[36] *Ibid.*, July 11, 25, 28, 29, 1875.

[37] The report was printed in the *Kansas City Times*, December 16, 1875, and in the *Daily Journal of Commerce*, December 17, 1875.

[38] The following expenditures had been recorded: for engineering expenses, $40,027; for construction, $480,938.83; for salaries and officers' contingent expenses, $200,150.00; for right of way, $53,022.43; and for tie-and-timber account, $34,109.18.

[39] *Daily Journal of Commerce*, December 17, 1875.

[40] *Kansas City Times*, December 17, 1875, January 10, 1876.

[41] Lopata, *Local Aid*, 102. Lopata's brief discussion of the Memphis road is often inaccurate.

[42] *Kansas City Times*, December 2, 1876, April 13, 15, 1877.

[43] Decision reprinted in *Kansas City Times*, November 20, 1877. This affirmed a state decision *State v. Greene* 54 Mo. 540–577, which discusses the legal issues surrounding the charter problem at length. Lopata, *Local Aid*, 101–127, traces the movement in the state during the 1870's to avoid payment on past bond issues to railroads.

[44] *Kansas City Times*, April 17, 1877.

[45] The Economic Base of Greater Kansas City, September 27, 1949, 165, unpublished manuscript prepared for the Federal Reserve System, used through permission of supervisory author.

[46] *History of Jackson County*, 191–193.

CHAPTER 10

[1] William Allen White, *Autobiography* (New York, 1946), 207–212, contains a moving sketch of Van Horn's later years as an editor. For examples of Van Horn's metaphysical editorials, see *Kansas City Journal*, November 19, 1893, February 11, 1894.

[2] *Kansas City Star*, February 11, 1892.

Bibliography

The following bibliography is selective and includes only materials cited in the text or books and articles that have contributed in a substantial way to the design of the study.

MANUSCRIPTS

THOMAS EWING, JR., PAPERS. Kansas State Historical Society, Topeka, Kansas.

W. G. AND G. W. EWING PAPERS. Indiana State Historical Society, Indianapolis, Indiana.

WILLIAM GILPIN PAPERS. Missouri Historical Society, St. Louis, Missouri.

HANNIBAL AND ST. JOSEPH BRIDGE CORRESPONDENCE. Archives of the Native Sons of Kansas City, Kansas City, Missouri.

JOHN JOHNSON MANUSCRIPTS. Private collection of Miss Frances Berenice Ford, Kansas City, Missouri.

JAMES F. JOY MANUSCRIPTS. Burton Historical Collections, Detroit Public Library, Detroit Michigan.

SAMUEL C. POMEROY PAPERS. Kansas State Historical Society, Topeka, Kansas.

JOHN W. REID MANUSCRIPTS. Private collection of Mrs. Frederick James, Kansas City, Missouri.

ROBERT T. VAN HORN MANUSCRIPTS. Archives of the Native Sons of Kansas City, Kansas City, Missouri.

ROBERT T. VAN HORN MANUSCRIPTS. State Historical Society of Missouri, Columbia, Missouri.

UNPUBLISHED GOVERNMENTAL AND
BUSINESS RECORDS

Minute Books of the Kansas City, Galveston, & Lake Superior Railroad Co. also the Kansas City & Cameron Railroad. Chicago, Burlington and Quincy Archives, Newberry Library, Chicago, Illinois.

Minutes of the Chamber of Commerce of Kansas City, Missouri, 1856–1879. Transcript. Archives of the Native Sons of Kansas City, Kansas City, Missouri.

Proceedings of the City Council of Kansas City, Missouri. Office of the City Clerk of Kansas City, Missouri.

Record of Ordinances of Kansas City, Missouri. Office of the City Clerk of Kansas City, Missouri.

Records of the Hannibal and St. Joseph Railroad Company. Archives of the Chicago, Burlington and Quincy Railroad Company, Chicago, Illinois.

Tax Book Containing 1857 and 1858 Kansas City Tax Records. Manuscript in the possession of Miss Frances Berenice Ford, Kansas City, Missouri.

The West Kansas City Land Company Minute Book, 1867–1894. Archives of the Native Sons of Kansas City, Kansas City, Missouri.

PUBLISHED GOVERNMENT DOCUMENTS

Missouri. General Assembly. *Report of the Committee to Examine into and Report upon the Condition of the Various Railroads in the State of Missouri, . . . Approved March 5, 1855.* (1855).

————. House. *Journal . . . First Session of the Twentieth General Assembly.* (1859).

————. Senate. *Statements and Testimony . . . Taken Before the Committee on Railroads and Internal Improvements of the Extra Session of the Thirty-Fourth General Assembly.* (1887).

U. S. *A Compilation of All the Treaties Between the United States and the Indian Tribes Now in Force.* (1873).

————. Census Office. *Eighth Census, 1860. Population of the United States in 1860.* (1864).

————. *Ninth Census, 1870. The Statistics of the Population of the United States.* Volume I. (1872).

————. *Tenth Census, 1880. Statistics of the Population of the United States.* Volume I. (1883).

————. Congress. *Congressional Globe.* 1849–1870.

————. House. *Report of the Special Committee Appointed To Investi-*

gate the Troubles in Kansas. 34 Cong., 1 Sess., H. Rept. 200, Serial 869. (1856).

————. Senate. *Report of the Committee on Post Office and Post Roads on the Expediency of Establishing a Mail Route to Oregon by Way of Panama.* 29 Cong., 1 Sess., S. Doc. 306, Serial 473. (1846).

————. *Report of the Committee on Post Office and Post Roads on the Expediency of Establishing a Mail Route from Missouri to Oregon.* 29 Cong., 1 Sess., S. Doc. 178, Serial 474. (1846).

————. *Report of the Select Committee on Transportation-Routes to the Seaboard with Appendix and Evidence.* 43 Cong., 1 Sess., S. Rept. 307, Serial 1589. (1874).

————. *Report of the United States Pacific Railway Commission.* 50 Cong., 1 Sess., S. Exec. Doc. 51, 9 vols., Serial 2504–2509. (1888).

————. Patent Office. Agriculture. *The Agricultural Capabilities of the Great Plains.* (1858).

LAWS AND DECISIONS

Kansas Private Laws.
Kansas Territorial Laws.
Laws of Missouri.
Missouri. *Compilation of the Laws in Reference to Such Railroads as Have Received Aid from the State.* (1859).
Missouri Reports.
Statutes of Territory of Kansas.
U. S. Circuit Court. District of Kansas. *Joseph Stewart vs. The Union Pacific Railway Company.*
————. *Statutes at Large.*

NEWSPAPER MATERIAL

Kersey Coates Clipping File. Kansas City Public Library, Kansas City, Missouri.
William Gilpin Clipping File. Kansas City Public Library, Kansas City, Missouri.
Independence Scrapbook. Archives of the Native Sons of Kansas City, Kansas City, Missouri.
Jackson County Scrapbook. Archives of the Native Sons of Kansas City, Kansas City, Missouri.
Kansas City Scrapbooks, No. 1 and No. 2. Archives of the Native Sons of Kansas City, Kansas City, Missouri.

Charles Kearney Clipping File. Kansas City Public Library, Kansas City, Missouri.

Scrapbook of John Calvin McCoy, A collection of newspaper reminiscences of McCoy; indexed. Kansas City Public Library, Kansas City, Missouri.

NEWSPAPERS

Atchison *Daily Champion.*
Jefferson Inquirer (Jefferson City, Mo.).
Jefferson City *People's Tribune.*
Kansas City *Enterprise.*
Kansas City *Western Journal of Commerce, Weekly Journal of Commerce, Daily Journal of Commerce.*
Kansas City Star.
Leavenworth *Daily Times.*
Liberty Weekly Tribune.
St. Joseph *Weekly Gazette.*
St. Louis *Missouri Argus.*
Washington, D. C., *National Intelligencer.*

UNPUBLISHED STUDIES

BENNETT, HOWARD F., The Hannibal & St. Joseph Railroad and the Development of Northern Missouri: 1847–1870. Ph.D. Thesis, Harvard University, Cambridge, 1950.

The Economic Base of Greater Kansas City, September 27, 1949. Manuscript prepared for the Federal Reserve System. In the possession of supervisory author.

FITZSIMMONS, MARGARET L., Railroad Development in Missouri, 1860–1870. M.A. Thesis, Washington University, St. Louis, 1931.

GEARY, DANIEL, Reminiscences of Fifty Years in Kansas City. Typescript, March 8, 1906. Archives of the Native Sons of Kansas City, Kansas City, Missouri.

OSBORNE, ETHEL, Missouri's Interest in the Trans-Continental Railroad Movement, 1849–1855. M.A. Thesis, University of Missouri, Columbia, 1928.

POWELL, DOROTHY E., History of the Hannibal and St. Joseph Railroad, 1847–1883. M.A. Thesis, University of Missouri, Columbia, 1942.

TEMPLIN, LUCINDA DE LEFTWICH, The Development of Railroads in Missouri to 1860. M.A. Thesis, University of Missouri, Columbia, 1915.

BOOKS AND PAMPHLETS

ARMITAGE, MERLE. *Operations Santa Fe.* New York, 1948.

Atchison, Topeka and Santa Fe Railroad Company. New York, 1864.

BANCROFT, HUBERT H. *History of the Life of William Gilpin.* San Francisco, 1899.

BELCHER, WYATT W. *The Economic Rivalry Between St. Louis and Chicago, 1850–1880.* New York, 1947.

BRAYER, HERBERT O. *William Blackmore: The Spanish-Mexican Land Grants of New Mexico and Colorado 1863–1878.* 2 vols. Denver, 1949.

CASE, THEODORE S., ed. *History of Kansas City, Missouri.* Syracuse, 1888.

CASTEL, ALBERT. *A Frontier State at War: Kansas, 1861–1865.* Ithaca, 1958.

CHANUTE, OCTAVE, AND GEORGE MORISON. *The Kansas City Bridge.* New York, 1870.

Charter, Treaty and Contracts of the Atchison & Pike's Peak Railroad. New York, 1863.

Chicago, Burlington & Quincy Railroad Company, Documentary History. 3 vols. Chicago, 1929.

CIST, CHARLES. *Sketches and Statistics of Cincinnati in 1851.* Cincinnati, 1851.

CLEVELAND, FREDERICK A., AND FRED W. POWELL. *Railroad Promotion and Capitalization in the United States.* New York, 1909.

COCHRAN, THOMAS C. *Railroad Leaders, 1854–1890, the Business Mind in Action.* Cambridge, 1953.

CONNELLEY, WILLIAM E. *Doniphan's Expedition.* Kansas City, 1907.

COPLEY, JOSIAH. *Kansas City and the Country Beyond.* Philadelphia, 1867.

DALTON, WILLIAM J. *The Life of Father Bernard Donnelly.* Kansas City, 1921.

DRAKE, B., AND E. D. MANSFIELD. *Cincinnati in 1826.* Cincinnati, 1827.

DURR, FRED. *Population and Labor Force.* Part IV in *Economic Development in South Central Kansas.* Lawrence, Kansas, 1957.

ELLIS, ROY. *A Civic History of Kansas City.* Springfield, Missouri, 1930.

FLINT, HENRY M. *Railroads of the United States.* Philadelphia, 1868.

GARWOOD, DARRELL. *Crossroads of America.* New York, 1948.

GATES, PAUL W. *Fifty Million Acres.* Ithaca, 1954.

GILPIN, WILLIAM. *Central Gold Region.* Philadelphia, 1860.

————. *The Cosmopolitan Railway.* San Francisco, 1890.

————. *Mission of the North American People.* Philadelphia, separate editions 1873 and 1874.

GOODRICH, CARTER. *Government Promotion of American Canals and Railroads 1800–1890.* New York, 1960.

GREELEY, HORACE. *An Overland Journey from New York to San Francisco.* San Francisco, 1860.

GRIFFITH, WILLIAM. *History of Kansas City.* Kansas City, 1900.

GRODINSKY, JULIUS. *The Iowa Pool.* Chicago, 1950.

————. *Jay Gould, His Business Career, 1867–1882.* Philadelphia, 1957.

HAFEN, LEROY, AND ANN W. HAFEN, eds. *Central Route to the Pacific by Gwinn Harris Heap.* Glendale, Calif., 1957.

HASKELL, HENRY C., JR., AND RICHARD B. FOWLER. *City of the Future.* Kansas City, 1950.

HEMPSTEAD, FAY. *A Pictorial History of Arkansas.* St. Louis, 1900.

History of Clay and Platte Counties, Missouri. St. Louis, 1885.

History of Jackson County, Missouri. Kansas City, 1881.

History of the Pacific Railroad of Missouri. St. Louis, 1865.

Industries of Kansas City, Board of Trade Review. Kansas City, 1879.

The Internal Improvement System of the State of Missouri Showing the Enormous Frauds Practiced in Obtaining and Expending State Aid. St. Louis, 1859.

KERR, JOHN L. *The Story of a Western Pioneer, the Missouri Pacific: an Outline History.* New York, 1928.

LOPATA, EDWIN L. *Local Aid to Railroads in Missouri.* New York, 1937.

[LYKINS, JOHNSTON]. *Railroads Chartered and Projected Centering at Kansas City, Mo., with Many Other Interesting Facts.* No place, no date.

MACKAY, ALEXANDER. *The Western World or Travels in the United States in 1846–47.* 3 vols. London, 1849.

MALIN, JAMES C. *Grassland Historical Studies: Natural Resources Utilization in a Background of Science and Technology.* Volume I, *Geology and Geography.* Lawrence, Kansas, 1950.

————. *Grassland of North America, Prolegomena to Its History.* Lawrence, Kansas, 1948.

————. *Winter Wheat in the Golden Belt of Kansas.* Lawrence, Kansas, 1944.

MASTERSON, V. V. *The Katy Railroad and the Last Frontier.* Norman, Oklahoma, 1952.

McCOY, JOSEPH G. *Historic Sketches of the Cattle Trade of the South and Southwest.* Kansas City, 1874.

Memoirs of Henry Villard. 2 vols. Boston, 1904.

MIDDLETON, KENNETH A. *The Industrial History of a Midwestern Town.* No. 20 in *Kansas Studies in Business.* Lawrence, Kansas, December, 1941.

MILLER, WILLIAM H. *History of Kansas City.* Kansas City, 1881.

————. *Second Annual Report of the Trade and Commerce of Kansas City, Missouri.* Kansas City, 1879.

MILLION, JOHN W. *State Aid to Railways in Missouri*. Chicago, 1896.

MOORE, POWELL A. *The Calumet Region*. Indianapolis, 1959.

MORGAN, PERL W. *History of Wyandotte County*. Chicago, 1911.

OVERTON, RICHARD C. *Burlington West*. Cambridge, Massachusetts, 1941.

PAINTER, URIAH H. *The Pacific Railroad, Congressional Proceedings*. West Chester, Penn., 1875.

PERKINS, ROBERT L. *The First Hundred Years, An Informal History of Denver and the Rocky Mountain News*. Garden City, 1959.

POMEROY, EARL. *In Search of the Golden West, The Tourist in Western America*. New York, 1957.

PRIMM, JAMES N. *Economic Policy in the Development of a Western State, Missouri, 1820–1860*. Cambridge, Massachusetts, 1954.

REED, LAURA C., ed. *In Memoriam, Sarah Walter Chandler Coates*. Kansas City, no date.

RICHARDSON, ALBERT D. *Beyond the Mississippi*. Hartford, Connecticut, 1867.

RICHARDSON, ELMO B., AND ALAN W. FARLEY. *John Palmer Usher, Lincoln's Secretary of the Interior*. Lawrence, Kansas, 1960.

RIEGEL, ROBERT E. *The Story of the Western Railroads*. New York, 1926.

ROBINSON, CHARLES. *The Kansas Conflict*. New York, 1892.

RUSSEL, ROBERT R. *Improvement of Communication with the Pacific Coast As an Issue in American Politics, 1783–1863*. Cedar Rapids, Iowa, 1948.

SHOEMAKER, FLOYD C. *Missouri and Missourians*. 5 vols. Chicago, 1943.

SMITH, HENRY N. *Virgin Land*. New York, 1957.

SPALDING, CHARLES C. *Annals of the City of Kansas*. Kansas City, 1858, reprinted in facsimile ed., Columbia, Missouri, 1950.

STEGNER, WALLACE. *Beyond the Hundredth Meridian*. Boston, 1954.

TAYLOR, GEORGE R., AND IRENE D. NEU. *The American Railroad Network, 1861–1900*. Cambridge, Massachusetts, 1956.

TAYLOR, GEORGE R. *The Transportation Revolution*. New York, 1951.

TROTTMAN, NELSON. *History of the Union Pacific*. New York, 1923.

United States Biographical Dictionary, Missouri Volume. New York, 1878.

WADE, RICHARD C. *The Urban Frontier, The Rise of Western Cities, 1790–1830*. Cambridge, Massachusetts, 1959.

WESTON, W., ed. *Weston's Gude to the Kansas Pacific Railway*. Kansas City, 1872.

WHITE, WILLIAM A. *Autobiography*. New York, 1946.

WHITNEY, CARRIE W. *Kansas City, Missouri, Its History and People, 1808–1908*. 3 vols. Chicago, 1908.

Wyandotte County and Kansas City, Kansas. Chicago, 1890.

ZORNOW, WILLIAM F. *Kansas, a History of the Jayhawk State*. Norman, Oklahoma, 1957.

ARTICLES AND PERIODICALS

BARNES, LELA, ed. "An Editor Looks at Early-Day Kansas: The Letters of Charles Monroe Chase." *Kansas Historical Quarterly*, 26:113–151 (Summer, 1960).

BECKMAN, PETER. "Atchison's First Railroad." *Kansas Historical Quarterly*, 21:153–156 (Autumn, 1944).

————. "The Overland Trade and Atchison's Beginnings." Essay VI in *Territorial Kansas, Studies Commemorating the Centennial* (Lawrence, 1954), 148–161.

"Bullene, Thomas Brockway." In Howard L. Conard, ed., *Encyclopedia of the History of Missouri*. 1:424 (New York, 1901).

"Cincinnati—Her Position, Duty and Destiny." *De Bow's Review*, 7:362–365 (October, 1849).

"Coates, Kersey." In Howard L. Conard, ed., *Encyclopedia of the History of Missouri*, 2:36–38 (New York, 1901).

CONNELLEY, WILLIAM E. "Characters and Incidents of the Plains." *Kansas State Historical Society Collections*, 10:111–119 (1907–1908).

————. "The First Provisional Constitution of Kansas." *Kansas State Historical Society Collections*, 6:105–106 (1897–1900).

COTTERILL, R. S. "The National Railroad Convention in St. Louis, 1849." *Missouri Historical Review*, 12:203–215 (July, 1918).

CRUISE, JOHN D. "Early Days on the Union Pacific." *Kansas State Historical Society Transactions*, 11:529–549 (1909–1910).

DE VOTO, BERNARD. "Geopolitics with the Dew on It." *Harper's Magazine*, 188:313–323 (March, 1944).

DOUGLAS, RICHARD L. "A History of Manufacturing in the Kansas District." *Kansas State Historical Society Collections*, 11:81–215 (1909–1910).

FARLEY, ALAN W. "Samuel Hallett and the Union Pacific Railway Company in Kansas." *Kansas Historical Quarterly*, 25:1–16 (Spring, 1959).

FITZSIMMONS, MARGARET L. "Missouri Railroads During the Civil War and Reconstruction." *Missouri Historical Review*, 35:188–206 (January, 1941).

GATES, PAUL W. "The Railroads of Missouri, 1850–1870." *Missouri Historical Review*, 26:126–141 (January, 1932).

GILPIN, WILLIAM. "The Cities of Missouri." *Western Journal and Civilian*, 11:31–40 (October, 1853).

GLAAB, CHARLES N. "Business Patterns in the Growth of a Midwestern City." *Business History Review*, 33:156–174 (Summer, 1959).

————. "Kansas City's Hannibal Bridge: Western Town-Booming and Eastern Capital." *The Trail Guide* (Kansas City), 4:1–16 (March, 1959).

————. "Visions of Metropolis: William Gilpin and Theories of City

Growth in the American West." *Wisconsin Magazine of History*, 45:21–31 (Autumn, 1961).

GLICK, GEORGE W. "The Railroad Convention of 1860." *Kansas State Historical Society Transactions*, 9:467–480 (1905–1906).

GOODRICH, CARTER. "American Development Policy." *Journal of Economic History*, 16:446–460 (December, 1956).

HENDERSON, HAROLD J. "The Building of the First Kansas Railroad South of the Kaw River." *Kansas Historical Quarterly*, 15:225–239 (August, 1947).

"History of the Kansas City Stockyards." *Hereford Swine Journal* (July 30, 1943).

"The History of Railroad Building into and out of Kansas City." *Kansas State Historical Society Collections*, 12:47–52 (1911–1912).

KLASSEN, JOE. "The Civil War in Kansas City." *Bulletin of the Missouri Historical Society*, 16:134–156 (January, 1960).

LANGSDORF, EDWARD, AND R. W. RICHMOND, eds. "Letters of Daniel R. Anthony, 1857–1862." *Kansas Historical Quarterly*, 24:6–30, 198–226 (Spring-Summer, 1958).

"Letters of John and Sarah Everett, 1854–1864, Miami County Pioneers." *Kansas Historical Quarterly*, 8:143–174 (May, 1939).

Missouri Valley Historical Society Annals. Vol. I (1921–1926).

PAYNE, MILTON J. "City of Kansas, Early Municipal History of." In Howard L. Conard, ed., *Encyclopedia of the History of Missouri*, 1:632–634 (New York, 1901).

POPPLEWELL, FRANK S. "St. Joseph, Missouri, As a Center of the Cattle Trade." *Missouri Historical Review*, 32:443–457 (July, 1938).

PORTER, KENNETH W. "William Gilpin: Sinophile and Eccentric." *Colorado Magazine*, 37:245–267 (October, 1960).

"Reid, John William." In Howard L. Conard, ed., *Encyclopedia of the History of Missouri*, 5:327–328 (New York, 1901).

RIEGEL, ROBERT E. "The Missouri Pacific Railroad to 1879." *Missouri Historical Review*, 18:3–26 (October, 1923).

————. "The Southwestern Pool." *Missouri Historical Review*, 19:12–34 (October, 1924).

SCOTT, JESUP W. "Westward the Star of Empire." *De Bow's Review*, 27:125–136 (August, 1859).

"St. Louis—Its Early History." *The Western Journal* 2:71–86 (February, 1849).

SPRING, LEVERETT W. "The Career of a Kansas Politician." *American Historical Review*, 4:80–104 (October, 1898).

TEGEDER, VINCENT C. "Lincoln and the Ascendancy of the Radicals in the West." *Mississippi Valley Historical Review*, 35:77–90 (June, 1948).

VEVIER, CHARLES. "American Continentalism: An Idea of Expansion, 1845–1910." *American Historical Review*, 65:323–335 (January, 1960).

Index